Arnold Suppan, Richard Lein (Eds.)

East European Identities in the 19th and 20th Century

EUROPA ORIENTALIS

herausgegeben vom

Institut für Osteuropäische Geschichte
an der Universität Wien

Band 8

LIT

East European Identities in the 19th and 20th Century

edited by

Arnold Suppan and Richard Lein

LIT

Umschlagbild: Idee und Layout:
Marija Wakounig, Georg Kastner und Richard Lein

Gedruckt mit Unterstützung des Bundesministeriums
für Wissenschaft und Forschung in Wien

Bibliographic information published by the Deutsche Nationalbibliothek
The Deutsche Nationalbibliothek lists this publication in the Deutsche Nationalbibliografie; detailed bibliographic data are available in the Internet at http://dnb.d-nb.de.

ISBN 978-3-643-50102-8

A catalogue record for this book is available from the British Library

Krotenthallergasse 10/8
A-1080 Wien
Tel. +43 (0) 1-409 56 61
Fax +43 (0) 1-409 56 97
e-Mail: wien@lit-verlag.at
http://www.lit-verlag.at

LIT VERLAG Dr. W. Hopf
Berlin 2009
Fresnostr. 2
D-48159 Münster
Tel. +49 (0) 2 51-620 32 22
Fax +49 (0) 2 51-922 60 99
e-Mail: lit@lit-verlag.de
http://www.lit-verlag.de

Distribution:
In Germany: LIT Verlag Fresnostr. 2, D-48159 Münster
Tel. +49 (0) 2 51-620 32 22, Fax +49 (0) 2 51-922 60 99, e-Mail: vertrieb@lit-verlag.de

In Austria: Medienlogistik Pichler-ÖBZ GmbH & Co KG
IZ-NÖ, Süd, Straße 1, Objekt 34, A-2355 Wiener Neudorf
Tel. +43 (0) 22 36-63 53 52 90, Fax +43 (0) 22 36-63 53 52 43, e-Mail: mlo@medien-logistik.at

In Switzerland: B + M Buch- und Medienvertriebs AG
Hochstr. 357, CH-8200 Schaffhausen
Tel. +41 (0) 52-643 54 30, Fax +41 (0) 52-643 54 35, e-Mail: order@buch-medien.ch

In the UK by: Global Book Marketing, 99B Wallis Rd, London, E9 5LN
Phone: +44 (0) 20 8533 5800 – Fax: +44 (0) 1600 775 663
http://www.centralbooks.co.uk/html

In North America by:

Transaction Publishers
New Brunswick (U.S.A.) and London (U.K.)

Transaction Publishers
Rutgers University
35 Berrue Circle
Piscataway, NJ 08854

Phone: +1 (732) 445 - 2280
Fax: + 1 (732) 445 - 3138
for orders (U. S. only):
toll free (888) 999 - 6778
e-mail: orders@transactionpub.com

Index of Contents

Preface by the Austrian Federal Minister of Sciences and Research

It is a great pleasure to present this volume of articles and reports, which results from the Annual Convention of the Centers for Austrian and Central European Studies at the University of Alberta in September 2008, to the scientific community. When the Austrian Ministry of Science and Research started its ambitious program to promote Austrian and Central European Studies in other parts of the world in the 1970s with the foundation of the "Center for Austrian Studies" at the University of Minnesota and the Austrian chair at Stanford University, nobody could foresee the exceptional success of this initiative. Today there exist six such institutions in four different countries (U.S.A., Canada, Hungary and Israel), which have proven to be of great significance not only for students of the host nations who want to learn about Austrian and Central European history, but also for young scholars who are eager to study in foreign countries and get in touch with the local scientific community. All of these colleagues conduct valuable research not only on the history of the former Austro-Hungarian Empire and its successor states, but also on recent conflicts in Central Europe as well as in other countries all over the world. Most of these young scholars have already undertaken interesting investigations with notable results and are looking forward to promising careers in research and teaching.

Unfortunately, until 2007 only little was known about the Center's students and their work in the scientific community, which is why their research remained mostly unnoticed by scholars in Austria as well as in other European countries. To improve the situation, the Austrian Ministry of Science and Research decided not only to bring the young scholars together in the course of the annual meeting of the Centers for Austrian and Central European studies, but to bring out their recent working papers in a special edition of the regular publication of the Institute for East European History at the University of Vienna, called *Europa Orientalis*. This is meant to give them the possibility of promoting their research outside their own Alma Mater. The first annual meeting of scholars and students in Minneapolis 2007 and the first subsequently published volume of working papers, *From the Habsburgs to Central Europe*, were such successes that our Ministry decided to carry on the initiative and to organize both meetings and publications on a regular basis. In this way we hope not only to assist students and young scholars in connecting to the international scientific community, but also to help further generations obtain a broader understanding of our common history.

Johannes Hahn, PhD

Federal Minister for Science and Research

Marija Wakounig

The Institute of East European History University of Vienna

The Institute of East European History in Vienna has continued its wide-ranging activities in the academic year 2008/09. Our most important tasks during that time were the introduction of the institute's new master study program "East European History" and the transformation of the basic study program "Historical Sciences" by the Faculty for Historical and Cultural Sciences due to the Bologna process. Although there is still some fine-tuning that needs to be done, both study programs were well accepted by students as well as professors and are considered to be a great success. We are also pleased to announce that the long-standing director of our Institute, Prof. Arnold Suppan, had been elected Secretary General of the Austrian Academy of Sciences. Fortunately for us, he has, despite his new demanding job, decided not to give up academia but to continue his research and his teaching at the University of Vienna. His post as director of the Institute was already taken over in February 2008 by Prof. Marija Wakounig and, as her deputy, Prof. Oliver J. Schmitt. In addition to that the Institute for East European History has furthermore organized numerous guest lectures, conferences and other scientifically related events, which were frequented by some well-known members of the international scientific community. These activities are also going to be continued in the upcoming academic year, to which we are, despite the present economic conditions, which unfortunately lead to budget cuts, looking forward with confidence.

Basic Facts

Personnel: 14 scholars (four full professors, four associate professors, three assistant professors, three assistants), four general employees, three part-time instructors;

Academia: approximately 1.500 students per semester, actually 25 PhD candidates, 50 diploma candidates;

Regular events: International Seminar for Students of the Historical Department of the University of Ljubljana, held every spring.

Regular publications: Europa Orientalis; Prague Papers on the History of International Relations (published together with the Institute of World History, Charles University Prague)

Library: 120,000 volumes; two librarians, one part-time employee;

Fields of research: Soviet Union, CIS, Russia, East Central Europe, Southeast Europe

Current Activities

Research Platform "Wiener Osteuropaforum"

We are pleased to announce that in 2009 the interdisciplinary research platform "Wiener Osteuropaforum", sponsored by the University of Vienna, had been established at our Institute. The aim of the newly founded platform is to bring together scientists from different fields of historical, juridical, cultural, geographical, political, lingual and theological sciences, who are conducting research on various topics related to Eastern Europe. The platform, which is headed by Prof. Oliver J. Schmitt together with Prof. Dieter Segert from the Institute for Political Sciences of the University of Vienna, at the moment consists of sixteen major scientists coming from eleven different subject areas. In addition to that, a large number of grad students and post-docs have declared their willingness to participate in the project and to contribute to their colleague's work by sharing their knowledge. In this way the platform's initiators hope to create a network between the participating colleagues in order to broaden their knowledge of Eastern Europe in the past as well as in present time and to develop future interdisciplinary research projects. The research platform, which will last at least for three more years, has furthermore announced that it will sponsor a wide range of programs and events in the upcoming years, reaching from guest lectures and seminars to interdisciplinary workshops and conferences.

Galicia" doctoral college (interdisciplinary)

The Institute for East European History is the leading institution of the interdisciplinary „Galicia" doctoral college, sponsored by the Austrian Science Fund (FWF). It consists of nine collegiates from six different countries, studying Slavic studies, German studies, East European History, Economic and Social History. The college was set up in November 2006 and has been recently renewed for another five years.

Guest Lectures

- „Der Anfang vom Ende? Wirtschaftsreformen in den 1960er Jahren in der SFR Jugoslawien“ (Prof. Aleksandar Jakir, Croatia), March 6, 2008.
- „Neuere Tendenzen in der russischen Historiographie“ (Dr. Michail Krom, Russia), April 3, 2009.
- „Die Okkupation Rumäniens durch die Mittelmächte während des Ersten Weltkriegs 1916-1918 (Lisa Mayerhofer, Germany), April 24, 2008.
- “Die christlich-orthodoxe Geschichtsschreibung im osmanischen Südosteuropa, 15.-17. Jhdt. (Konrad Petrovszky, Germany), May 8, 2008.
- „The National Awakening of the Mongols and the Heritage of Tchingiz Khan” (Dr. Vsevolod Bashkuev, Russia), May 6, 2008.
- „The Concept of „Freedom of Conscience“ in Tsarist Russia“ (Prof. Paul Werth, USA), May 19, 2008.
- „Die Frage der Bevölkerungszahlen auf dem Balkan und die Bedeutung der osmanischen Quellen“ (Doz. Mehmet Hacisalihoglu, Turkey), June 26, 2008.
- „Die rechtliche und kirchliche Lage der Walachen in der österr. Militärgrenze nach den Statuta Valachorum (Prof. Petar Vrankic, Germany), March 30, 2009.
- „Die Turksprachen: Ein Überblick” (Prof. Claus Schönig, Germany), April 23, 2009.
- “Die Deutsche (Karls-)Universität vom Münchener Abkommen bis zum Ende des Zweiten Weltkrieges. Universitätsleitung und Wandel des Professorenkollegiums” (Doz. Alena Míšková, Czech Republic) May 4, 2009.
- „Ideology and Alliance Politics: Reflections on the Rise and Demise of the Sino-Soviet Alliance” (Prof. Chen Jian, USA), May 13, 2009.
- “Kulturelle Begegnungen” (Prof. Ingeborg Baldauf, Germany), May 28, 2009.

- „No Saint: Jozef Tiso, 1887-1947“ (Prof. James Ward, USA), June 22, 2009.
- „Geschichtsschreibung und Erinnerungskultur in Bosnien-Herzegowina 1878 bis 1941“ (Dennis Dierks, Germany), June 24, 2009.

Conferences

- „Vampirismus und magia posthuma im Diskurs der Habsburgermonarchie im 18. und 19. Jahrhundert“ (Prof. Christoph Augustynowicz together with the Institute of East European History), July 2 - July 4, 2009.
- „Prozesse ukrainischer Nationsbildung“ (Prof. Andreas Kappeler together with the Institute of East European History), October 1 - Oktober 3, 2009.
- “The Revolutions of 1989” (Prof. Arnold Suppan together with the Austrian Academy of Sciences) October 1 - Oktober 3, 2009.

Other major events

- Book Presentation: „Quo vadis EU? Osteuropa und die EU-Erweiterung“, ed. by Iskra Schwarcz and Arnold Suppan, June 13, 2008.
- Film presentation: „Peace Kicking Mission“, directed by Peter Waldenberger, January 12, 2009.
- Book presentation: „Humanismus bei den Slovenen. Slovenische Humanisten bis zur Mitte des 16. Jahrhunderts, ed. by Marija Wakounig, June 6, 2009.
- Book presentation: „Imperienvergleich. Beispiele und Ansätze aus osteuropäischer Perspektive, ed. by Guido Hausmann and Angela Rustemeyer, September 29, 2009.

Main Publications 2008/2009

- Emilia Hrabovec, Beata Katrebova-Blehova (Eds.), Slowakei und Österreich im 20. Jahrhundert. Eine Nachbarschaft in historisch-literarischer Perspektive, Europa Orientalis 3, Wien/Berlin 2008.
- Iskra Schwarcz, Arnold Suppan (Eds.), Quo vadis EU? Osteuropa und die EU-Erweiterung, Europa Orientalis 5, Wien/Berlin 2008.

- Oliver Jens Schmitt, Kosovo. Kurze Geschichte einer zentralbalkanischen Landschaft, Wien/Köln/Weimar 2008.
- Arnold Suppan, Richard Lein (Eds.) From the Habsburgs to Central Europe. The Centers for Austrian and Central European Studies, Europa Orientalis 6, Wien/Berlin 2008.
- Oliver Jens Schmitt, Skënderbeu, Tiranë 2008.
- Marija Wakounig (Ed.), Primož Simoniti – Humanismus bei den Slovenen. Slovenische Humanisten bis zur Mitte des 16. Jahrhunderts, Österreichische Akademie der Wissenschaften – Zentraleuropa-Studien 11, Wien 2008.
- Arnold Suppan, Wolfgang Mueller (Eds.), Peaceful Coexistence or Iron Curtain? Austria, Neutrality, and Eastern Europe in the Cold War and Détente, 1955-1989, Europa Orientalis 7, Wien/Berlin 2009.
- Oliver Jens Schmitt, Gherardo Ortalli (Eds..), Balcani occidentali, Adriatico e Venezia fra XIII e XVIII secolo. Der westliche Balkan, der Adriaraum und Venedig (13.-18. Jahrhundert), Österreichische Akdemie der Wissenschaften – Schriften der Balkan-Kommission 50, Venezia/Wien 2009.
- Oliver Jens Schmitt, Eva Anne Frantz (Eds.) Albanische Geschichte. Stand und Perspektiven der Forschung, Südosteuropäische Arbeiten 140, Regensburg 2009.
- Oliver Jens Schmitt, Skanderbeg. Der neuen Alexander auf dem Balkan, Regensburg 2009.
- Guido Hausmann, Angela Rustemeyer (Eds.), Imperienvergleich. Beispiele und Ansätze aus osteuropäischer Perspektive. Festschrift für Andreas Kappeler, Forschungen zur osteuropäischen Geschichte 75, Wiesbaden 2009.

Gary Cohen

The Center for Austrian Studies (CAS) University of Minnesota

PROGRAMS AND INITIATIVES IN 2008

The Center for Austrian Studies sponsored a wide range of programs in 2008, despite the challenging economic conditions which universities and research institutes faced in the United States and throughout the world. Critical to the Center's mounting these programs was the ability to secure supplemental funding from outside the University of Minnesota. As a result, we were able both to enhance the best elements in our established programs and to add new initiatives which broadened the work of the Center.

Ongoing programs and collaborations

As in the past, Center offered a diverse range of lectures, literary readings, and musical performances open to the campus and Twin Cities communities, with some thirteen events in addition to the 24th Annual Robert A. Kann Memorial Lecture. The richly varied subjects included art history, cultural studies, social and political history, music history, sociology, and international relations. The presentations demonstrated clearly the vitality of the research being devoted at present to Austrian and Central European questions as well as the high levels of current artistic endeavors in that part of the world. The Center's close cooperation with many other departments, centers, and individual colleagues in the College of Liberal Arts as well as other segments of the University of Minnesota contributed to the high intellectual interest of the our programs and to the diverse audiences which they attracted.

The Center's long history of collaborations with Austrian and Central European universities and individual scholars bore fruit in the return of distinguished figures who are old friends of the Center as well as the participation of individuals new to the Center and the University of Minnesota. Siegfried Beer, who gave the 2008 Kann Lecture, Anton Pelinka, Oliver Rathkolb, and Gerald Stourzh are well known figures in Austrian scholarly circles who have each contributed to previous Center programs. The Austrian Fulbright Visiting Professor during the spring 2008 semester, the sociologist Christian Fleck, was also a welcome returnee to the Twin Cities campus. On the other hand, the distinguished Austrian-born author, editor, and translator Sissi Tax, the Graz sociologist Max Haller, and the Slovene historian Andrej Rahten visited the University of Minnesota campus for the first time, bringing fascinating new perspectives and drawing new audiences.

The Center's publications in 2008 also demonstrated the strength of our continuing activities. Daniel Pinkerton produced two issues of the Austrian Studies Newsletter with the wide range and freshness of content which have become a hallmark of this internationally circulated publication. Volume 39 of the Austrian History Yearbook, edited by Pieter Judson, offered a rich array of new scholarship.

The Center also produced a new volume in its book series, Austrian and Habsburg Studies (Berghahn Books), Embodiments of Power: Building Baroque Cities in Europe, edited by Gary B. Cohen and Franz A. J. Szabo. Central European Studies, a book series at Purdue

University Press for which Center director Gary Cohen serves as associate editor, published three new books in 2008: two on the collapse of socialist Yugoslavia and its aftermath and the Swedish historian Fredrik Lindström's Empire and Identity: Biographies of the Austrian State Problem in the Late Habsburg Empire.

The Center's support for new scholarship on Austria and East-Central Europe also takes the form of organizing biennial book and dissertation prizes, sponsored generously by the Austrian Cultural Forum, and the R. John Rath Article Prize for the best article in each annual volume of the Austrian History Yearbook, supported by gifts from the late Prof. Rath, his family, and friends. Aided by distinguished juries of scholars from Europe and North America, the Center awarded all three prizes at the end of 2008. Deborah R. Coen was awarded the ACF prize for best book, David W. Gerlach won the ACF prize for best dissertation, and Patrice M. Dabrowski was awarded the Rath Prize.

Thanks in large part to the efforts of the Center's administrative manager, Linda Andrean, we have increased in recent years our programming for public audiences outside the immediate University of Minnesota community. Professional development workshops for teachers in middle and high schools have become a regular feature of the Center schedule in the last several years. In April 2008 Linda Andrean, together with colleagues from the Institute for Global Studies and the Center for Holocaust and Genocide Studies at the University of Minnesota and from the Minnesota State College and University System, organized a highly successful workshop entitled "The Ethics of Medicine: The power to heal, the power to harm," in connection with a traveling exhibit from the U. S. Holocaust Memorial Museum, "Deadly Medicine."

Conferences and new initiatives

The Center for Austrian Studies launched several important initiatives in new directions during this last, which promise to bear fruit in various ways into the future. In March 2008, the Center, with support from the Austrian Federal Ministry of Science and Research, the European Studies Consortium at the University of Minnesota, and other units in the university, sponsored an international scholarly symposium, "Social Policy in the New Europe: The Experience of Austria and the Smaller EU Members." A remarkable array of distinguished university scholars and public policy practitioners from Austria, the Netherlands, Finland, and the United States presented papers; and we expect to publish a volume of essays deriving from this symposium.

With major support from the Horst M. Rechelbacher Foundation as well as other organizations, including the Austrian Lebensministerium and the Federal Ministry of Science and Research, the Center staged in September 2008 a major public forum, "Climate Change, Sustainable Agriculture, and Bioresources." This forum brought together renowned experts from universities, non-profits, and government agencies in Minnesota, Austria, and Germany to present the findings of recent scientific research, agricultural experimentation and development, and policy studies on climate change and modes of sustainable production. Hundreds of professors, students, researchers, and members of the general public attended the sessions. For the first time, the Center expanded its reach by producing, in cooperation with Twin Cities

Public Television (TPT), a thirty-minute television program based on interviews with presenters from the forum, entitled, "Food, Fuel, and Climate Change: An Austrian-American Forum." This film has been broadcast repeatedly on public television in Minnesota, and the DVD will be distributed to schools and nonprofit agencies. Later in 2009, it will be available for streaming on the internet from the websites of The Minnesota Project and TPT. By taking advantage of multiple media outlets, CAS has made tens of thousands of people aware of what Austria and America are doing in this vital field.

The Center's new initiatives during 2008 also included preparations for a new multi-year team research project entitled "Understanding the Migration Experience: The Austrian-American Connection." Funded by a generous gift from the Dietrich W. Botstiber Foundation, the research, data collection, and analysis phase will begin in January 2010, with a team of researchers including Dr. Annemarie Steidl and Dr. Wladimir Fischer from Vienna and Prof. James Oberly from the University of Wisconsin, Eau Claire. The Immigration History Research Center and the Minnesota Population Center at the University of Minnesota will cooperate in this project.

Amir Eshel

The Stanford University Forum on Contemporary Europe Stanford University

In its Program on Austria and Central Europe, the Stanford Forum on Contemporary Europe (FCE) at the Freeman Spogli Institute for International Studies (FSI) is proud to report a full year of programming, including research seminars, an international conference, the Distinguished Visiting Austrian Professorship, and a robust scholarly exchange.

Public Speaker Series

- Michael Eskin, Columbia University, Wake Up Call: Grünbein, Descartes, Pushkin
- Anton Pelinka, Central European University, Budapest, Europe and the U.S. After the U.S. Presidential Election
- Istvan Deak, Columbia University, The Worst of Friends: The Many Layered Struggles of Germany's Eastern and Southeastern European Allies for Local Dominance and Ethnic Cleansing, 1938-1945; and Freedom Fighters or Terrorists? Collaboration, Resistance, and Retribution as Illustrated by the Incidents at Oradour in France, Via Rasella in Rome, and Ujvidék/Novi Sad in Hungary/Yugoslavia
- Charles Ingrao, Purdue University, Confronting the Yugoslav Controversies: Can Scholars Make a Difference?
- Wolfgang Mueller, Austrian Academy of Sciences, The USSR and European Integration
- Piotr Mitzner, Cardinal Stefan Wyszynski University, Warsaw, A Trap: What Temptations Did Stalin Offer Polish Writers?

Contemporary History and the Future of Memory Symposium, including Istvan Rev, Central European University, Budapest, A History of the Emergence and Phenomenal Success of Memory as a Discursive-Frame

Mikolaj Kunicki, Notre Dame University, From Hegemony to Demise: The Politics of Lustration and the Crisis of the Church in Post-Communist Poland

Stanford University - University of Vienna Biannual Conference

In March 2009, The Forum on Contemporary Europe hosted the international conference, "Austria and Central Europe Since 1989: Legacies and Future Prospects," the third and final installment in the series of biannual conferences to study the political and cultural landscape of Austria and Central Europe since 1945. While the previous conferences focused on Central Europe during the period of the post-war up to 1989, this year's conference gathered leading scholars and public figures to discuss the exciting developments of our contemporary era and to offer comments on future prospects for the region.

The conference offered multi-disciplinary views of Central Europe today. Addressing topics from the area stretching from the Baltics to the Balkans, speakers focused on Austria as well as Hungary, the Czech Republic, Poland, and the counties of former Yugoslavia. Presentations explored political, economic, social, and cultural facets of the region's larger dynamic. Among the milestone changes during this period which were highlighted were Austria's (and other Central European countries') ascendance to the European Union, the disintegration and reconfiguration of Balkan nations, the collapse of the Soviet Bloc, and the great mobility of goods and labor through the region and new forms of social and cultural interaction.

Conference participants included:

Keynote Speakers

- Emil Brix, Ambassador, Director General for Cultural Affairs, Foreign Ministry for European and International Affairs, Austria
- Martin Weiss, Consul General of Austria, Los Angeles
- Arnold Suppan, Generalsekretär, Austrian Academy of Sciences
- John Boyer, Professor of History, University of Chicago

Panelists and Panel Chairs

"Memory" -- Chair: Norman Naimark, Professor of History, Stanford University

- Wolfgang Mueller, Research Scholar, Austrian Academy of Sciences
- Arnold Suppan, Generalsekretär, Austrian Academy of Sciences

- "Security" -- Chair: James Sheehan, Professor of History, Stanford University
- Hanspeter Neuhold, Professor of Public International Law and International Relations, University of Vienna
- Erwin Schmidl, Head of the Contemporary History Unit, National Defence Academy Vienna
- Coit D. Blacker, Professor of International Relations and Director, Freeman Spogli Institute for International Studies, Stanford University

"Law" -- Chair: Helen Stacy, Lecturer, Stanford Law School and Fellow, Freeman Spogli Institute for International Studies

- Michael Gehler, Professor of History, University of Hildesheim
- August Reinisch, Professor of European, International and Comparative Law, University of Vienna
- Eva Brems, Professor, Human Rights Centre, Ghent University
- Manfred Nowak, Professor, Ludwig Boltzmann Institute of Human Rights/UN Special Rapporteur on Torture

"Culture in New Europe" -- Chair: Amir Eshel, Professor of History and German Studies and Director, Forum on Contemporary Europe, Stanford University

- Kristin Rebien, Professor of German Studies, San Diego State University
- Andreas Stadler, Director, Austrian Cultural Forum New York
- Adrian Daub, Assistant Professor of German Studies, Stanford University

"Culture and Global Europe" -- Chair: Amir Eshel, Professor of History and German Studies and Director, Forum on Contemporary Europe, Stanford University

- Guenther Stocker, Privatdozent at Institute for German Studies, University of Vienna
- Marton Dornbach, Assistant Professor of German Studies, Stanford University
- Russell Berman, Professor of Comparative Literature, Stanford University

"Economics" -- Chair: Christophe Crombez, Visiting Professor, Forum on Contemporary Europe

- Bernhard Ramsauer, CEO, Sal. Oppenheim jr. & Cie. KGaA
- Timothy Josling, Professor Emeritus of Food Research, Stanford University

New Publication on Austria and Central Europe Since 1989

The Forum is pleased to collaborate with conference contributors to develop a forthcoming publication, with the tentative title "Austria and Central Europe Since 1989: Legacies and Future Prospects."

Distinguished Visiting Austrian Chair

This year FCE is pleased to host distinguished Professor Astrid Fellner (Associate Professor, Department of English and American Studies, University of Vienna) within Stanford's Department of Comparative Literature. As her residence at Stanford comes to a close, Professor Fellner delivers the following report:

When I arrived at Stanford University at the end of December 2008, I was thrilled to be able to teach at such a renowned institution, and I was eager to find new venues for joint research. As an Austrian Americanist I have the benefit of knowing both cultures and I felt very privileged to have the possibility of teaching and working on transatlantic cultural crossings of "American culture" at Stanford. And indeed, Stanford was the ideal institution for me to pursue my research in the processes of cultural transfer between the U.S. and Austria and to teach courses on multicultural issues in Europe and the influences of Americanization in Austria.

While holding the Distinguished Visiting Austrian Chair, I taught two classes in the Department of Comparative Literature. In the first quarter I taught a class entitled "Borderland Identities and Cultural Hybridity Between Europe and America." In this class we compared texts by Afro-German, Turkish-German, and Austrian people of color writers with U.S. Latina as well as African American writers, paying attention to the different ways in which these texts address the relationship between home, identity, community, and nation. In the Spring Quarter, I offered a course "CSI Vienna? U.S. Cultural Exchanges in Austria since the 1980s," which formed part of a larger international team-teaching project called "American/Cultural Studies as a Transnational Project" between Stanford, U of Vienna and Bradley U (Peoria, IL). The Stanford students had the opportunity to engage in collaborative work with students from the University of Vienna and BU via the Learning Management System "Sakai." As it turned out, this collaboration was truly rewarding. Since two of my graduate students from the University of Vienna were able to visit Stanford on a short-term research grant from Austria, they could also participate in this course, which turned this class into a site of cultural exchange. With kind support of the FCE, I organized a presentation at Haus Mitteleuropa on May 20, 2009, where my Stanford students together with the visiting student from U of Vienna presented their projects. The collaborative student projects and pictures of this event can be found at: http://www.univie.ac.at/Anglistik/TransatlanticDialogues/classes.html

In addition to establishing a contact between American and Austrian students and fostering direct cross-cultural dialogue in my classrooms, I launched a research collaboration on "American culture" and its global dimensions in Europe. Together with colleagues from Great Britain, the Netherlands, and Slovenia, I am now working on a project called "Imagining America in Austria: The Contact Zones of Popular Culture," which is looking at how "America" has functioned as an intermediary in the production of popular culture in Austria and how this production has been mediated on local, regional, national, and European levels through the knowledge work of "coolness" as an affective force. Looking into the dynamic cultural processes of how American music and cultural icons have been appropriated in Austrian culture and how products of mass culture, like Facebook or Starbucks have become ambivalent symbols of "America" in everyday life in contemporary Austria, this project focuses on the conjunction between the appeal of "American" culture and the marking of identity as "American."

During my residence at Stanford, I collaborated with a number of scholars in the Dept. of Comparative Literature and in the English Department and I was also able to attend a series of lectures and workshops, which gave me the great opportunity to meet other scholars. In addition to the professional work relationships I formed with colleagues, I have also developed personal friendships with some colleagues that allowed me to feel like a part of the Stanford community. I have learned a great deal from my stay at Stanford and will certainly have a lifetime of memories.

The Forum looks forward to welcoming incoming Distinguished Visiting Austrian Chair Professor Siegfried Fina (Associate Professor of European Union Law and Technology Law, University of Vienna), in January 2010. Professor Fina's visit will be jointly supported by the Forum on Contemporary Europe and the Stanford Law School.

Advanced Graduate Student Travel Fellowship

The Forum on Contemporary Europe will sponsor short-term research visits by the following Stanford advanced graduate students and junior faculty at the University of Vienna during the Summer and Fall of 2009:

- Kate McQueen, Graduate Student, German Studies, Literature and Journalism in Fin de siécle Vienna, 1890-1920
- Iga Zelazny, Graduate Student, Art, The Cult of the Cross in Byzantium
- Cristina Bonnet-Acosta, Graduate Student, Spanish, Re-writing Heimat: The Emerging Transnational Writings of Immigrants in Austria
- James Mace Ward, Assistant Professor, History, Political biography of Jozef Tiso
- Adrian Daub, Assistant Professor, German Studies

Stanford University – University of Vienna Scholarly Exchange

The Forum awarded multiple advanced graduate and post-doctoral research residencies to allow scholars from the University of Vienna and other Central European institutions to conduct research visits to Stanford University. FCE was pleased to host six such visitors during 2008-2009, and looks forward to continuing to expand this scholarly exchange in future years:

- Herbert Lachmayer, Visiting Professor, Comparative Literature, Da Pointe Institute
- Wolfgang Mueller, Research Scholar, Austrian Academy of Sciences
- Georg Schiemer, Ph.D. Candidate, Philosophy, University of Vienna
- Thomas Martinek, Ph.D. Candidate, English, University of Vienna
- Marko Schauwecker, Ph.D. Candidate, Law, Ludwig Maximilians University
- Katharina Noussi, Ph.D. Candidate, Political Science, University of Vienna

Franz A. J. Szabo

The Wirth Institute for Austrian and Central European Studies University of Alberta

Wirth Institute's ambitious program continues into its eleventh year

On September 5, 2008, the Wirth Institute for Austrian and Central European Studies formally celebrated the 10th anniversary of its establishment. To mark the event the Institute organized a special anniversary ceremony to which local, national and international dignitaries as well as the campus community and the general public were invited. The Institute also published a 76-page booklet entitled "Ten Years Wirth Institute," which was distributed to all guests attending the anniversary ceremony.

The anniversary celebrations also included a series of signing ceremonies with the Austrian, Czech and Hungarian governments to strengthen ties between these countries and the University of Alberta and to entrench or renew various fellowship programmes of the Institute. Other events of the day included the opening of two major exhibitions organized by the Institute, a high-level public policy roundtable discussion and a ceremonial banquet. After celebrating its tenth anniversary in September 2008, the Wirth Institute moved into its eleventh year with an ambitious program, which included five major conferences, a University of Vienna study-tour workshop on the Canadian West, a complete retrospective of the films of Michael Haneke, as well as the usual array of lectures, round-table discussions and concerts.

The largest of the conferences was the 7th Biennial Conference of the European Community Studies Association of Canada (ECSA-C), which the Wirth Institute brought to Edmonton for the first time in its 13-year history on September 25-27, 2008. Founded in 1995, the Association has developed into the leading professional association for the study of Europe in Canada. ECSA-C seeks to promote the study and understanding of the European Union and European affairs. The conference, entitled "The Maturing European Union," addressed the opportunities and challenges in the maturing European Union and focused on important aspects of European integration such as continuity and change in European institutions, the relationship between the member states and Brussels, key policy areas within the Europe, European migration, citizenship and identity, the economics and politics of enlargement, and the EU's role in the global arena. While the European Union's institutions and culture of Europeanness have matured, it is often argued at the same time that the project of European integration has reached a turning point. The over 80 participants from Europe and North America thus variously assessed the imperatives of institutional renewal and maturation set off against the challenges of enlargement.

In addition to this major conference, the Wirth Institute also hosted the second annual meeting of Austrian Centres, organized and funded by the Austrian Federal Ministry for Science and Research, on September 7-8, 2008. Shortly thereafter, on September 16, the Institute organized a symposium as part of an interdisciplinary field trip of the Center for Canadian Studies at the University of Vienna, reversing our usual role of bringing Central European subjects to Canadians by bringing Canadian subjects to visiting Europeans. In addition to a group of 25 students and professors from Vienna, the symposium, entitled "Social and Cultural Interaction and Literary Landscapes in the Canadian West," was also attended by numerous local students and faculty. Its objective was to introduce new aspects of the early history of Alberta and the Canadian West and to review the present-day literary landscape of Alberta.

In addition to hosting conferences in Edmonton, joint projects with other institutions in Canada, the United States and Europe are periodically planned. In the 2008-2009 academic year three such conferences were organized nationally and internationally. On September 19-21 the Institute co-sponsored a conference with the School of Music of the University of Victoria, entitled "Bartók's String Quartets: Tradition and Legacy." This conference brought together internationally recognized music theorists, musicologists, performers, and composers from North America and Hungary to participate in an interdisciplinary conference focusing on these remarkable works. The conference considered both the imprint of folk and classical traditions on Bartók's string quartets, and the ways in which his quartets influenced those of later composers. The conference included performances by the Lafayette String Quartet. On October 2-4 the Institute also co-sponsored a conference marking the 40th anniversary of the Prague Spring with the Munk Centre for International Studies of the University of Toronto. A broad range of scholars, government officials and public intellectuals examined both the roots and consequences of the Prague Spring, highlighting some of the optimistic expectations and sobering realities of that time in Cold War history. Finally, on June 12-13, 2009, the Institute mounted a joint conference with the Center for Urban History of East

Central Europe, L'viv, Ukraine. This was the Wirth Institute's first co-operative venture with an academic institute in Western Ukraine. The conference focused on social control and sexuality in the cities of Eastern and Central Europe during the long nineteenth century with a special focus on the practices and discourses of the "deviant". Topics included homosexuality, prostitution, sex crimes, "crimes of passion", and white slaving.

The Wirth Institute chose to mount its second conference on the Austrian School of Economics, "What is so Austrian about Austrian Economics," in Mississauga, Ontario, this year, in an effort to bring this biennial event to different parts of Canada. The conference took place on October 17-18, 2008, in the midst of the current economic crisis, so that in addition to its focus on epistemic, programmatic, theoretical and policy dimensions of Austrian economics, the issue of the applicability of Austrian analytical tools to the current recession was also widely discussed.

In March 2009 the Wirth Institute mounted a major retrospective of the films of Michael Haneke, screening his entire output up to that point over a period of two weeks in conjunction with Edmonton's Metro Cinema. The films of this austere Austrian filmmaker, who almost gives a new definition to "uncompromising," lacerate with purist zeal the environment of numbness, moral laziness, ethical cowardice, thoughtlessness and self-serving collusion with the vast edifice of vacuous materialist comfort of contemporary society.

The many lectures presented by the Institute every year were highlighted by the annual Toby and Saul Holocaust Lecture – this year presented by Gerhard Weinberg on the theme "Kristallnacht November 1938: As Experienced Then and as Seen Now," – guest lectures by University of Vienna professors Arnold Suppan and Wynfrid Kriegleder and the Franz Schubert Institute's Deen Larsen, as well as an array of lectures by various ambassadors, including the new Austrian ambassador to Canada, H.E. Dr. Werner Brandstetter, the Slovenian Ambassador, H.E. Tomaž Kunstelj, and the Canadian ambassadors to Poland and Hungary, H.E. David Preston and H.E. Pierre Guimond respectively. Also visiting the Institute for the first time was the new Czech ambassador to Canada, H.E. Karel Žebrakovský.

Lively roundtable discussions also highlighted both the 10th anniversary celebration and the Haneke Film Festival. In the former case, Dr. Katalin Bogyay, Hungarian Secretary of State for Education, Dr. Vlastimil Růžička, Czech Deputy Minister of Education, Krzysztof Kasprzyk, Consul General, Polish Consulate General, New York, and Dr. Carl Amrhein, Provost and Vice-President Academic, University of Alberta discussed "Implementing a Society of Knowledge in an era of Social Transformation." The two roundtable discussions at the Haneke Film Festival were entitled "Anger and Provocation in the Cinema of Michael Haneke," and "Ethics and Politics in the Cinema of Michael Haneke," and included a broad array of University of Alberta scholars.

Concerts included the conclusion of the Institute's Haydn Mass series with Pro Coro Canada with a performance of the "Harmonie" Mass, and recitals by the blind Hungarian pianist, Tamás Érdi, and the Prague-based Panocha String Quartet. Recurring concerts included the Institute's annual Christmas concert with participation of Austrian, Czech, Hungarian, Polish and Slovak community choirs from Edmonton and Calgary, the Institute's annual co-operative venture with the Alberta Baroque Ensemble (this year's concert, entitled "The Austrian Connection," included works by Leopold and Wolfgang Amadeus Mozart, Albrechtsberger and Stamitz), and the annual recital by the winners of the previous year's Johann Strauss Foundation scholarships.

The two exhibitions that the Wirth Institute mounted in conjunction with its tenth anniversary celebration were "Masterpieces of Graphic Art from the Slovak Republic," which was co-sponsored with the Embassy of the Slovakia, and "Legacy of Empire: Treasures of the University of Alberta Libraries Central European Collection." It is well-known that the resources of the University of Alberta Libraries comprise the second largest – and first in volumes per student – research collection in Canada and represent one of the major collections in the world (the University of Alberta was recently ranked 13th largest research library in the world, well ahead of such well-known universities as Princeton). Perhaps less well-known, however, is that it includes the most outstanding collection of Austrian, Habsburg and Central European materials in Canada, and is among the four leading libraries in this field in North America. The University of Alberta also houses Canada's most extensive university map collection, which contains a significant series of maps of Central Europe not available anywhere else on the North American continent. The unique strength in Austrian and Central European subjects of the University of Alberta Libraries dates to the 1960s and has at its heart the acquisitions of two major Austrian collections: the famous "Priesterseminar" library of the Archbishop of Salzburg, purchased in 1965, and the library of the Viennese Juridisch-Politische Leseverein, purchased in 1969. The "Legacy of Empire" exhibition highlighted some of the unique treasures of these collections.

Finally, the proceedings of the Institute's September 2003 conference, "Embodiments of Power: the Baroque City in Austria and Europe," were published this past year as: Gary B. Cohen and Franz A.J. Szabo, eds., Embodiments of Power: Building Baroque Cities in Europe (Oxford & New

York, 2008); the proceedings of the April 2005 conference, "The Cinema of Central Europe," were published this past year as: Wacław M. Osadnik and Irene Sywenky, eds., Central European Cinema Today: Beyond Words and Images, in a special issue of the Canadian Review of Comparative Literature, Vol 34, No. 3 (2007), pp. 253-360; proceedings of our Institute's October 2005 conference, "The Austrian School of Economics" were published this past year as: Roger Koppl, ed., Explorations in Austrian Economics, Vol. 11 of Advances in Austrian Economics (Bingley, UK, 2008); and a guide to the film festival dedicated to the films of Michael Haneke was published as: William Beard, ed., The Films of Michael Haneke (Edmonton, 2009).

Franz A.J. Szabo

Director,

Wirth Institute for Austrian

And Central European Studies

Günther J. Bischof

Center for Austrian Culture and Commerce - CenterAustria University of New Orleans

2007/2008 Celebrating Ten Years of CenterAustria

THE UNIVERSITY OF NEW ORLEANS
CENTER|AUSTRIA
1997 - 2007
10
YEARS

CenterAustria celebrated its 10-year anniversary throughout the 2007/08 academic year with a series of academic conferences, concerts, lectures and celebrations.

Festivities were initiated with our partners at the University of Innsbruck and the City of Innsbruck in early September with a reception in the University's grand offices in the old city's Claudiana. The occasion was the annual joint symposium between the Universities of Innsbruck and New Orleans. The Canada Center of the University of Innsbruck, directed by Ursula Mathis-Moser, made the local arrangements and co-organized the conference on the topic of Acadians and Cajuns: The Politics and Culture of French Minorities in North America (for a conference summary see http://www.centeraustria.org/acadians-cajuns/). The University of Moncton in Canada was a partner too. A conference volume edited by Ursula Moser-Mathis and Günter Bischof, Acadians and Cajuns. The Politics and Culture of French Minorities in North America/Acdiens et Cajuns: Le Politique et culture de minorités francophones en Amérique du Nord (canadiana oenipontana, vol. 9) (innsbruck university press in 2009) was published.

In February 2008, Erhard Busek, former vice chancellor of Austria and the European Union's coordinator of the Stability Pact in the Balkans, delivered a lecture on "Nation Building in the Balkans in the 21st Century." Eva Nowotny, the Austrian Ambassador to the U.S., and Andreas Stadler, the Director of the Austrian Cultural Forum in New York, were in attendance as well as Karlheinz Töchterle, the Rektor of the University of Innsbruck, and Franz Mathis, the coordinator of UNO activities in Innsbruck. The ten year anniversary was celebrated with a ceremony in which Gordon "Nick" Mueller, the founding director of CenterAustria deliverd the keynote address. Fritz Plasser, the University of Innsbruck's Dean of the Political Science and Sociology, and coeditor of the joint annual publication Contemporary Austrian Studies was also present to launch volume XVI The Changing Austrian Voter.

At the same time 30 students studied at UNO through the annual Austrian Student Program, directed by Ellen Palli, throughout the month of February.

In late February 2008, a workshop on "The Abolition of Slavery in the British Empire" was organized with Wolfgang Zach, chair of the University of Innsbruck's English Department, with scholars from Innsbruck, UNO and Vanderbilt University.

The arts were part of this year of intensive exchanges with Innsbruck. The City of Innsbruck sponsored the annual exhibit of two Tyrolese artists at UNO's Fine Arts Gallery in November 2007 with drawings and installations by Roland Maurmaier and Philip Haselwanter. In early March 2008 the Innsbruck Ensemble für Modern Musik visited New Orleans for concerts and workshops and at UNO Music Department. Horst Burmann from the City of Innsbruck's Cultural Office was our principal partner in organizing these events.

In early April a joint conference on "The Prague Spring and the Soviet Invasion of Czechoslovakia in 1968" was staged in New Orleans in cooperation with the Ludwig Boltzmann Institut für Kriegsfolgen-Forschung (Institute for Research on the Consequences of War). Petr Kolař, the Czech Ambassador to the U.S., graciously opened the conference. Scholars from Germany, Russia, Austria, Great Britain and the United States analyzed this tragic Cold War event (for a summary of conference proceedings see http://www.hnet.org/~german/pdf/20080417_prague_spring.pdf)

This conference was a result of an international research project by Stefan Karner's Boltzmann Institut in Graz on the Prague Spring, in which CenterAustria was the American partner. The English publication of these conference papers will be published later in 2009 in Mark Kramer's "Harvard Cold War Studies Series" with Rowman & Littlefield.

In mid-May, a joint symposium was organized in cooperation with the Austrian Marshall Plan Anniversary Foundation and Dieter Stiefel of the Institute of Social and Economic History of the University of Vienna on "Images of the Marshall Plan" in Vienna (the summary of the conference is available at

http://www.h-net.org/~diplo/reports/PDF/ImagesOfTheMarshallPlan.pdf). The conference volume will be edited by Günter Bischof and Dieter Stiefel and will be published in the TRANSACTLANTICA series of the StudienVerlag Innsbruck.

Next to these special activities, ceremonies and conferences, a number of special lectures were organized and attracted considerable attention:

- Andrea Grisold and Wolfgang Maderthaner (Vienna): Austria's Economic and Social Performance 2000-2006 within a European Context

- Andreas Pribersky (Vienna/UNO) and Alla Rosca (Moldova State University/UNO): Competing Memories? Remembering the Holocaust and the Gulag in Europe after 1989 (Annual Marshall Plan Chair Lecture)

- Helge Pharo (Oslo): The Politics of the Nobel Prizes

- Barbara Stelzl-Marx (Graz): The Red Army in the Postwar Occupation of Austria, 1945-1955

- Marion Wieser (Innsbruck/UNO): Religion and Politics in Recent American Elections

The student exchanges remain at the heart of the University of Innsbruck's partnership with UNO. During the academic year of 2007/2008 25 Innsbruck students studied at UNO for a year or a semester. Among them Hannes Richter and Urusula Daxecker who completed their PhDs in Political Science at UNO. The annual "Austrian Student Program" brought another 30 students from all over Austria to UNO for a month-long "Schnupperstudium in American Studies. In addition, Andreas Pribersky from the Department of Political Science of the University of Vienna served as the Marshall Plan Chair; Marion Wieser from Innsbruck's Department of Political Science was completing her dissertation on "Religion and Politics in Recent American Elections" as the Ministry of Science Fellow.

Moreover, a new book by two distinguished Austrian diplomats, published in Günter Bischof's Transaction Publishers series "Studies in Austrian and Central European History and Politics", was launched in October at UNO

CenterAustria has never organized so dense a schedule of activities and special events in one year. It would not have been possible without the hard work of the 2008/9 CenterAustria team Gertraud Griessner, Marion Wieser and Sandra Scherl (UNO) and Hannes Richter (Designer and Webmaster, Berlin), as well as the help from Franz Mathis, Ellen Palli and Horst Burmann in Innsbruck. The regular financial support of the Austrian Marshall Plan Foundation and a special grant from Austrian Ministry of Science/OEAD made it all possible. Susan Krantz, Dean of the College of Liberal Arts at UNO, and Matthias Schennach at the University of Innsbruck's Auslandsamt, were strong supporters of our programs too.

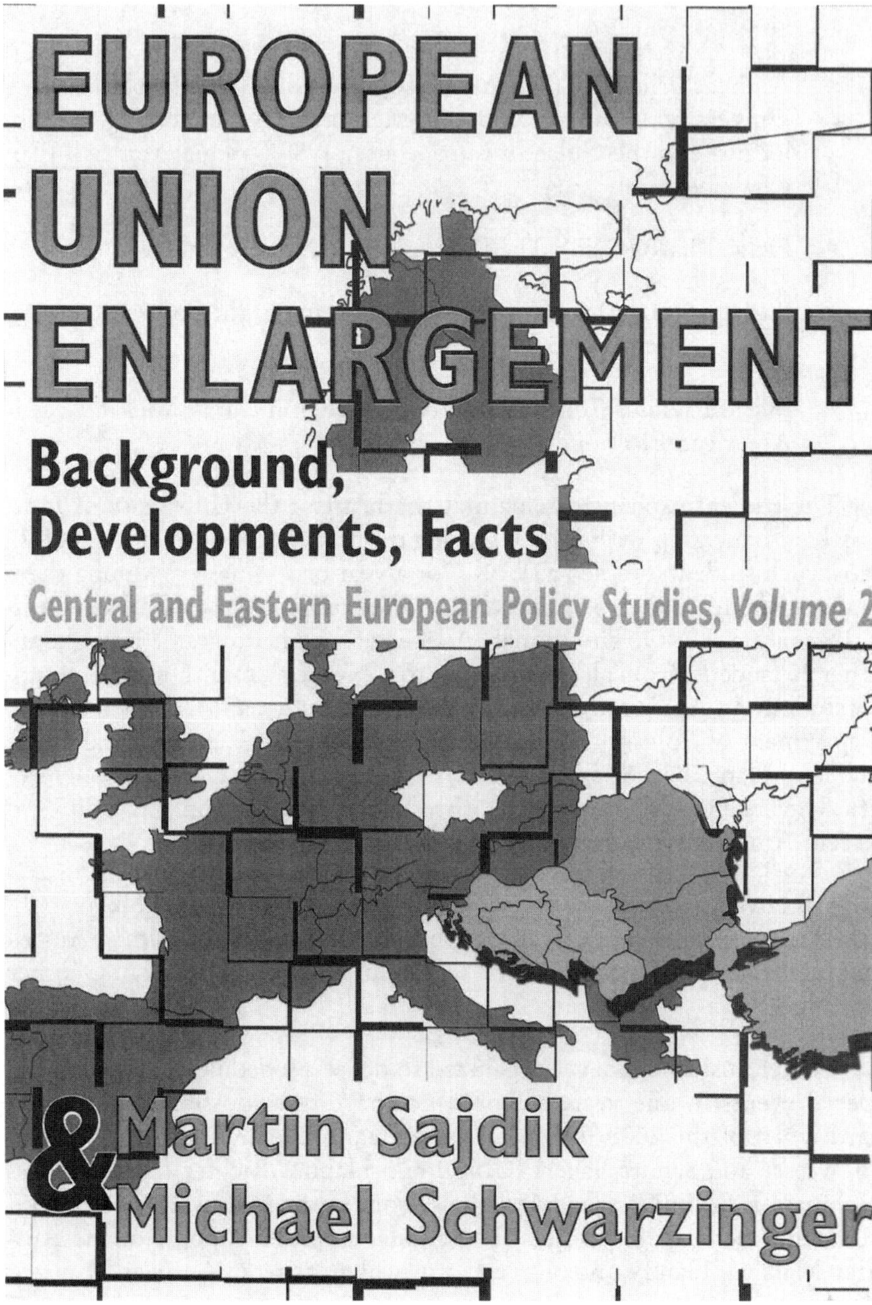

Elisheva Moatti

Center for Austrian Studies The Hebrew University of Jerusalem

The Center for Austrian Studies at the Hebrew University was established in May 2001 as a joint initiative of the Austrian Ministry of Foreign Affairs, the Austrian Ministry of Education, Science and Culture and the Friends of the Hebrew University in Austria.

Its goal is to promote Austrian studies and Austrian culture in Israel at the academic level, to establish and maintain contacts between Israeli and Austrian scholars and students by organizing symposia, lectures, conferences and workshops on Austrian issues. "Austrian studies" is understood in the broad sense of the word, rather than being narrowly defined as a concentration on the geographic area covered by the present Republic of Austria. The focus envisioned consists in interdisciplinary, broad Central European area studies with an Austrian core.

In May 2005, the Center for Austrian Studies was affiliated, together with the Helmut Kohl Institute for European Studies, the Marjorie Mayrock Center for Russian, Eurasian and East European Research, the Paul Desmarais Center for the Study of French Culture, and the Center for the Study of Italian Culture, into the European Forum at the Hebrew University, a framework that serves as epicenter for all the centers, chairs, funds and foundations active within the university dealing with research and teaching on issues related to Europe and the European Union. In October 2007, a new Center was added to the European Forum, the DAAD Center for German Studies. The European Forum is a trans- and multidisciplinary institution operating under three Faculties: Social Sciences, Humanities and Law.

The Center for Austrian and Central European Studies emphasizes the role of the Republic of Austria in the EU enlargement and integration processes and the role of the City of Vienna as a cultural center in European history. Attention is given to the Jewish population of the Habsburg Empire and its multifaceted impact on European culture, especially thanks to the Aaron Menczer Fund and the municipality of Vienna. The Center sponsors graduate courses about Austria, organizes international conferences and series of lectures, promotes research projects and publications of books, "Conference and Lecture Series" and "Working Papers". This broad area of interest and research gives the Center for Austrian Studies a greater visibility in research as well as in teaching, in Israel and abroad.

The activities of the center extend to teaching and research on the one hand, and to public relations in the broad sense and exchange programs with Austrian universities on the other hand. A special emphasize is put on personal encounters. This is achieved by international conferences, organized the Center for Austrian Studies, which provide an exceptional framework, especially for graduate students and young scientists, to make personal contacts with their colleagues from the respective other country. In addition, these conferences allow the Israeli public to participate, thereby broadening and deepening the knowledge about Austria in Israel.

The last year, the center organized a workshop and two international conferences with the support of the Austrian Ministry for European and International Affairs. The research workshop "The Holy Land and Europe" (April 29-May 1, 2008) was planned as part of a research project launched in 2007 entitled 'Sites of Memories and Memories of Sites.' The project explores the multi-layered interconnection and close interdependence existing between sites in the Holy Land and their images in Europe as instruments of memory.

The specific aim of the workshop was to establish a network of partners from Israel and Europe, to draw a plan for future cooperative research and to develop appropriate financing strategies. Apart from staff and graduate students of the Hebrew University, headed by Prof. Bianca Kühnel, scholars from four European countries were invited to participate: Prof. Milan Pelc, Institute of Art History, Zagreb; Prof. Marina Vicelja Matijašić, Department of Art History, University of Rijeka (Prof. Matijašić was unable to attend due to illness); Prof. Bruno Reudenbach, Department of Art History, Hamburg University; Maria Dorninger (University of Salzburg); Hanna Vorholt (British Academy) and Annette Hoffmann (Max Planck Kunsthistorisches Institut, Florence)

During the workshop's three days, the participants presented their particular fields of research and their relevance to the project theme. In addition, the participants had the chance to visit the holy sites in Jerusalem, guided by Dr. Lily Arad, Dr. Anastasia Keshman and Dr. Galit Noga-Banai - all from the Art History department at the Hebrew University, and active participants in the project.

After getting acquainted with the partners in the project and with the holy places, the participants were ready to plan future action. An outline of common interests and goals was agreed upon, which includes projects such as exchange programs for students and scholars, study trips to the sites included in the program participants' research, and participation in and organization of seminars, symposia and conferences. Two forms of immediate action were defined: an extension of the partners' circle and the identification of sources of financing. The participants seemed to be excited about the project, and enthusiastic about working together.

The international conference "Ottoman Roots of Contemporary Realities: The Middle East and the Balkans Compared", held at the Konrad Adenauer Conference Centre at Mishkenot Sha'ananim (January 18-20, 2009) explored the common history of the Balkans and the Middle East, spanning over four hundred years, which are characterized by Ottoman control and influence. The importance of the Ottoman legacy for shaping the contemporary Balkans is evident; as Balkan specialist Maria Todorova notes, "it seems that the conclusion that the Balkans are the Ottoman legacy is not an overstatement." The various Ottoman features of the contemporary Balkans can be traced in different cultural spheres: from languages to local cuisines; from contesting historical memories to architecture and social and administrative structures. However, clearly the most important reflection of Ottoman domination in the region is the development of Islam and its various local features. As for the Middle East, although the presence of Islam predated the arrival of the Ottomans, the long period of Ottoman rule shaped some of the major political, institutional, legal, and religious features of the modern Middle East.

Over the past two decades, numerous studies have explored the various cultural, religious, and political aspects of the Ottoman heritage in each of these two regions. There is still, however, a dearth of comparative studies that deal with the common features of the Ottoman presence while, in tandem, highlighting the unique cultural aspects. Probably because of the different languages needed to study the two regions, and the prevalence of the nation-state as the main research frame, study of the Balkans and study of the Middle East have developed separately from each other, with only few attempts to examine the two regions using a comparative approach. The proposed joint research project aims to fill this gap by comparing the various aspects of Ottoman heritage in the Middle East and the Balkans and investigating their relevance to contemporary Muslim and non-Muslim societies living in these former areas of the Ottoman state. The project will assemble historians, anthropologists, philologists, specialists of literary, art, and architecture studies from Austria, Germany, Israel, Turkey, and different Balkan states. We hope this will enable us to form a research community that will cooperate further in the future.

At the end of the academic year, the international conference "1989-2009: Twenty Years to the EUnification of Europe" (June 14-14, 2009) examined the 20 years after the breaking of barriers, which eventually brought about the unification of Eastern and Western Europe, this conference has indeed stressed that the EU is still facing many internal and external challenges. Some would call them failures, but I would prefer to call them by the more optimistic word - challenges. We need more time to be able to evaluate whether those are indeed failures the EU has not been able to address or perhaps they are prolonged "transition periods". I also think the EU is sometimes blamed for failures for which it does not have the means (be it financial, administrative or technical) or the prerogatives to address those.

As the German Chancellor, Angela Merkel, said in a speech on Europe to members of her conservative Christian Democrat party (CDU) in Berlin, the EU needs to "consolidate" before enlarging any further. "No one is well served in a Europe that can't keep up with integration and takes on too many new members too quickly."

A recent research found out that after 5 years to the fifth biggest enlargement, the EU's decision-making process was not harmed, at least not in numbers. The EU has adopted as many decisions in a composition of 27 MSs as it did when it was composed of 15 Western MSs. At least in quantity there is no decrease, as some pessimists doomed. This is an optimistic message.

But the next phase of the research should carefully examine the quality of those decisions. Has - or to what extent - the common denominator lowered? Has indeed the focus of attention shifted, and to where? It would be worth to map this.

But to conclude such a multi-disciplinary international conference that combines political science, policy studies, law, economy, sociology, history, and art disciplines by lecturers from all around the EU, Israel and the US and Canada, I would not like to concentrate only on such institutional aspects.

There are many challenges to pick from. I would like to address one failure in particular, which I prefer to call a challenge. It is one of the most daring challenges the EU have been addressing and will have to address for many years to come – the lack of European demos, not in the sense of a nationhood building, but even in the sense of civic identification with the EU's goals; some sense of proud in the EU achievements. This should be achieved at the level of the ordinary European citizen, and also at the level of some senior governmental ministers.

As we heard throughout the conference this is a troubling aspect that is not developed enough in the EU, and it is unclear to what extent the different main players in the integration process are interested to develop. Though what I am referring to is not an identity which would replace the national one, but would come in addition to it, as another layer of identity. In a Multi-level governance as the EU is multi-level identity is required.

Internally, the challenge of transformation in each of the ten new Central and Eastern European Countries to stable democratic rule has been accomplished. As Prof. Frank Schimmelfenning said, the EU was not the main agent of democratization in the critical phase of 1989-1991. This fulfilled the first condition of accession maturity in the level of democracy. Prof. Tibor Palankai introduced the next phase of EU "membership maturity" – the capacity to take advantage of EU economic policies.

Four of the new MSs joined the euro and completed a higher level of membership maturity, while 8 others will have to struggle to achieve that (even more today with the current economic crisis). 9 new MSs joined Schengen, achieving a higher level of personal integration of free movement, removing the last brick of harsh past communist reality of dividing borders between East and West Europe.

But Prof. Palankai actually finished his lecture with a not so optimistic note, that the EU integration's economic gains are hardly felt by the majority of people, which explains the growing negative attitudes and diminishing support for EU integration. Prof. Mitchell Orenstein demonstrated this point even further, and Prof. Shlomo Avineri also pointed to the losers of EUnification. This is another dare challenge the EU should face in the new MSs in order to raise support and identification with the EU and the integration process.

But this lack of EUropean identity is an EU wide phenomena, common in the veteran MSs as well.

As the lecture by Dr. Martin Koopman showed, political will, both from the French and the German side is also a necessary and perhaps even essential component not to the "natural" advancement of the integration process, but to great leap forwards as the Maastricht Treaty with EMU, CFSP and JHA gave base to.

As Prof. Jan Zielonka said, enlargements can be costly to the deepening of the integration process. The first enlargement of the EU to the UK is such an example. The opt-outs champions, the UK and Denmark (and also Ireland), belong to this enlargement. They joined the EC when it was not even a common market, and already their vision of it was of a mere free trade union.

In many respects, the EU is building a new "Tower of Bable", but manages to do it while speaking dozens of languages, not one or 6 as Dr. Jan Fidermuc suggested it should. This is actually a good example to the EU's motto "unity in diversity". To have only few official EU languages may bring a more efficient EU but not an inclusive one, and I think the cost of disenfranchisement should not be calculated only in economic figures, but in EU identity and loyalty terms as well.

One language will not bring a united EU sense of community, on the contrary. And anyway the "Brussels" language of acronyms is troubling enough in the distance it puts between the ordinary citizen and its understanding the Brussels' jargon.

As we heard from Ettore Deodato, SMS has become the "common language" of young Europeans. This is the generation the EU has difficulties conveying the advantages of the integration project to. Where the EU is quite clearly failing is the creation of a true "tower of Babel" kind of demos, the "we feeling" which raise loyalty, even if "only" a civic and not a cultural one.

We began the conference with asking how can more unity live side by side with preserving diversity? Cultural diversity should be maintained and even encouraged. It is one of the "natural advantages" the EU has to offer, but unity is needed in many other fields.

Prof. Vlasta Kunova stressed that the unification of Europe by EU law is a positive continuation of the first European unification by Roman Law. But this is a peaceful legal Eunification process on paper which is not enough.

As Prof. Jan Zielonka said, the EU integration project is not about conquering new territories. It is about conquering new public policies spheres. In some respects enlargement helps to widen the integration process to more policy fields. Lior Herman showed us how the new MSs can "breathe life" and be leading players in new common market trade in services, as healthcare, promoting a de-jure integration policy field into a de-facto increasing/growing reality. Once more it demonstrates the functional aspect of integration - that in spite the lack of political will integration can advance and have a spill-over effect. In that respect widening can bring more horizontal deepening, but it did not build common civic identity and feelings of solidarity. On the contrary.

Much more time will be needed to "conquer" the identity of the EU citizens. The integration process represents a backlash at nationhood that was to blame for causing WWII. Despite that, for the past 5 or 6 decades nations and national myths have remained at the very centre of identity building, as Evgeny Finkel's presentation demonstrated. The European integration process, which brought peace and prosperity to citizens of west and then east Europe, has not yet been able to foster their loyalty. This is the missing element in the integration process.

There is no doubt that protection of the environment can become a major part of a person's identity and self-definition, as Mark Volovici and Michal Goren claimed. The question is how much 'European' can such identity be? The question arises which myth or ideology can the EU adopt for building its civic identity and feelings of loyalty?

Democratization is also not unique to the EU, and as Prof. Frank Schimmelfenning convincingly established, the EU is not even the central agent of democratization it was thought to be in the CEECs who entered the EU.

If we can indeed learn something from the confusing moto of "unity in diversity" it is that the EU common identity should not, or even cannot be founded on a cultural base, but instead needs to find a civic common meeting-ground.

In that respect the collapse of the USSR was indeed a loss of the unifying "other" the EU had, but it may be replaced with any mass murder, either by the Nazi regime or by Russia, which can serve (and is serving) as EUrope's "other". The problem is it is too far away from the minds and hearts of the young generation of Kantian Europe.

Educational exchange programs in the EU are one tool to encourage an "ever closer union". Erasmus and Tempus are a very good agent of "kosher slaughter" of stereotypes of neighboring EU countries, but it is a much weaker vehicle of promoting some pro-EU integration attitudes among its participants. The young generation in the EU that is leaving in the Kantian world the founding fathers of the EU carefully built, are more skeptical of the integration process. This is not such a positive prospect for future European integration.

The EU has been a great success story, as Prof. Paul Landvai said, but it's a myth that is not told enough to the children of EUrope. Such unifying vision is missing, instead the thrilling processes that begun in 1989 on the Eastern parts of Europe brought back fault lines to the EU, as Amb. Dr. Emil Brix has stressed. I'm sorry the final message of this conference is less optimistic than what I would have liked it to be.

The intensive courses too, given by guest lecturers from Austria, further the personal encounters and offer an excellent opportunity for scientists from Israel and Austria to initiate common research projects.

Dr. Jasmine Dum-Tragut from the Department of Linguistics at the University of Salzburg offered an intensive course on "Armenia Today – Viewed from a Linguistic, Cultural, Ethnic, and Religious Viewpoint".

Over the past seventeen years of independence Armenia has changed its political, demographic, and economic face. These changes, which were explained in an introduction to the course, have also affected other aspects of life in Armenia:

- The Armenian language – for example, by a rigorous de-Russification in many domains, a strengthening of Armenian in school teaching and mass media, a noticeable convergence with Iranian Armenian vernacular and even with Western Armenian, and a purification and at the same time modernization of the lexicon.

- The Armenian culture – for example, by a "clash" of traditional Armenian culture with Western lifestyle and mentality; a loss of traditions on the one hand, and a rather chauvinistic return to traditional values and attitudes on the other.

- The Armenian Apostolic Church – for example, by reform movements in the clergy, an opening of the church to the common people, an uphill struggle with sects in all regions of Armenia, with a re-Christianization of the Armenian people after seventy years of atheistic communist life.

- The minorities of Armenia – for example, by demographic changes through mass immigration of Azeris during the Karabakh conflict; the change of the public laws concerning minority language teaching and even exercise of freedom of religion, at least with respect to Christian minorities; and the changed status of minorities such as the Christian Assyrians or the Armenian Jews.

The course provided insight into the linguistic, cultural, and religious problems of present-day Armenia.

Photographic or film (documentation) material, reports from mass media, and above all the personal experience of the lecturer gained during numerous campaigns of fieldwork in Armenia, contributed to this intensive course.

The contacts established between Dr. Dum-Tragut and the faculty of the Hebrew University of Jerusalem during her stay at the Center for Austrian Studies led to a joint research project. In the framework of this research project, Dr. Dum-Tragut will visit the center again in November 2009.

Prof. Dr. Anne Betten, Paris-Lodron-Universität Salzburg gave a course on "Language and Migration".

Migration as a worldwide phenomenon in present days gets increasing attention from different disciplines, including linguistics where "language and migration" and "contact linguistics" are well established fields of sociolinguistic research. Changes of culture and especially language -- or rather the varying forms of bi- and multilingualism (including pidgins) -- resulting from migration have a great influence on the construction and definition of the (new) identities in the new surroundings of individuals and entire ethnic groups. This process can be regarded either as personal loss or enrichment; the second generation often develops „mixed" identities of their own, which are linguistically expressed by deliberate code-mixing (‚hybrid' languages) in their peer-groups.

The seminar introduces positions and methods of actual sociolinguistic research on these topics, including empirical field work with examples from pilot-studies in Europe and in Israel. The students are expected to contribute with own recordings of narrative interviews (‚language-biographies') which are typical for the multicultural roots of the Israeli society.

The different exchange programs are another crucial element in the Center's program. The Austrian Ministry of Science and Research is sending a lector the Center for Austrian Studies who teaches courses on Austrian subjects, not covered by the faculty of the Hebrew University of Jerusalem, and participates in different research projects.

Dr. Heidemarie Uhl from the Austrian Academy of Science offered a seminar on "Memory in Europe since 1945: Transformations of Memory, Representations of Remembrance".

The European landscape of memory of 1933-1945 has changed significantly within the last two decades. In the words of Tony Judt, we can speak of the decline of the post-war myths which had constituted much of collective memory in the European nations since 1945, and of a new culture of memory which focuses on the Holocaust. This transformation process can be described in a series of national variations, but also bears a set of transnational resemblances: In post-war Europe, all countries – except the German Federal Republic – declared themselves as victims of Nazi suppression and terror. The national cultures of memory were mostly dedicated to the victims of political (and national) persecution and to the heroes of resistance. The remembrance of the Jewish victims of the Nazi regime, on the other hand, was on the margins of public and official memory, conducted mostly by the Jewish communities. Today European memory of this historical period shows a different picture: Holocaust remembrance days, national monuments for the murdered Jewish citizens in European capitals – like Berlin and Vienna - and cities, new Memorial Museums and exhibitions in memorial sites are indicators for the relevance of the Holocaust in European memory. Furthermore, on a global scale the awareness for the Holocaust as the historical point of reference for the universal values of civilization – human rights, civil rights – has grown. "The Holocaust (Shoah) fundamentally challenged the foundations of civilization" is the introductory statement of the Declaration of the Stockholm International Forum on the Holocaust (1998). This was the founding act for the ITF Task Force for International Cooperation on Holocaust Education, Remembrance, and Research, an international board which has meanwhile been joined by 26 countries. In Europe, the transformation described above is the result of numerous conflictual discussions and struggles for memory. And Holocaust memory is still confronted with counter memories which claim an alternative victim status – especially in the post communist countries where the victims of communism in many cases are in the center of official and public memory. The course will concentrate on the process of transformation which has shaped the new European culture of remembrance since the 1980s. This change of paradigm affects the academic historical master narratives as well as public discourse, official forms and rituals of remembrance and material representations of memory in public space like monuments. Our starting point will be an introduction to theoretical and methodological approaches to the concepts of "collective" (Maurice Halbwachs) and cultural memory (a term coined by German historian Jan Assmann). Case studies which cover different forms of "cultural memory" (Jan Assmann) – from documentary films to monuments, museums and memorial sites - will provide insight into similarities and differences of European Holocaust memory: Are there differences between "perpetrators societies" - Germany and Austria – and occupied countries? Has the "negative memory" (Volkhard Knigge, director of Buchenwald memorial), dealing with the guilt of societies, become the role model for European memory? And can we observe a new cultural border between "western" and post communist countries; is this particular form of memory now reproducing the borders of the cold war? In this new culture of remembrance, art plays a crucial role. The challenge to represent the unrepresentable, to give Holocaust remembrance an aesthetic representation, has produced some of the most discussed works of art on an international level. Holocaust remembrance in the arts will also be a focal point of this course. These topics will be framed by a question which serves as a leitmotif of the analytical approach to a European memory which is focused on the Holocaust: what are the political, social, cultural and epistemological backgrounds for the transformations in European/global memory which can be observed since last decades of the 20th century?

The support of research projects is another vital aspect of the activities of the Center for Austrian Studies. A group research project "Consuming Memory and Constructing Identities in Modern Europe", headed by Prof. Bianca Kühnel, Prof. Vered Vinitzky-Saroussi, Dr. Irit Dekel, is conducted in cooperation with Dr. Heidemarie Uhl from the Austrian Academy of Sciences.

Since the establishment of the group in December 2008, the group's members have met routinely every two weeks to discuss its research prospective. During the meetings the participants have introduced their own research and offered their methodological and theoretical perspectives. The group has elaborated widely on issues such as encounters with memory artifacts in everyday activities, on intentional vs. un-intentional memory artifacts and on the relations between memory and movement. The main aim that the group posed to itself is to prepare a research proposal for an extensive and up-to-date research in the field of collective memory studies. Currently the participants work on an application to external foundations, to be submitted during the next academic year.

For some of the meetings, the group has invited collective memory experts for consultation and for further input. Among them: Prof. Dr. Heidemarie Uhl from the Austrian Academy of Sciences and the prominent psychologists Prof. Dr. Barry Schwartz. With Prof. Uhl, the group has established wider relations and it currently plans to collaborate with a parallel group that she directs in Vienna. In October 11-14, 2009, the research group will meet in Vienna with Austrian colleagues and conduct a research workshop at the Austrian Academy of Science.

On top of this, the group has become a fertile ground for some of the participants' individual research, some of which became material for presentations in conferences.

Individual research projects, supported by the Center for Austrian Studies are:

- Riety van Luit, PhD student at the Mandel Institute of Jewish Studies,
- Legatio ad Imperatorum: The Austrian State Facing Three Shtadlanim and Organized Communal Resistance against the German Jewish Schools and the Abolishment of the Galician Kahal (1790-1793),
- Sara Yanovsky, PhD student at the European Forum,
- Taking Responsibility and Action – Jewish Education in Vienna 1918-1938,
- Erzsebet Mislovics, PhD student at the Department for the History of the Jewish People and Contemporary Jewry,
- Two Centuries of a Hungarian Jewish Family: A Prosopographic Study of the Munks,
- Anat Varon, PhD student at the European Forum,
- Jewish Intellectuals in Vienna between the Two World Wars,
- Dr. Louise Hecht, Post-doctoral student at the Department of Jewish History,
- From Vienna to Jerusalem: The Journalist, Poet, and Politician Ludwig August Frankl von Hochwart (1810-1894),
- Sharon Gordon, PhD student at the Department of History,
- Carl Menger and Viennese Modernism.

Thanks to the generous help of the Austrian Ministry of Science and Research, the Austrian Ministry for European and International Affairs, the Austrian National Bank, several Austrian universities, and the Friends of the Hebrew University in Austria, the Center for Austrian Studies can send each year 49 students to intensive language courses to different Austrian universities, for periods up to two months.

For more information on the Center for Austrian Studies at the European Forum at the Hebrew University, please visit our website: www.cas.huji.ac.il.

Dieter A. Binder

Central European Studies Andrássy Gyula University Budapest

The Dean's Report

Number of students:

1st year: 14

2nd year: 7

Basic Information:

New course enrolments for the year 2008/09: 20, 1 Erasmus Student from Germany, 2 Erasmus Students from Turkey (Ata Türk University) accepted.

Postgraduate School (PhD history): 1. Viva voce accepted in May (Dr. Marta Fazekas); 3 students in the Postgraduate School under the supervision of the Faculty

Accreditation: Since accreditation had been pronounced open with March 2008 as the time limit, adjustments had to be made to the suggestion of Acquin in September 2007 and these were re-submitted: Acquin responded by accrediting the current Master Programme until 2012 in December 2007.

Accreditation submitted for the Master Programme "Central European History".

Faculty publications: The thesis by Dr. Fühner (Jewish Policy under Maximilian I.) has been published so far; now in preparation at the press is work by Mrs Kovacs (The Peace Movement in Central Europe in the 20th Century), Mrs Cserni (Feminism in Eastern Europe), and Mrs Götz (Conflict Management in the Example of Kosovo).

The Faculty has organised the following symposia in cooperation with the Kulturforum Österreich (Director Dr. Elke Atzler):

"Vom Ankommen und Weggehen – Arrivals and Departures" (the final contributions to this symposium on migration held in autumn 2007 – the "Migrations Symposion" is currently being called, publication in the Faculty series will follow in autumn 2008.)

"Die Politik des Fussballs – The Politics of Football" (publication of this symposium held in spring 2008 will be in a special edition of the journal Drei Raben, Budapest, 2008.)

Research projects:

- Sport and Myths (Associate Professor Dr. Georg Kastner): The results are now being prepared for the press with publication in 2009.
- Postdoctoral project Kastner: Hungary 1956 and the UN
- Eurolab (an international conference in cooperation with Dr. Elke Atzler, Kulturforum, to be held in September 2008 with speakers from France, Lithuania, Romania, Bulgaria, Italy, the UK and Austria.) financing: EU – sponsorship funds

Monographs by members of the Faculty: 3

- István M. Féher: Schelling – Humboldt. The Outlook for Hermeneutics. Frankfurt/Main: Lang 2007, 268 pages.
- Andreas Oplatka: Magyar határnyitás 1989. szeptember 11. nulla óra. Budapest: Helikon 2008, 344 pages.
- Dieter A. Binder: Skrivna Druzba. Zgodovim in simbolika prostozidajev. Celjska: Mohorjewa 2008, 313 pages.

Publishing activities for essay anthologies etc. 1

Arnold Suppan, Marija Wakounig, Georg Kastner (eds.): Osteuropäische Geschichte in Wien – East European History in Vienna. 100 Years of Research and Teaching at the University. Innsbruck - Vienna: Studienverlag 2007, 450 pages.

CEEPUS application for 2008/09 approved: AT-0305-01-0809 – Reason, Myth, Religion. The Task for Philosophy and Theology Today

(Participants: University of Vienna, University of Vienna, Faculty of Philosophy and Educational Sciences, University of Vienna, Faculty of Roman Catholic Theology, Institute for Christian Philosophy, University of Zagreb, Institute of Philosophy, Pázmány Péter Catholic University, Faculty of Humanities, Eötvös Loránd University, Institute for Philosophy, Andrássy Gyula University, Budapest, Faculty of Central European Studies (Professor Dr. István Féher), Warsaw University, Institute of Philosophy, University of Wroclaw, Institute of Philosophy, Adam Mickiewicz' University of Poznan, Instytut Filozofii UAM Zaklad Etyki, The University of Bucharest, Faculty of Philosophy, University of Ljubljana, Faculty of Theology, Unversity of Prishtina)

Excursions:

Faculty Excursion: This year's Faculty Excursion took place in the first week of May 2008 with 25 participants (the route: Budapest, Transylvania, Sekler-Land, Moldavian monasteries, Cernowitz with a trip to the Kamieniec Podolski region – Bessarabia). Student participation was financed by an Austrian grant and a small personal contribution of the students themselves plus a donation from the Visegrad Fund.

Swiss excursion June 2008: Professor Oplatka and Associate Professor Oplatka shared the responsibility for arranging this trip on the part of the Faculty.

Open prize contests: An open academic prize context was held by the Faculty for the academic year 2007/08 open to students of all faculties. This was won by Rahel Herrmannova (Slovakia, Visegrad scholarship holder), she will present and discuss her prize winning essay within the scope of a panel submitted by Associate Professor Kastner for participation at the annual congress of the German Studies Association in Minneapolis, USA in October. Her participation at this international congress will be made possible by financing from the BMfWuF Vienna that made the travel grant available for the prize essay.

a. A current cooperation with the Eötvös Loránd University Budapest for the purpose of establishing the department of "Cultural Studies".

As a result of the time intensive work required for the programme of studies area within the Hungarian framework specifications we established that the personnel resources of the Faculty/the University were inadequate for the project.

Faculty staff members:

- Faculty Professors: 6 (3 Hungarian, 1 Swiss, 2 Austria) of these 3 AT, financed by Hungary, a Swiss private foundation and by Austria.
- Associated Professors: 3 (1 Hungarian, 1 Swiss, 1 Austria) of these 3 AT, financed by Hungary, a Swiss private foundation and by Austria.
- Assistants: 2 (1 Hungarian, 1 German), financed by Austria.

Lisa A. Peschel
(University of Minnesota)

Survivor Testimony on the Cultural Life of the Terezín Ghetto, 1945-47

Finding a Place in Postwar Czechoslovakia

The testimony of Holocaust survivors is a thoroughly hybrid genre: it is always both a constative utterance that conveys information about the survivors' experience, and a performative utterance that attempts to create effects in the present. The performative most frequently associated with the survivors is one described by psychiatrist Dori Laub in which, while narrating their own objectification in the camps, they restore their destroyed subjectivity by becoming speaking subjects.[1] In this article, however, I examine a different type of performative: testimony by survivors whose subjectivity was not destroyed by their wartime experiences, but who found it threatened in the postwar period as various barriers blocked their re-integration into the society where they felt they belonged. In postwar Czechoslovakia, Czech-Jewish survivors created narratives about the Terezín ghetto with which, I argue, they carried out the discursive work of attempting to reintegrate themselves into the social body. To do so they drew on a particular topic that, considering the widespread and intense interest in Czech-language culture after the war, could have engendered feelings of solidarity from their fellow Czechs: testimony about their participation in the cultural life of the ghetto.

Two book-length works show this performative at work in narratives written by survivors over sixty years of age, whose formative experiences included World War I and the establishment of Czechoslovakia as an independent state. The pressures this generation faced included legal problems with citizenship and restitution of property, and discursive pressures to affiliate to new postwar ideals of "Czechness" (various manifestations of Czech nationalism) and "leftness," (a range of progressive political stances)—ideals that represented a radical narrowing of the range of identifica-

1 See, for example, his essays Bearing Witness, or the Vicissitudes of Listening and An Event without a Witness: Truth, Testimony and Survival in: Shoshana Felman and Dori Laub, M.D., Testimony: Crises of Witnessing in Literature, Psychoanalysis, and History, New York 1992, 57-74 and 75-92.

tions that had been acceptable in the prewar multinational Czechslovak state.[2]

Their works emerged within the framework of a popular postwar genre, the so-called "prison literature" [vězenská literatura] published by Czechoslovak survivors of various Nazi prisons and concentration camps. In this field of literature, which according to journalist Vacláv Běhounek had grown, by fall 1947, to over one hundred works, survivors of Terezín had published five book-length accounts: a number which he states, in comparison with the amount of literature written by survivors of other individual prisons and concentration camps, left the ghetto relatively well documented.[3]

These examples of prison literature are by no means the only extant narratives about the ghetto from this period. Survivors wrote accounts that appeared in various postwar periodicals, and additional narratives, not intended to circulate publicly, were created and collected as part of the "Documentation Action" organized by the Jewish Religious Community.[4] The book-length works examined here, however, represent a particular venue in which they pursued their goal of reintegration: a literary form in which, unlike magazine or newspaper articles, the survivors maintained a fair degree of control over the style and content of the narrative. The pressures established by the expectations of the readers they hoped to reach, however, played a significant role in shaping those narratives.

In other words, these authors did not become a counter-public, creating works intended only for their own group and assumed to be unacceptable or of no interest to a wider public; their narratives appear to be crafted with the larger non-Jewish Czech public in mind. For example, both authors conformed to the style of prison literature established quickly after the war, which required authors to adopt a relatively objective first-person voice that narrated the events they had experienced in a journalistic

2 In September 1946, the Ministry of the Interior issued an order that clarified the position of "people of Jewish origin" regarding their citizenship. Until this point, Czechoslovak Jews who had selected „German“ or „Jewish“ rather than „Czech“ or „Slovak“ nationality in the 1930 census had encountered various difficulties in confirming their citizenship status, which in the worst-case scenario could have resulted in deportation.

3 Vacláv Běhounek, Naše vězenská literatura, in: Kytice, 2/9, Prague 1947, 385-96. The works about Terezín that Běhounek mentioned were Psychology of Life in the Terezín Concentration Camp by Professor Emil Utitz, Ghetto of our Days by Mirko Tůma, Three Years in Terezín by Anna Auředníčková, Terezín Torso by Irma Semecká, and A Jewish Tragedy by Rabbi Dr. Richard Feder.

4 The Jewish Religious Community announced this effort in the first postwar issue of their newsletter. See „Dokumentární Akce ŽNO v Praze“ in: Věstník židovské obce náboženské v Praze, Prag, 01.09.1945, 8.

[reportážní] style. Regarding the content, each dealt to a greater or lesser degree with their status (wartime and postwar) as Jews, but both engaged with the same objects of feeling—that is, topics associated with a strong emotional response—that had been established as valuable in postwar periodicals: Czechness/leftness as national/political ideals, wartime suffering, and Czech culture, especially theater.

How did these survivors craft their narratives, and especially their descriptions of the cultural life of the ghetto, to pursue their goal of reintegration?

Anna Auředníčková (born 1873, age 70 at deportation, died 1957) moved mostly in German-speaking circles but was fluent in both languages. She was a well-known translator of Czech literature into German, popularizing numerous Czech authors, including Karel Čapek, for German-language readers. Auředníčková, a widow and a baptized Catholic whose late husband was not Jewish, was deported alone to Terezín on August 3, 1942. Her daughter, whom she mentions frequently in her narrative, was apparently not classified as Jewish by the Nazi racial laws.

Her book, Three Years in Terezín, was one of the earliest accounts of the ghetto. It was published (in Czech) in 1945, as the first book in the series Current Affairs and Documents [Aktuality a Dokumenty] by publisher Alois Hynek, with illustrations by Terezín survivor Leo Haas.[5]

Auředníčková, writing in the immediate postwar period when the fate of Czechoslovak Jews of German nationality was most uncertain, belonged to the group of survivors who most urgently needed to demonstrate their affiliation to Czechness: those with a known relationship to German-language culture. Facing the radical devaluation of her prewar cultural affiliations and perhaps manifestations of anti-Semitism as well, she attempted to construct a viable postwar subject position by emphasizing her affiliation with Czech-language culture in the ghetto—a performance with the potential to shape the public of her readers into a group that would accept her as a fellow Czech.

The text on the book jacket, as a narrative strategically intended to appeal to the potential reader, framed her narrative in terms common in postwar discourse:

5 Haas and several other artists were arrested in the Terezín „affair of the painters“ when their drawings depicting true conditions in the ghetto were discovered. They were transferred to the Terezín Small Fortress in July 1944 and deported on October 3, 1944 to Auschwitz.

"Auředníčková, famous as promoter of Czech literature abroad, has translated more than seventy Czech writers. [...] She relates without exaggeration [...] the Terezín hell: suffering, hunger, fear of transports, of death, horror of abuse and torture and hope in a happy ending and a better future. The story is remarkable for the underground movement, in which the author carried on with the promotional work for Czech culture, as she was employed her whole life."[6]

The reader expecting descriptions of suffering and horror might have been surprised by her chapters titled "Sport in Terezín," "People Who Interested Me," and "Small Joys in Terezín." Those accustomed to political prisoners' accounts may have found it difficult to classify an extensive and apparently openly conducted public lecture series as an "underground movement." Her own narrative diverged from the received narrative that readers had been led to expect by the book jacket text, reshaping two objects of feeling: the ghetto itself, and the forms that resistance, i.e. an "underground movement," could take. Her intense performance of affiliation with Czech culture, however, corresponded with the claims of the book jacket text and with narrative forms already familiar from the discourse in contemporary periodicals.

Her performance of belonging began with the first sentence of the book, when she immediately renounced any aspirations to status based on the specific features of her suffering. She identified Terezín as "mild ... in comparison with so many other places where there was no hope of return, where only death meant freedom from torture."[7] She placed herself as one of a group of fellow Czech sufferers just a few lines later, when she described the moment her transport order was delivered: "Just its [the doorbell's] ringing meant fear—fear was the keyword of that terrible period. The Germans wanted to strike terror in all whom they oppressed. I was afraid, like millions of others during those years."[8] Thus she emphasized not the specificity of Jewish deportations but the fear shared by all Czechs during the Nazi occupation, creating a "we" by positioning herself in solidarity with non-Jewish as well as Jewish readers.

Indeed, the collective narrative Auředníčková created was clearly about the "we" of "we Czechs" rather than "we Jews." Her rhetorical performance of belonging to Czechness saturated the narrative from its smallest details (for example, frequent use of personal pronouns and possessives such as "we Czechs" and "our excellent artists") to its broadest themes (the Czech

6 Anna Auředníčková, Tři léta v Terezíne, Prague 1945, book jacket.
7 Ibid., 5.
8 Ibid.

cultural life of the ghetto and her dedication to Czechoslovak presidents Masaryk and Beneš). Throughout the book she occasionally made gestures toward leftness, writing, for example, that when a fellow prisoner suggested she should be classified as a "prominent," which would have given her access to better housing and increased rations, she answered that she would not accept such a special position: "I was always socially oriented, and in Terezín I wanted only to serve the poor and try to distract the sick and blind."[9] In spite of additional attempts to affiliate herself with leftist characteristics, her unmistakably bourgeois prewar past, a past she described in great detail in her narrative, provided her with limited room to manueuver in terms of refashioning herself as a socialist. However, there was one valid non-socialist subject position still remaining to postwar Czechs. Although she never overtly stated a political affiliation, she did provide enough information for readers to assume she may have been associated with the People's [Catholic] Party [Československá strana lidová]. As she revealed several pages into her narrative, she was a baptized and practicing Catholic who participated actively in the religious life of Christians in the ghetto.[10]

By establishing herself as a Catholic, she not only removed another potential barrier to "otherness" between herself and non-Jewish Czechoslovaks, most of whom were at least nominally members of the Catholic church, but provided a reason why, unlike the other authors of Terezín testimony, she expressed no opinion about Jewish identity or about anti-Semitism.[11] With the paradoxical narrative situation she created—the events she described, as her readers well knew, were determined by her Nazi-imposed status as a Jew, yet she herself never mentioned any relationship to this imposed identity—she performed an option for her readers: that they could take interest in her story and circulate it further as a part of the shared narrative of the Czechs' wartime past, while regarding her Jewishness-by-race as irrelevant.

Auředníčková made no attempt to conform to the "model ghetto" narrative that identified Terezín mainly as an instrument of Nazi propaganda—a narrative that appeared frequently in the pages of the Communist Party newspaper Rudé právo, [Red Truth], the postwar daily with the largest circulation. She devoted only a few mentions and two pages to a description of the Nazis' most notorious use of the ghetto as propaganda: the June 1944 visit of a commission from the International Red Cross.[12] In her narrative, the cultural life of the ghetto was identified not with the objectification of

9 Ibid., 33.
10 Ibid., 35.
11 In the 1930 census, 73.5 percent of Czechoslovak citizens had registered as Catholics.
12 Auředníčková, Tři léta, 31-32.

the Jews through "command performances" for international visitors but as the key to a tremendously rewarding restoration of her own subjectivity in the ghetto.

Auředníčková arrived during a period when the ghetto's resources were strained to the breaking point: in the summer and fall of 1942, thousands of elderly Jews from Germany and Austria were deported to Terezín, the mortality rate skyrocketed, and the Jewish leadership focused intently on saving the youth. Auředníčková described the first weeks of hunger and loneliness in Terezín as an experience that brought her to the brink of suicide. Trying to find a way to occupy herself with useful work, she volunteered to darn stockings for the nurses in a Terezín clinic. One day a nurse she admired asked her about her life before the war, and that conversation led to a casual invitation to speak to a group of Terezín nurses about her literary work. She was soon speaking to groups of adults and young people on a regular basis. Records preserved in the Terezín Memorial support her claim that "in all I entertained listeners 348 times."[13]

Auředníčková wrote of her affiliation with Czech culture not only as a lecturer but as an audience member. She did not write about Terezín theater specifically, explaining that, although she would have liked to attend the operas Bartered Bride [Prodaná nevěsta] and The Kiss [Hubička], both works of deep national significance for Czechs, she was afraid that, because her father had been on the board of the Czech National Theater, "my strong memories would be too overwhelming; in Prague during the whole time of German terror I was not allowed to go to the theater."[14] She was, however, aware of works being staged in the ghetto, and implied their resistant nature by mentioning that the Nazis tolerated performances of plays by Karel Čapek, author of two of the best-known anti-fascist plays of the late 1930s, because "they did not know the meaning" of his works.[15]

13 Ibid., 35. A list of her lectures is published in Elena Makarova, Sergei Makarov, and Victor Kuperman, University over the Abyss, Jerusalem [2]2004, 432-33.

14 Ibid., 40. As she specified, her father was a member of the Staročeské Družstvo [Old Czech Society] that administered the Czech National Theater from its founding until 1900. In an episode that demonstrates the long-established connection between Czech theater and politics, the Old Czech Society, associated with the Old Czech Party, was replaced in 1900 due to the rising political fortunes of another party, the Národní strana svobodomyslná [National Party of Freethinkers], whose members were known as the Mladočeši [Young Czechs], by a new administrative body under their control, the Společnost Národního divadla [Society of the National theater].

15 Ibid., 39. Čapek's plays The White Plague (1937) and The Mother (1938) were both staged at the National Theater in Prague.

Some of her most vivid descriptions were devoted to the experience of hearing Czech music in the ghetto. While acknowledging that the Czech cultural life was not the only national cultural life in the ghetto, she performed her own affiliation clearly:

"I heard beautiful concerts, evenings of chamber music, which were truly a pleasure. Those good musicians were for the greater part my [Czech] countrymen. It was a holiday when, for an over-full hall, they played Dvořák, Smetana; works of composers of other nationalities were however played as well. But when some Dvořák quartet or Smetana's "From My Life" sounded, we, the Czechs, were ecstatic.[16] If Ančerl conducted Czech compositions, the audience was glad; it was not only a pleasure for our hearing but our spirits quivered at the sound, full of longing and love for the beloved homeland."[17]

As a rhetorical performance of affiliation to Czechness, this passage includes several tactical features: she placed herself in the audience among "we, the Czechs," and invited readers to share in the pleasure that the titles of these works, well-known objects of feeling, evoked, as well as national pride in Karel Ančerl, a conductor for Czechoslovak Radio and in the beloved prewar Liberated Theater of Jiří Voskovec and Jan Werich. The emotional intensity of this paragraph—pleasure to the point of ecstasy—invited the readers' spirits to vibrate in sympathy with the prisoners', to share in a moment of communitas inspired by their common love for "the beloved homeland."

Her passionately performed devotion to Czech culture, however, did not come without a personal cost: in her narrative, she was silent about her equally passionate devotion to German-language culture. Although she did mention attending German-language lectures by speakers such as Rabbi Dr. Leo Baeck and Professor Emil Utitz, tailoring her descriptions to demonstrate how their talks would appeal specifically to Czechs, she did not mention her participation in other aspects of the ghetto's German-language cultural life. Other sources suggest just how much that involvement meant to her. For example, her fellow prisoner Philipp Manes, an active organizer of German-language culture in the ghetto and Auředníčková's contemporary, described in his diary a successful staged reading of Goethe's Faust, part II, in July of 1944.[18] Reporting that the audience was struck by "beauty

---

16 Z mého života is the name of Smetana's String Quartet No. 1 in E minor.

17 Auředníčková, Tři léta, 36.

18 Manes was born in 1875 and deported to the ghetto with his wife Gertrud from Berlin on July 23, 1942. Both perished after their deportation from Terezín to Auschwitz on October 28, 1944 (the last of the fall 1944 wave of transports).

of the language" and "deeply gripping final scenes," he reproduced, with great pride, the text of a letter from a spectator, Auředníčková herself:

"The Faust evening was, for me and the whole circle of my friends, a great pleasure. [...] The wonderful words of Goethe are always an experience [...] even the unbearable heat could not dampen my enthusiasm. I thank you ... that you devote yourself to such performances, that with such humble means you bring the listeners into another world."[19]

In his own estimation, "When one of the most important women in the Czech lands, who has lived in [the realm of] art for fifty years, speaks in this way, I am allowed to be a little bit proud of my work."[20] Thus while Manes confirmed the important prewar subject position that Auředníčková described in her own narrative, he simultaneously provided a counter-narrative to her own. In her postwar narrative, she apparently did not feel it suitable to reveal that she had a circle of German-speaking friends in the ghetto with whom she also shared feelings of solidarity and pleasure and that her attachment to German-language art, which inspired similar emotional reactions of transport "into another world," was as strong and authentic as her connection to Czech-language culture. Instead, she represented the German language only as a useful conduit for her work of transmitting Czech culture to non-Czech speakers. In her book, although she mentioned meeting Manes and trying to obtain a ticket to Faust, she did not describe her attendance, much less her reaction. Rather she focused on the fact that he shared a surname with renowned Czech painter Josef Manes (1820-1871) and that he immediately invited her to lecture to his audience about Czech literature, an invitation she accepted right away since "it was already my intention."[21]

Compared with the emotional intensity of her descriptions of the cultural life, Auředníčková narrated the liberation itself practically as a non-event. There is no climatic, victorious moment in her text; her testimony transitions directly from rumors regarding Nazi plans to kill the prisoners at the very end of the war, to the SS officers fleeing the ghetto, to the doctors and nurses, including Russians, who arrived to care for the sick prisoners and thus prevented typhus from spreading further.[22] This, however, is by no means the end of her narrative. Almost fifty additional pages follow in which she described other features of life in the ghetto. The chapter titled

19 Philipp Manes, Als ob's ein Leben wär: Tatsachenbericht Theresienstadt 1942-1944, Berlin 2005, 346.

20 Ibid.

21 Auředníčková, Tři léta, 43.

22 Ibid., 57.

"People Who Interested Me" fits to some extent into the genre "testimonials to the fallen", a narrative form which was richly represented in postwar public discourse, but others, such as "Sport in Terezín" and "Small Joys in Terezín", appear to be frankly fond recollections of life in the ghetto itself.

Most striking is her penultimate chapter, titled "What My Listeners Most Wanted to Hear", which represents a remarkable re-staging of her own performance activity in the ghetto. Here she related various stories she had told in Terezín—stories she had apparently selected not only for their popularity in the ghetto, but based on what might also interest postwar listeners: stories of President Masaryk, whose memory remained an important symbol across the political spectrum, and her encounters with other prewar personalities, especially those from theater.[23] She devoted two pages to vivid personal anecdotes about actors of the Czech National Theater, and in somewhat less lively prose, perhaps as a gesture to postwar cultural interests, described speaking to her Terezín listeners about the "the crown of all actorly art", Russian theater.[24]

On the final page of her narrative she joined her own experience of the end of the war with a narrative meaningful to most non-Jewish Czechs: the Prague Uprising. A young Czech, a friend of her daughter's who brought her packages after the SS fled the ghetto, was killed during the fighting in the last days of the war. She devoted the last three sentences of her narrative to him: "He defended Prague on the barricades with weapons in his hand [...] and he fell. One of the heroes of our revolution. I gratefully remember him [...] who heroically fought for our freedom."[25] On one hand these lines, with their phrases "our Prague", "our revolution" and "our freedom" again performed affiliation with other Czechs. On the other, the question of naming this event had important political overtones, and her choice of "our revolution," the name preferred by the Communists, ended her narrative on an appropriately leftist note.

Auředníčková, in spite of the book jacket's mention of "a better future," made no mention at all of her life after the war. Considering the pain of postwar return that many survivors encountered, this is not completely surprising. The tone of one review, however, suggests that the lingering of her narrative in Terezín itself may reflect a certain attachment to those last

23 As Bradley Abrams points out, due to the first president's extraordinary status, „all political factions sought to claim Masaryk as their own, whether [...] their world views corresponded with his [...] or not." Bradley Abrams, The struggle for the soul of the nation : Czech culture and the rise of communism. Lanham, Md. 2004, 119.

24 Auředníčková, Tři léta, 106.

25 Ibid., 115.

months when her prewar past was still considered socially relevant; that is, why her penultimate chapter may function as a performance of nostalgia not only for the prewar period in which she enjoy contact with these luminaries, but for her months in Terezín, when she shared these memories with eager listeners.

Although her book was well received by some reviewers, it was harshly criticized by others.[26] For example, a journalist for Hlas osvobozených [Voice of the Liberated], the newspaper of the Union of Liberated Political Prisoners (which included Jewish members), published the following review, titled simply "Three Years in Terezín," on September 13, 1946, apparently some months after Auředníčková's book appeared in print.[27] In it he accused her of not providing enough information to orient "the uninformed reader" and argued that she "trivializes tragic events by dismissing them with just a few lines, or she does not mention them all." Displaying some apparent class hostility as well, he commented sarcastically, "We expected even more moving chapters, for example, about the shining social relations of fifty years ago or those page-long life histories of meaningless people!" Ultimately, he described the problem as one of responsibility and accountability:

"But those who come before the public with their experiences from such a tragic time must be aware that all things printed create a document of the period, and that they are answerable for the truth of their information and the impression that they convey to the reader. And because this author's concept distorts the picture of such great suffering, we must object against such a way of writing.... Today we know that Terezín was a waiting room to the gas chambers. Germans there played out for the world a farce about humanitarian treatment of the Jews and made of it a huge stage, upon which the prisoners played their miserable role, so that they could later be murdered."[28]

The author clearly had an expected narrative in mind, but instead of the story of "great suffering" and the prisoners' "miserable role," he had read the story of a seventy-year-old German-speaking bourgeois woman's successful fight to re-establish her subjectivity and obtain a subject position of some status in an environment where many of her contemporaries died within weeks after arriving. What elicited this degree of censure? Considering the high status of narratives of martyrdom in postwar society, did he

26 Běhounek mentioned about twelve authors, including Auředníčková, who wrote "the best book about their imprisonment". Běhounek, Literatura, 388.

27 Ay, „Tři léta v Terezíně", in: Hlas osvobozených, Prague, 13.09.1946, 2.

28 Ibid.

fear that the suffering of the former political prisoners as a group, suffering that served as a valuable form of political capital, might be brought into doubt through Aured's narrative? that the image the Union promoted, of the brave, anti-fascist political prisoners as martyrs in the camps, might be undermined by her testimony, which basically described the narrative recreation of her bourgeois prewar world within the space of the ghetto? Regardless of the reasons for his censure, her recent role as a lecturer in the ghetto, and even potential hopes for a similarly respected position as a storyteller in postwar Czechoslovakia, were sarcastically dismissed. For the public of Hlas, Auředníčková had clearly violated not only their expectations but their demands regarding how Terezín should be represented in the postwar public sphere; therefore, she should be silent.

Emil Utitz (born 1883 in Prague, age 59 at deportation, died 1956) was apparently bilingual but conducted most of his professional activities in German. Everything he wrote through 1938, including his last pre-war work, Writings of the Prague Philosophical Circle [Schriften des Prager Philosophischen Cercles], was published in that language. Utitz was a professor of psychology and aesthetics before the war.[29] He taught in Germany at the universities in Rostock and Halle but was forced to leave his position after Hitler came to power in 1933; he returned to Prague and taught at the German university there. He was deported to Terezín on July 30, 1942, where he became head of the ghetto library and supervised a branch of the lecture series.

His book, Psychology of Life in the Terezín Concentration Camp, was published in Czech—his first work in that language—by the Worker's Press (Prague), which was linked with the Social Democratic Party, in 1947 and in German by the Continental Edition Verlag (Vienna) in 1948. No translator is indicated in the Czech edition. Utitz divided his brief account—only 61 pages—of the psychology of Terezín prisoners into fifteen short chapters according to specific phenomena in the ghetto, such as "Rumors", "Work Morale" and "The Building of Groups." Illustrations were by Heilbrunn, Otto Ungar and Leo Haas.[30]

Utitz's own stated goal was to create a scholarly account of Terezín as a social and psychological phenomenon, but his work remains completely

29 See, for example, his works The Artist [Der Künstler] (1925), History of Aesthetics [Geschichte der Aesthetik] (1932), and Person and Culture [Mensch und Kultur] (1933).

30 No further information is available on Heilbrunn. There were 22 adult male prisoners by that name in Terezín. Ungar, like Haas, was arrested and deported to Auschwitz in the Terezín „affair of the painters." He was liberated at Buchenwald but died in a clinic at Blankenheim on July 25, 1945.

accessible to the lay reader. Unlike Auředníčková, Utitz did not employ his first sentence to place himself in relation to the past shared with Czech non-Jews, but to place his own book in relation to the already-existing literature:

"About concentration camps in general and about Terezín in particular much has been written. I dare to increase the number of these publications [...] for the reason that I believe, thanks to my profession as psychologist and philosopher, that I am able to communicate something scientifically interesting."[31]

Utitz's narrative, although he, like Auředníčková, was a Czechoslovak Jew known for his affiliation with German-language culture, conveyed no sense of urgency about performing affiliation to Czech-language culture. Perhaps in keeping with his stated aim of objectivity he did not focus exclusively on Czech-specific performances of identity, instead describing the full range of national and political orientations represented in the ghetto. He also made no attempt to compare the Terezín prisoners' suffering (or his own personal suffering, or any generalized notion of Jewish suffering) with the suffering of other postwar Czech groups. Nevertheless, within the framework of his objectivity, he managed to make his own affiliations, as well as his opinions regarding the postwar situation of the Czechoslovak Jews, vividly clear.

The narrative of Terezín as the "model ghetto" was obviously known to him, and throughout his own narrative he countered the portrayal of the prisoners and their institutions as mere pawns of Nazi propaganda. In a three-page introductory chapter, "The Environment," he immediately established the difference between Nazi intent and prisoners' experience: "For us it was important to create truly functioning institutions; the Germans envisioned the theatrical magic of outward appearance, to influence foreign visitors."[32] Providing an example drawn from his own work as head of the ghetto library and organizer of public lectures, he described how the Nazis exploited the lectures as an "advertisement" to be displayed for visitors, yet constantly threw obstacles in the prisoners' path by threatening them with prohibitions, which they avoided by giving false titles to talks on potentially provacative topics.[33] Thus he revealed the fundamen-

31 Emil Utitz. Psychologie života v Terezínském koncentračním táboře. Prague, 1947, 7.

32 Utitz, Psychologie, 7-10, 9.

33 Ibid., 9. Ruth Bondy points out that a lecture originally titled „On the Building of Palestine" was renamed „Jacob at the Well" in the version of the lecture schedule submitted to the Nazi leadership. Ruth Bondy, "Elder of the Jews:" Jacob Edelstein of Theresientstadt. Trans. Evelyn Abel, New York 1989, 326.

tally doubled nature of many of the institutions in the ghetto: while they ultimately did serve propaganda functions for the Nazis, they also served important functions for the prisoners themselves.

In this particular example he also established the lecture series as a site of resistance, where prisoners actively deceived the Nazis in order to protect the integrity of their own public sphere as a space of agency where they were able to achieve their own goals. However, Utitz's description of a site often mentioned in the "model ghetto" narrative, the ghetto coffee house, suggested a more subtle form of resistance. While conceding that it was established as part of the Nazi program of deception—an "insane idea" of the German leadership, coming at a time when there was a severe housing shortage—he described the important role it began to play for the elderly and other prisoners:

"It offered the opportunity to creep out of their overcrowded housing, to chat, to hear music and page through old yellowed illustrated magazines. Many welcomed it as something that did them good, to be able to sit on a proper chair. Some evenings the youth recovered from the effort of their work with cheerful cabaret performances. What was thought up as bold farce could somehow be turned to the benefit of all."[34]

Regardless of Nazi intention, the Jews in effect took ownership of these and other spaces that were forced upon them as part of the propaganda effort. Within such spaces they were abel to continue, to some extent, in their normal practices from prewar life, even within the abnormal environment of the ghetto.

After brief chapters on "Changes in Character," "Rumors," and "Escape into the Past," Utitz engaged again with the cultural life of the ghetto in a two-page chapter entitled "Images of the Future."[35] Here he argued that people's hopes for life after the ghetto were intimately tied with expectations that they would return to their pasts—that is, to a world just like the one they had left behind. He described performance as a way in which they simultaneously accessed the lost, fervently missed world of the past and projected themselves into their envisioned postwar lives. In the process of

34 Utitz, Psychologie, 26.

35 Ibid., 23-24. In "Changes in Character" (11-16) Utitz described, for example, the useful numbness that helped prisoners bear their own powerlessness (15). "Rumors" (17-19) in Terezín, with their usual content regarding the rapidly approaching end of the war, constituted their own form of world-making. "Escape into the Past" (20-22) described an intensely performative notion in which people exchanged narratives of their prewar lives with their fellow prisoners, telling stories which sometimes matched and sometimes far exceeded the conditions of their pre-Terezín existence.

noting Austrian, Czech and Zionist Jews' attachment to their own cultural forms, his personal affiliation became clear as well:

"If the sentimental song "In the Prater the Trees Bloom Again" was sung, almost all the Viennese men cried, and even more the Viennese women. Memory and hope [of returning] merged, painful memory and tiny, quivering hope."[36]

The glorious concert performance of Bartered Bride was, for the numerous Czechoslovaks, a joyful act of worship. When the sparkling melodies sounded, full of life, the bright tears ran down their cheeks. Prague, so close yet so unreachably far, home [domov], the firm tie of belonging. In taking it in, inhaling this strong, healthy, stirring music, the confidence of return; the vision of the Moldau with the old stone bridge and rows of statues of the saints, and high above it the cathedral and castle. There should wave, and will wave again, our own flag [naše vlajka]. And for the Zionists, the singing of their Hebrew songs and their characteristic circle dances were a holy prophesy, that one day they will be able to kiss the longed-for soil of Palestine; that they will reach, after a thousand years of wandering, their goal in the land of their fathers.[37]

In spite of Utitz's overall goal of objectivity, his description of Bartered Bride dominated the paragraph. Although he began by speaking of the Czechoslovaks in the third person, not immediately claiming the affective memories as his own, he described the powerful nostalgia for Prague, and even the vivid visual imagery evoked by the strains of Smetana's music, and ultimately placed himself within the "we" of "we Czechoslovaks" with his phrase, "our own flag." In the end, his stirring description was just as emotional as Auředníčková's expression of "longing and love for the beloved homeland," and had the potential to work in the same way for a non-Jewish Czech reader: to create a sense of solidarity through shared attachment to Prague as object of feeling, a shared urge to protect the city against those who would claim it with a foreign flag.

In the next chapter, entitled "Work Morale," Utitz again engaged with the double nature of ghetto institutions, arguing that, "behind the Potemkin facades that the German leadership energetically conjured up lay hidden [...] much honest work."[38] He counted among the "laborers" in the ghetto those whom the postwar Communists called "cultural workers":

36 The Prater is the most famous park in Vienna, mentioned in numerous songs, plays, and literary works.

37 Utitz, Psychologie, 23.

38 Ibid., 25-33, 26.

"It was no pleasure for small groups of artists to go into the houses of the sick and elderly, into crowded, poorly ventilated, stinking rooms, constantly subjected to the risk of infection."[39]

In this portrayal of art as a social service, as a good to be distributed to the needy, Utitz presented a complex reply to the postwar debate regarding the role of culture: should artists serve the party as the Communists demanded by engaging politically with postwar reality, or should art remain a realm of free expression? Utitz in effect turned their formulation inside out. Artists engaged with the reality of the old people's misery by providing them with something they desperately needed: an escape into nostalgia and fantasy. In a later chapter, describing artists who became conceited about their positions in the ghetto and did not want to participate in activities such as performing for the sick, he wrote, "The danger developed that from this service to the public would emerge a kind of l'art pour l'artismus."[40] Thus he pointed out, in effect, a "third way": a role for art, neither as direct engagement with reality nor as complete freedom from it, but as a socially conscious practice that would serve "each according to his needs," acknowleging that engagement with reality was not in every audience's best interests. In fact, considering the Jewish leadership's focus on youth, which translated into lower rations and poorer housing for the elderly, such performances represented one of the few manifestations of solidarity and compassion their fellow prisoners could express without jeopardizing the goal of helping the youth survive the war.

After brief chapters on "Dishonesty", "Courage" and "Erotics and Love," he engaged with the topic of "Group formation".[41] In a politically evenhanded way he expressed admiration for both the Communists and the Zionists for their exemplary sense of solidarity with other prisoners, whom they regarded respectively as fellow victims of fascism or fellow Jews.[42] He recognized these and other forms of group identity, such as religious practice, that were based on self-affiliation.[43] However, he refused to describe the Jews an essentialized group, finding the the ghetto itself the best evidence against a definition of Jewishness based on so-called racial features:

39 Ibid., 28.

40 Ibid., 55.

41 Ibid., 34-36, 37-42, 43-46, 47-51.

42 Ibid., 47. This comparison was not as inflammatory as it might have been in prewar years. During the few postwar years when Stalin hoped that Israel might become a socialist state, Communists stopped condemning Zionists as "Jewish bourgeois nationalists."

43 Ibid., 53.

"I often ask myself if the uninitiated would recognize all present as Jews—according to the Nuremberg laws. The differences were so marked [...] we should not underestimate the enormous role played by tradition, experience, upbringing, environment and culture. The race-fanatics have forgotten this."[44]

It is not surprising that, in an era when the Jews' fate had been determined by externally opposed racial laws, Utitz would take advantage of every chance to counter such classifications. However, he did not resist the urge to identify one Jewish characteristic as something that has gone "right into the blood": a specifically Jewish relationship to suffering, and corresponding ability to bear hardship and disappointment.[45]

Utitz devoted an entire short chapter to "Cultural Efforts".[46] In it he distinguished between the Czech- and Hebrew-language vs. the German-language performances:

"The latter relied upon professional actors with routine habits, which led to ham acting and bad provincial style, for it was not possible simply to bring the environment of our large scenes into those conditions. [...] The Czech and Hebrew theater was led by young directors who worked with enthusiastic amateurs. That was the right path, by which excellent things were achieved."[47]

This type of comparison appears frequently in the testimony of younger survivors; in fact, criticism of the German-language "bourgeois" theater by young Czech-Jewish leftists was sometimes so biting that it appeared to be motivated by their own desires to place themselves in a specifically Czech and leftist subject position rather than by any sincere engagement with the German-speaking artists' work.[48] Utitz's evaluation, however, appears more as a practice associated with his professional identity as professor of aesthetics, especially since he even acknowledged, in a way that younger survivors rarely did, that the German-speaking actors might be from "our large scenes": that they might be German-speaking Czechoslovak Jews instead of "Germans". In addition, although he did claim that the Czech Jews

44 Ibid., 47.

45 Ibid., 41.

46 Ibid., 52-55.

47 Ibid., 54.

48 Notes for such a critique written by prisoner Pepík Taussig in the ghetto itself recall the tone of Ay's critique of Auředníčková and exhibit similar expressions of national and class antagonism. See Josef Taussig, O terezínských kabaretech, in: Miroslav Kárný, Jaroslova Milotová, Eva Lorencová, (Eds.), Terezínské studie a dokumenty 2001, Prague 2001, 310–346.

were the leaders in the areas of music, theater and cabaret, he did not credit this position to innate superiority or greater talent. Instead he listed a host of factors that contributed to the more vigorous Czech cultural scene, such as the retaining of talent due to a lower level of prewar emigration and a greater feeling of comfort and ownership: Terezín, for the Czech Jews, was "the last remnant of home," where they stood "in a common front with their compatriots against the invaders and oppressors".[49] Thus he encouraged Czech readers' pride and emphasized the Jews' feelings of solidarity with them, without encouraging nationalist bigotry or appearing to engage in it himself.

Utitz also wrote of the temporary relief and even the sense of liberty the prisoners experienced when engaged in cultural activities and praised the artists who provided it: "What a mood, what jokes, irony, humor poured out in the cabarets! For so many hours of relief and cheer, thousands thank those improvising artists."[50] Expanding upon the affective experience, he described a sense of pleasure that was difficult to place within any particular political framework, but it was clear that he considered pleasure an end, a good, in itself, and the artists' role in providing it as a socially valued contribution.

Utitz, like Auředníčková, did not describe his postwar experience. However, three short final chapters were followed by a two-page conclusion, in which he engaged briefly but directly with the question of postwar Jewish fate.[51] As he described, shortly after the liberation, the owner of the building in Terezín where Utitz was living appeared and struck up a conversation:

"He was avidly interested in our fate, because he was in no way an anti-Semite; during the war he had supported Jews as much as he could. He asked about the size of the losses and the number of those who remained alive. My answer did not suit him, and very surprised he wanted an explanation: "I always considered the Germans an exceedingly thorough nation; why have they not made a completely clean slate of it?"[52]

Utitz concluded with the hope that the "question of such a laughably small minority" would soon be solved, since "beatings and blows inflicted by enemies cause far less pain than injuries from people with whom we

49 Utitz, Psychologie, 48-49.

50 Ibid., 65, 55.

51 Ibid., 67-68. The chapters are "Vanity and Delusions of Grandeur," (56-59), "Provisional Existence" (60-62), and "Spiritual contagion," in which he described certain Jewish leaders' adoption of the ways of their oppressors (63-66).

52 Ibid., 68.

fought as brothers, in times of need, on the same front".[53] Thus, with this final episode, he subtly challenged his fellow Czechs to consider whether they had not also, even inadvertently, expressed the kind of sentiments that caused the survivors so much pain and made their attempts at postwar reintegration so difficult.

In a review published on June 10, 1947 in Právo lidu [Truth of the People], the daily newspaper of the Social Democractic party (which also controlled the press that published Utitz's book), the writer praised Utitz for his "scientific specificity and objectivity" and for writing the first book in the Czech language "that looks at this familiar subject from a higher perspective than the narrowly personal."[54] Although he named the topics of several of the chapters he did not engage with the contents in depth, calling that a "specialist affair for psychologist and sociologists." However, he again pointed out the value of providing the reader with "some truth, generally applicable, not only about the individual, but something which would finally have greater use for humanity than simple descriptions of various horrors."[55]

Thus, although Utitz received neither exceptionally enthusiastic response nor censure regarding his theses on the prisoners' behavior in this review, his postwar performance of scholarship was lauded; the review at the very least suggested that he would recover his prewar subject position as a respected researcher.

* * *

The testimony of these older survivors, while both pursued the goal of reintegration into the postwar Czechoslovak social body, revealed differing patterns of affiliation and renunciation in response to the pressures on their narratives. Both, to some degree, renounced or at least underplayed their attachment to German-language culture in order to perform their affiliation with specifically Czech culture, and made at least symbolic gestures toward affiliation with characteristics associated with leftness. Regarding Jewish identity or related suffering, Auředníčková, as a baptized Catholic, apparently felt no need to remark upon it. Utitz, while writing about various ways that Jews performed a range of political, religious and national group identities and simultaneously resisting any externally imposed definitions of Jewish identity, did make explicit although restrained statements on the postwar status of the Jews. Apparently aware that focus

53 Ibid.
54 „Psychologie života v terezínském ghettu." In: Právo lidu, Prague, 10.06.1947, n.P.
55 Ibid.

on their own suffering would not serve their goal of reintegration, both attempted to generate solidarity by presenting their persecution in a way that included them within the Czech community of sufferers.

Neither supported the narrative sanctioned by the Communists—that of the ghetto as a "huge stage, upon which the prisoners played their miserable role"—devoting little attention to the visit of the International Red Cross comission and focusing instead on the many ways in which they exercised agency in the ghetto. Why not affiliate with this narrative that may have gained them some status, since it had clearly been given the stamp of approval by the most powerful postwar political party? Based on their narratives, I believe the memories of their successful fight for agency in the ghetto simply meant too much to them for them to renounce it voluntarily, especially in a postwar period when their subjectivity was threatened by the loss of family, friends, language, social position, political and professional status and perhaps even citizenship. Affiliating with a narrative that argued for their complete objectification would have required denial of both their past and present subjectivity—and not just their own but that of their fellows who had perished and could not longer speak for themselves.

In their narratives, the cultural life of the ghetto represented one of the most active fields of agency; for example, it played a prominent role in Utitz's depictions of various types of self-selected group identification. However, on a personal level, both performed an intensely emotional relationship with specifically Czech culture. For this generation, the affective performance in their narratives—the performance of a choice, in the ghetto as a space of limited agency, to affiliate themselves actively and proudly, as performers and spectators, with Czech culture—may have been the single most productive postwar tactic they could have employed. Considering the diversity of their linguistic and political positions, it would have been difficult for them to perform convincingly the dominant forms of Czechness and leftness required in the postwar period. Therefore, rather than appealing to commonality—to a shared set of postwar ideals or goals—they appealed to groupness: a sense of affective linking through the shared emotional experience of pleasure generated by common objects of feeling.

Pleasure funtions as a rhetorical strategy by opening boundaries, by creating a "we" of shared enjoyment, by inviting the reader to affiliate with the same object of feeling, creating a sense of groupness and belonging.[56] However, there is an excess in these narratives that is difficult to explain in terms of tactics alone. Both survivors mentioned pleasure even when it was not "necessary"—that is, in contexts where it was not directly linked with

56 Sara Ahmed, The Cultural Politics of Emotion, New York 2004, 164.

Czech culture. For example, Auředníčková wrote at one point, simply, "there were more and more listeners and the success made me happy."[57] Utitz, in addition to exclaiming about the pleasure generated by the humor of the cabarets, called the entire cultural life "a surprisingly cheering picture."[58]

As Běhounek pointed out in his survey of postwar prison literature, one of the functions of testimony was its ability to confirm for prisoners that they had really experienced what they remembered experiencing: by reading the testimony of others, they were able to verify memories that their postwar listeners may have found difficult to believe.[59] In postwar Prague, perhaps confronted by suspicious reactions to a narrative that seemed not too monstrous but, especially in relation to others' accounts, too positive to be true, the survivors may have begun to doubt the reality of events that they had regarded as a remarkable achievement and source of pride. Perhaps these superfluous mentions of pleasure were intended, not for non-Jewish Czechs, but for each other, for their fellow survivors, as a reminder that, ironically, one of the last places where they had not been required to renounce valuable aspects of their personal linguistic, cultural and political affiliations was in the ghetto.

57 Auředníčková, Tři léta, 25.
58 Utitz, Psychologie, 65.
59 Běhounek, Literatura, 393.

David Schriffl
(University of Vienna)

Austrian-Slovak Relations from 1945 to 1968. Cooperative Neighbours or impassable Border?

Introduction

Why to analyze Austrian-Slovak relations when a sovereign Slovakian state did not exist between 1945 and 1968? Slovakia merely had two periods in modern history existing as a sovereign state, namely between 1939 and 1945 and since 1993. But does that mean it didn't exist as an entity or factor of influence for Austrian politics, economics, and culture?[1] Modern historiography tends to analyze mostly the relations between sovereign states In most cases Czechoslovakia and Prague are brought into focus when looking at the history of Austria's northern neighbouring state.[2] By doing so, we risk to neglect important developments and facts in terms of Austria's foreign relations. The major goal of my dissertation-project is to close this gap.

Files related to this object can be found both in Slovakian archives and in the Austrian State Archive. In the Austrian State Archive the documents of the Austrian general consulate in Bratislava/Pressburg and the files of the Federal Chancellory/Department for Foreign affairs and later the Austrian Ministry of Foreign Affairs are the main source for my efforts in writing a history of the relations in the period between the end of the Second World War and the Prague spring in 1968. Since Slovak subjects were part of the documents referring to Czechoslovakia as a whole it is necessary to search a large number of files in order to locate those being significant for the subject. On the (Czecho-) Slovak side the competence on foreign affairs was concentrated in Prague. Therefore most documents concerning cross-border activities should be held in the central archives. Certainly many files

1 For the influences of Viennese Nationalsocialist authorities on the formation of the Slovak State in 1939 cf. David Schriffl, Die Rolle Wiens im Prozess der Staatswerdung der Slowakei 1938/39. Europäische Hochschulschriften, Reihe 3: Geschichte und ihre Hilfswissenschaften 1001, Frankfurt am Main/Berlin/Bern/Bruxelles/New York/Oxford/Wien 2004.

2 Cf. for example Paul Ullmann, Eine schwierige Nachbarschaft. Die Geschichte der diplomatischen Beziehungen zwischen Österreich und der Tschechoslowakei von 1945 - 1968. This is a lucid recently published work focussing on the diplomatic ties between Austria and Czechoslovakia.

related to Austria can be found there, some of them even covering Slovak affairs. However, it is impossible to get a clear and complete picture of the contacts between Austria and Slovakia only by doing so. For this purpose – aside from the mentioned Austrian holdings – the files of Slovak authorities are more adequate. Although a large number of Slovak files have to be taken into consideration in order to extract the significant ones, I was able to locate interesting documents shedding light on the Austrian-Slovak relations.

The space available is too short to depict all aspects and developments of the Austrian-Slovak relations. Therefore I will deliver some insights of my research in this article.

The establishment of Austrian diplomatic representation in Slovakia

Czechoslovakia was – except for the Great Four – the first country to establish diplomatic relations with Austria. Already in June 1945, the former Austrian legate in Prague Ferdinand Marek, who had remained in throughout the war in former Czechoslovakia, was accepted as Austria's diplomatic representative by the Czechoslovak authorities on a provisional basis.

An Austrian consulate in Bratislava had already existed before 1938 and there was no doubt at the Ballhausplatz that an Austrian office was to be re-established after 1945. The situation of the German-speaking minority in the country and the problem in reaching a distinction between them and Austrian citizens was one of the reasons leading to the installation of this liaison office. The distance between Prague and Bratislava was – especially considering the difficult traffic conditions shortly after the war – too far, thus making it impossible for the Prague office to take care of Austrian citizens residing in Slovakia. An Austrian office in Slovakia was opened two months later with the aim of supporting persons in possession of the Austrian citizenship. Therefore a representative was needed. Already as early as 2 July 1945 the chemist Paul Meyersberg reported for the Austrian government from Slovakia. Paul Meyersberg wanted to support the Viennese government as much as he could, but refused to hold an official position.[3] One of the first aims was to find a person acceptable for the Slovak authorities. The first candidate was Sisinio Pretis-Cagnodo. He was an estate owner in the village of Bodok near Topoľčany. Furthermore he was an anti-fascist combatant during the Slovak National Uprising in 1944 and had even been awarded a Partisan decoration in September 1945. Therefore Vi-

3 Meyersberg an StKa-AA, 1945 Juli 2, Austrian State Archive (hereafter ÖStA), AdR, StKa-AA, Gr.Zl. 641-pol/45, Zl. 396-pol/45.

enna regarded him better than acceptable to the Slovak authorities. But his land was confiscated by a Soviet officer and Pretis-Cagnodo was imprisoned for a short time and left Slovakia eventually.[4] This illustrates the situation of Austrian interests and its colony in Slovakia very well: within a short period only, Pretis-Cagnodo turned from being a candidate for the position of the Austrian diplomatic representative in Bratislava into a refugee.

A new candidate had to be found. The general suspicion of Slovak authorities against the German-speaking minority as a whole and hence against Austrians residing in the country was their alleged or true fascist attitude and collaboration with the German enemy. Thus a representative was needed whose distance to the National Socialist ideology was undoubted. Because of the short distance and the close personal ties between Vienna and Bratislava, the sought-after person was located through Viennese contacts. The plenipotentiary in Prague had already declared that he would be unable to find such a person due to the distance between the Czechoslovak capital and Bratislava. Ing. Friedrich Lenhardt, a businessman who had resided in Bratislava already before 1938, finally seemed to be acceptable for the Slovak authorities. In the eyes of the Federal Chancellory – Department of Foreign Affairs this was also due to his Jewish forebears who were mentioned by Lenhardt himself as an argument for the non-existence of contacts to national-socialist authorities.[5] His private house in Bratislava served as the first Austrian representation in Slovakia as early as September 1945. Although he wasn't a professional diplomat, his task was mainly to intervene for Austrians who had become victims of displacement and dispossession, and often had been placed in one of the camps erected for the unwanted German-speaking minority. Ironically enough, one of the victims of dispossession and flight reporting to Vienna in a list assembled by Lenhardt was the already mentioned Pretis-Cagnodo.[6]

Lenhardts position as a representative of the Austrian plenipotentiary in Prague was named "Beauftragter für die Slowakei"/delegate for Slovakia; a denomination Slovak politicians stipulated because of its similarity to the Slovak denomination of the ministers in the local government and because the normally used word "Vertreter" wouldn't have had enough political impact.[7] That indicates how Slovak politicians tried to use the ties to their

4 Aktenvermerk „pro domo", Rechtliche Stellung und Behandlung der österr. Staatsangehörigen i.d. Slowakei (Baron) Pretis – Linhardt, 1945 September 8, ÖStA, AdR, StKa-AA, Gr.Zl. 641-pol/45, Zl. 1005-pol/45.

5 Aktenvermerk, 1945 November 8 and 9, ÖStA, AdR, StKa-AA, Gr.Zl. 641-pol/45, Zl. 1334-pol/45.

6 Auszug Nr. 1 Lenhardt an Rechtsdienst der StKa-AA, 1945 September 16, ÖStA, AdR, StKa-AA, Gr.Zl. 641-pol/45, Zl. 1889-J/45.

7 Vollgruber an StKa-AA, 1945 October 12, ÖStA, AdR, StKa-AA, Gr.Zl. 641-pol/45, Zl. 1483-pol/45.

western neighbour in order to strengthen the aspired autonomous position of Slovakia in the Czechoslovak republic.

In 1947, he was replaced by the professional diplomat Karl Nedwed since on 22 October 1947 the status of the office was elevated to a general consulate, thus unfolding a wide variety of activities in Slovakia. Beside the classic consular activities, the promotion of economic and cultural exchange was an important field of activity – as was the collection of insight information in a country soon to be separated from the west by the newly erected iron curtain.

I was lucky to find a very interesting example for the – at least in this case – active way of collecting sensible information through employees of the general consulate.

Karl Rajnoch, an Austrian citizen, was born and brought up in Slovakia. He maintained close ties to the Catholic Church and was an employee of the Austrian representation since 1945. In 1950, he used his contacts to initiate an underground survey conducted with roughly 200 people in now communist Slovakia about the population's attitude towards the regime and the question whether Slovakia should be autonomous or independent. The outcome indicated – not surprisingly – a strong rejection of the communist regime. But it also showed that even in the "working class" only 55% at that time approved of the ruling system. And all parts of the population – except the "working class" – strongly demanded a sovereign Slovak state. But two thirds of the working-class members were reluctant to give a concrete answer to this question.[8] The 1950s have been a time of intense ideological conflict with the west and a totalitarian system of surveillance targeting Czechoslovakias own citizens. Political and religious opposition was persecuted just as fractions within the ruling communist party in many ways. Employees of foreign representations often were accused of espionage against the People´s democracy. The Bishop Michal Buzalka was one of the closest contacts of Karl Rajnoch. In a trial against three Slovak Bishops - one of them was Buzalka - Rajnoch was also accused of espionage. He and another employee of the Austrian consulate were arrested in November 1950, brought to trial and sentenced to prison. During a conversation with the interim head of the Czechoslovak Ministry of Foreign Affairs Zděnek Fierlinger, the Austrian legate in Prague Meinrad

8 Basic data extracted from: General Consul Nedwed to Austrian MFA Gruber (Verschluss), 1950 March 22, ÖStA, AdR, BMAA, II-pol, Tschechoslowakei 3, GZ. 120.655-pol/50, Z. 122.364-pol/50. More detailed data will be published in my article: Austria and Czechoslovakia, under Specific Consideration of Austrian-Slovak Relations 1945-1989. in: Arnold Suppan - Wolfgang Mueller (Eds.), Austria and Eastern Europe, 1955–1989, Europa Orientalis No. 7, and will also be part of my thesis.

Falser protested because the arrest had been carried out „(...) with brutal violence, without warrant and without identification of the officials (...)" which would „(...) definitely not be beneficial to the neighbourly relations to Austria. (...)"[9] The protest had no effect and Rajnoch had to serve his sentence in the prison of Leopoldov.

The expulsion of the German-speaking minority and Austrian nationhood

The main conflict between the neighbouring countries was and remained up until 1968 and beyond the expulsion of the German-speaking minority including Austrian citizens from Czechoslovakia and their expropriation. The problem later even sharpened when German-speaking refugees were naturalized in Austria under a law that was passed in 1954[10]. Shortly after the war the Czechoslovak authorities displaced and dispossessed - according to the so called "Beneš-decrees" - German-speaking persons without drawing a distinction relating to the citizenship of the affected person. The Austrian government and representatives tried to improve the situation by reaching the consent of the Czechoslovak authorities that Austrian citizens would be spared from displacement and dispossession. Although the conflict focused on the Czech lands rather than in Slovakia (due to the higher number of refugees, historical prejudices, and disputes dating back to the years before 1918), it was easier to get the wanted covenant from Prague than from Bratislava. While the ministry of the interior in Prague under Vaclav Nosek already assured protection for Austrian citizens as early as in June 1945, the Slovak authorities didn't want to comply.

In November 1945, the Slovak "Council of Representatives" which acted as the local government for Slovakia decided to formally adopt Noseks directive but also decided to confidentially "(...) give instructions to all ministries to proceed with all Austrian citizens the same way as with citizens of German nationality".[11]

After the Austrian side constantly had intervened for better treatment of its citizens, the Slovak National Council as the legislating institution in Slovakia declared in April 1946: "The Slovak National Council doesn't feel authorized to take up a position whether an Austrian nation exists or not. (...) The Slovak National Council does not intend as a consequence of the implementation of this nationality to change its attitude to the property of

9 Falser an Gruber, 1950 December 5, ÖStA, AdR, BKA-AA, II-Pol, Gr.Zl. 120.883-pol/50, Zl. 71-P/50.

10 BGBl Nr. 142/1954. Erwerb der Staatsbürgerschaft durch Volksdeutsche.

11 Decision Council of Ministers, 1945 November 5, Slovak National Archives (hereafter SNA), Úrad predsednictva Zbor Povereníkov, Box 3.

any foreign citizens who have been categorized up to now as members of the German nationality."[12]

In fact the measures to ensure the safety of Austrian citizens and their property in Slovakia officially came into effect later than in other parts of the country. This seems surprising at first sight, considering the rather positive attitude of the Slovak politicians towards Austria and its representatives (except for exponents of the Communist Party and the Partisan movement applying their anti-German resentment also against Austria). Nevertheless, it is obvious to me that the Slovak conservative parties (especially the Democratic Party) felt under pressure to adopt main parts of the Communist program, particularly its anti-German attitude, in order not to loose their influence in the Slovak political system. This thesis might help to understand why many measures haven't been carried out as strict as the quoted decisions would insinuate. An interview with the already mentioned Karl Rajnoch showed that in his memory the treatment of Austrians definitely did differ from other German-speaking people.

However, the decisive factor in the treatment of Austrians was the political background of the Slovak official who dealt with the plaintiff's application. Communists in general seem to have decided more often in favour of dispossession than conservative officials.

The displacement and dispossession of Austrian citizens and later the naturalization of such German-speaking refugees led to diplomatic tensions that lasted until the mid-seventies. Due to this problem, Austria and Czechoslovakia didn't elevate their representations to embassies. Legations were located in Vienna and Prague in a time when the exchange of ambassadors already was the usual way to administer normal and friendly diplomatic ties.

But there are certain differences between Slovakia and the rest of the country related to the treatment of the German-speaking minority. These differences also had an impact on the mutual images between Austria and Slovakia respectively Austria and the Czechs.

In the western part of Czechoslovakia the determining factor was, as expected, the higher number of persons who were affected and the density of their former settled territory, but the respective roles of the two groups of German-speaking minorities between 1938 and 1945 also contributed to the difference. The utilization of the "Sudeten Germans" in the Czech areas and the "Karpathen Germans" in Slovakia as instruments of Germany's

12 Decision of the Presidium of the Slovak National Council, 1946 April 12, SNA, Úrad predsednictva SNR, 1944-1960, Box 4.

foreign policy caused a national trauma in the western part of the country. The German settled territories were incorporated into Germany already in October 1938 and on 14 March 1939, the already diminished rest of Bohemia, Moravia, and Silesia became part of Germany as "Reichsprotektorat Böhmen und Mähren". In contrast, the same German policy using the minority in order to influence the interior politics of Czechoslovakia led to the establishment of a sovereign Slovak state on 14 March 1939. Furthermore large numbers of German-speaking citizens were expelled at the end of the war from the territory of todays Czech Republic, whilst the biggest part of Slovakia's German-speaking population already had been evacuated by German authorities before the fascist Slovak state perished. Therefore, the later expulsions affected many fewer people and did not play such a prominent role in Austria's view of Slovakia as in its picture of the Czechs.

The ideological conflict and its impact on the relations

The conflict in terms of nationality was – at least in the first decade after the war – closely connected to the ideological conflict. The expulsion of the German-speaking minority in Czechoslovakia after 1948 meant in many ways the subjugation of communist ideology under nationalist "necessities". Whilst the communist ideology theoretically argued that national conflict is an evil of capitalistic societies, in Czechoslovakia it actually combined the anti-fascist struggle with an anti-German struggle. Concepts of an ethnic "homogeneous" country, i.e. Czechoslovakia without Germans and Magyars, were served by the communist party and the Partsian movement to gain the consent of broad masses before coming into power in 1948.

A symbol for this merger of nationalism and communist ideology were the festivities in Devín. This medieval ruin served as a lieu de memoire already in the 19th century. Located at the eastern shore of the river March next to its confluence with the Danube, it marked the western border of the Hungarian kingdom within the Austro-Hungarian monarchy. In 1896, the government in Budapest erected a statue to commemorate the millennium of Hungary which was destroyed in 1921 by unknown perpetrators. From 1945 to 1951, the Czechoslovak government used the amphitheatre which had been erected in 1939 by German authorities[13] for its purposes. To commemorate the "apostles of the Slavs" Kyrill and Method, an "All-Slavic-Day" (Všeslovanský deň) was held every year attracting thousands of attendants. These manifestations answered several purposes: Shortly after the war they were to strengthen the alliance between Czechs and Slovaks

13 From the 22nd of November 1938 Devín/Theben was part of Germany. Cf. Schriffl, Rolle, 187-190.

after the end of the fascists Slovak Republic and to demonstrate the "Slavic antifascist coalition". Therefore it had a strong anti-German connotation displayed just on the border with the Second Austrian Republic considering itself as the first victim of Nazi-Germany. Furthermore, the communists could display their growing power within the Czechoslovak testimony of friendship and alliance with the Soviet-Union which led to harsh criticism by non-communist politicians and in the press.[14] From 1948 to 1951, the now ruling Communist party underlined its leading role in the state in line with the festivities in Devín and combined the well-known part-of-the-program anti-German attitude with its programmatic anti-Fascism. Consequently, communist propaganda led to a merger of ethnical and ideological conflicts, hence a worsening of the relations between Austria and Czechoslovakia.

This conflict was a major factor in the decline of the quality and quantity of cross-border contacts, mainly in terms of political and civil contacts on "lower levels". The erection of a totalitarian regime with a different social system and the assimilation of Czechoslovakia in the Soviet sphere of influence were mainly responsible for the decline of cross-border relations. The erection of a specially secured border zone with restricted access for civilians stopped the manifestations in Devín. In a phase of severe tensions and especially rigid restrictions from 1952 to 1959 no "All-Slavic-Days" were celebrated there.

Cultural cooperation, cross-border traffic and econmy

The "iron curtain" between Austria and Slovakia minimized local contacts for many years. Especially in the years after 1948, ideology not only led to criticizing Austrian politics but also Austrian culture and denying the close ties connecting both territories over centuries.

Before 1938, many Slovaks used to work as farm hands mainly in the northeastern part of Lower Austria or as merchants selling fruits and vegetables in Vienna. In the years of 1945 and 1948 this interchange was stopped in a way that symbolizes the change in the relations quite accurately.

The first setback was caused by the above mentioned national conflict. Slovak workers were "repatriated" and often replaced by the expelled Germans who were now used as cheap labourers.

14 Gabriela Kiliánová, Ein Grenzmythos: Die Burg Devín. in: Hannes Stekl - Elena Mannová (Eds.), Heroen, Mythen, Identitäten. Die Slowakei und Österreich im Vergleich, Wiener Vorlesungen Konversatorien und Studien Bd. 14, Wien 2003,69.

The second factor – ideology – was responsible for the plans to change Slovakia from an agricultural into an industrial country. Massive investments in industry caused a higher demand for workers in the industry.

The third factor was the simple cut-off of cross-border traffic for normal citizens as a result of the erection of the iron curtain.

The fields of cross-border traffic and cultural cooperation can also be taken as indicators for the intensity of ideological conflicts. In years of moderate liberalization during the early sixties, the activities of the Austrian General Consulate increased in terms of issuing visa and the arrangement of cultural contacts at "lower levels", e.g. publishers, theatres, local media, and others.

Visitors from Slovakia had the possibility to become acquainted with Austria and especially Vienna as tourists. Although Austrian visitors spent more money visiting Slovakia than Slovak tourists visiting Austria these trippers must have been a certain economic factor. In 1968, Viennese department stores were allowed to display advertisments in the Slovak daily newspaper "Pravda", the main organ of the Slovak communist party. These developments are reflected in the activity of the Austrian General Consulate. From 1 January to 23 November 1965, the representation in Bratislava issued 16,016 visas for trips to Austria. In the same period in 1966, the general consuls' employees already granted 24,289 visas.[15] After the invasion of the Warsaw Pact in Czechoslovakia and the phase of "normalization" these numbers declined drastically. People who had formed their own picture of the life in a western country aside from Communist propaganda were again imprisoned in their own country.

The Austrian General Consul Ernst Ploil was even able to arrange the translation and performance of modern Austrian literature – which was promoted until 1968 under the internal title "Austrian drama for Slovakia".

In the phase of moderate liberalization there was a strong interest in the culture of the western neighbour which could be promoted through private initiative – something that was very rare in the decades after 1948. Ploil tried to deliver the desired literature also to universities, the Slovak "ministries", academies, journalists, composers, and "(...) many other persons whose sympathy for Austria is well known.(...)"[16]

15 Report, 1966 November 23, ÖStA, AdR, Generalkonsulat Pressburg, S/I/1, Z. 16.237-A/66.

16 1965 August 12, ÖStA, AdR, Generalkonsulat Pressburg, K/III/1, Zl. 5085-A/65.

A special event in the promotion of the cross-border relations were guest performances of Austrian theatres – like the Volkstheater/People's theatre in December 1964 – and artists in Slovakia. Especially the Viennese ice revue which gave guest performances in Bratislava in 1963 seemed to be some kind of "ice-breaker" between the neighbours. A total of 260,000 visitors from all over Slovakia – including the leading politicians of the country like Alexander Dubček – saw the performances. The capital Bratislava in comparison had at that time approximately 280,000 inhabitants. The Austrian general consul reported that the revue was "(...) the best political promotion that has been made here for Austria since 1945".[17] There were also other festivities, such as a dancing contests between Bratislava and the Austrian cities Graz and Linz, and mutual visits of philharmonic orchestras and much more.

Needless to say that the archival documents reflect the changes in the relations not only in quality but also in quantity. Before the invasion of 1968, many files documenting the above mentioned contacts can be found. Concerning literature the end of this positive period is indicated by the fact that for the years between 1969 and 1976 only one single activity can be found and it is not related to the promotion of modern literature but to the possible erection of a memorial for Franz Grillparzer in the Slovak town of Sliač.

The moderate liberalization of the early sixties also stipulated more intense contact between governmental authorities across the bordering river March. The successful negotiations concerning technical corrections of the state border on the March River were – especially in comparison to earlier decades – conducted in an atmosphere of friendly cooperation. The work of the responsible commissions was supported by the Austrian General Consulate in Bratislava. Other areas of cooperation, such as international collaborations between institutions below the state level, were also assisted by the Austrian representation in Slovakia. For example, the consulate passed on information relating to a planned law for disaster control between the Slovak National Assembly and the Tyrolean provincial government.[18] Thus, it must be stated that in these years, questions concerning the Austrian-Slovak border region did not shadow the ties between Prague and Vienna. Rather, the Vienna-Bratislava region was a source of key dealings in this period. Therefore, it might come as less of a surprise that the March River border commission was an important sign of better

17 Wiener Eisrevue: Auftreten beider Gruppen in der ČSSR. Generalkonsulat Pressburg an BMAA Wien, 1963 August 17, ÖStA, AdR, Generalkonsulat Pressburg, Veranstaltungen, Zl. 2142-A/63.

18 Austrian General Consul Bratislava to Tyrol provincial government, 1966 April 26, ÖStA, AdR, Generalkonsulat Pressburg, C/III/4, Z. 1.575-A/66.

bilateral relations, and that, as mentioned above, Bratislava was chosen as the site for the first meeting of the foreign ministers of the two countries. It is an interesting coincidence that the dispute over Czechoslovak territorial claims in the first years after the war, mainly along the March River, had symbolized the deterioration of the bilateral relations, whereas the successful negotiations over minor corrections along the same border in 1968 marked their improvement.

The economic exchange was less affected by these measures. While there was a decline in the years after the war due to the loss of the German-speaking minority being responsible for many economic cross-border activities – the subsequent years brought an increase in transnational commerce. One reason for this fact might be that major parts of the industries of both countries were nationalized and therefore able to cooperate, even in times of political shock and while working in different social systems. Statistics between 1967 and 1971 show continuously strong increases in trade between Austria and Czechoslovakia.[19]

Nevertheless, research on the economic exchange between Austria and Slovakia is quite difficult because of the structure of Czechoslovak foreign exchange. In the years after the war, specialised companies for carrying out foreign trade existed in Slovakia. But already in 1951, all competences related to foreign trade were centralized in Prague. Therefore it is difficult to localise documents to develop a special history of foreign trade of Slovakia with Austria after that time. The existing documents are in examination by Slovak historians, but most of the files related to Austria have vanished.[20] As far as the Austrian side is concerned, statistics on bilateral trade were established without a distinction between Slovakian trade figures and those related to the rest of Czechoslovakia.

Mutual images

1. Shortly after the war the image of Austria was primarily defined as an occupied former part of Nazi-Germany. The image of the citizens of Slovakia's western neighbouring state was that of participants on Germany's war. The members of the German-speaking minority – no matter whether Austrian citizen or not – were considered as fascists and traitors

19 Ullmann, Nachbarschaft, 316.

20 Cf. L´udovit Hallon, Miroslav Londák, Sources and Possibilities of Research on Slovak-Austrian Economic Relations after the Second World War. in: Gertrude Enderle-Burcel - Dieter Stiefel - Alice Teichova (Eds.), Zarte Bande. Österreich und die europäischen planwirtschaftlichen Länder, Mitteilungen des Staatsarchivs, Sonderband 9, 291-302.

to Inter-war-Czechoslovakia. Therefore Austria's efforts to protect some of those people as her own citizens were reckoned as attempts to protect fascists and traitors. In terms of the mutual images the first phase between 1945 and 1948 must be seen as characterized by the "national conflict". It is interesting to see here an asymmetry in the perception of the question of German-speaking individuals in Slovakia. Whilst the Austrian authorities - according to the conception of the Austrian state and nation as the "first victim" of German National Socialism - expected the foreign authorities to except their citizens from the persecution as fascists and traitors, especially the Slovak authorities refused to do so (cf. Dokument oben). Whereas the Austrian side accepted the persecution of individuals who were reasonable suspected of having committed war crimes, the Slovak side secretly even declined to spare Austrians from the treatment intended for "Germans" as a whole.

2. The media communicate mutual images the neighbours had of each other. Especially in the early fifties the Slovak press - not surprisingly - promoted the ideological conflict. Main themes were the "reactionary forces" in Austria and their influence in politics and the comparison of the "workers paradise" to the suffering in a capitalist country.

3. Since the early sixties more moderate tones could be noted even in the party press like the "Pravda" the organ of the Slovak Communist party. Possibilities of cooperation and the search for analogies with the neighbour seemed to be more interesting than conflict or ideology. Titles like "Austria our neighbour" or "The triangle Vienna-Bratislava-Brno. New aspects of Austrian-Czechoslovak cooperation." speak a clear language. And in 1968 even advertisements of Viennese department stores for visitors from Slovakia were allowed to be published in the main organ of the Slovak Communist Party.

With higher numbers of television sets on both sides of the bordering river March since the early sixties, the Austrian Broadcasting Corporation played an increasing role as well for the Czechoslovak citizens as a source of information from the west as for the Communist politicians as an offence to the party's monopoly of information and therefore its power to create a certain image of the west. ORF´s television programmes could be received in western Slovakia and its radio programmes in the whole country. The loss of the monopoly is indicated in the fact that the sales figures of the Austrian communist newspaper "Volksstimme/Peoples voice" - the only admitted Austrian gazette - rose every Thursday when the program of ORF was part of it. Slovak politicians were aware of the problem but had obviously a strange explanation for the success of ORF in Slovakia - the poor quality of Slovak television.

I was able to locate Slovak documents from 1958 where it is stated that the number of television sets in Slovakia would rise from 20,000 in 1958 to 328,000 in 1965 and therefore measures were necessary to ensure that the citizens receive the Slovak programs and not the Viennese television. In December 1958 the "Council of Representatives" adopted a secret memorandum of its chairman in which one can read that "The content of the broadcasts of the Viennese television is from an ideological standpoint destructive, because it affects the mindset of the citizens in a negative way."[21] Therefore steps should be taken to ensure that the television sets in public buildings and private houses cannot receive the Austrian broadcasts and to improve the quality of the Slovak television programmes. The success of these measures was meagre and the success of Austrian television programmes uncontested.

As already described above, especially in the mid-1960s more Czechs and Slovaks were able to travel to the West than ever before – for the Slovaks this meant Vienna – and they were able to get a picture of the capitalist lifestyle and the advances of Western economy. In this regard, even Austrian highways had a high architectural value for the Slovak audience.[22]

Austria as a possible model in both the economic and political dimension, i.e. the combination of prosperity with a position between the power blocks, held a strong appeal for its neighbors. Not coincidentally, the Hungarian and Czechoslovakian reformers of 1956 and 1968 saw Austria's neutrality as a prototype for their own attempts to leave the Soviet sphere of influence. Thus, Austria became ever more a role model for Czechs and Slovaks, in contrast to the negative image that had been cultivated by their regime.

Summing up, one can say that prejudices and negative images, some that had already originated in the nineteenth century, were utilized on the Czechoslovak side in connection with the communist ideology in order to justify the regime's policies. But we can also see the image of Austria developing in Czechoslovakia towards a political and economic paradigm. Changes in these views took place in periods of more intense cross-border exchange of culture, media and tourism. The views described in 1. of this chapter basically represent the first ten to fifteen years after the war, 3. has described the trends from the 1960s.

---

21 Secret decision related to problems with Viennese television, 1958 December 4, SNA, Úrad predsednictva Sboru Povereníkov, Box 374.

22 Karl Peterlik, Komplexe Beziehungen. ČSSR, in: Oliver Rathkolb - Otto Machke - Stefan August Lütgenau (Eds.), Mit anderen Augen gesehen. Internationale Perzeptionen Österreichs 1955-1990, Wien/Köln/Weimar 2002, 626.

1968

The 1968 invasion naturally meant a decrease in contacts through culture and tourism. Most people coming to Austria in the years and decades after the abatement of the Czechoslovak reformist movement were refugees. The "normalization," i.e. the rigidification of the Communist regime, led to a worsening of relations between Austria and Czechoslovakia. This freezing atmosphere didn't improve until the mid-1970s in the climate of international détente.

For most Czechs and Slovaks who fled their country in 1968, their stay in Austria was only temporary – they emigrated on to Western Europe or the United States, regardless of whether they arrived in 1945, 1948 or 1968. In fact, there is a similarity between the "waves" of refugees in 1948 and in 1968. In both cases, the reasons for leaving were primarily political, and most of the refugees did not stay in Austria, which was only their first emigration stopover. Especially in 1968, most of the refugees soon returned to Czechoslovakia. For them Austria was merely a sort of observation post from which they could wait and watch the continuing developments in their home country. This can be seen in coeval diplomatic reports, as for example those from the Austrian General Consulate in Bratislava. Austria was and still is proud of having admitted these refugees in 1968, but Austrian foreign policy functionaries in Vienna were also aware of the limitations of possible Austrian assistance. Pointing out the obvious fact that many Czechoslovaks were likely to enter Austria with temporary visas to wait for further developments in order to decide whether to finally emigrate overseas, apply for asylum or to return, the Austrian Ministry of Foreign Affairs stated in October 1968 that the refugees would be without funds and would expect help. It therefore instructed the legation in Prague and the general consulate in Bratislava to "explain to each visa applicant, with the necessary emphasis, that he could not expect free accommodation or provisions through relief organizations, because all available accommodation possibilities had been exhausted."[23] The general consulate complied with these instructions by posting an information board in its waiting room. Brezhnev had decided that Czechoslovak citizens would be allowed to leave the country after the invasion because of the uncertainty as to how opponents of the invasion should be treated during the phase of "normalization." Especially after 30 August, the numbers of refugees increased greatly and tent camps were even set up in Vienna, a situation that may have contributed to the above-mentioned instructions by the Viennese authorities. According to reports by the Austrian Ministry of the Interior, from August 21 until October 1968 approximately 96,000

23 Austrian MFA to General Consulate Bratislava, 1968 October 4, ÖStA, AdR, Generalkonsulat Pressburg, S/I/1, Z. 69.718–68.

Czechoslovak citizens had entered Austria from Czechoslovakia and some 60,000 through Yugoslavia as a consequence of the invasion. In the same period, 129,000 had returned to their home country, most of them having stayed in Austria for only a few days. In October approximately 7,000 still remained in Austria and 2,248 had asked for political asylum.[24] This illustrates the role of Austria as a stopover and observation post during the crisis. All this underlines my thesis of the importance of contacts on "lower levels." In Slovakia, many of these contacts were supported and some even initiated – particularly from the early 1960s until the 1968 invasion – by the Austrian General Consulate in Bratislava.

But even during the military invasion of Czechoslovakia itself the Austrian General Consulate didn't cease to play its role as a link between Austria and Slovakia. On 21 August 1968, its building was cordoned off by the police and even Austrian citizens weren't able to enter it. General Consul Ploil organized convoys bringing Austrian and other western citizens to the border near Berg the minute the Soviet tanks vacated the bridge over the Danube to Petržalka. Staging area for the foreigners was the hotel Devín in the Slovakian capital. In an interview Ploil stated that every day two or three convoys organised by his office would reach the border, a part the General Consulate had to play as the only western diplomatic representation in Slovakia.[25]

Fig.1: © ÖNB/Wien FO402231/03

24 Ullmann, Nachbarschaft, 208. Jozef Rydlo speaks in a recently published article of nearly 30,000 Slovak refugees who left their country via Austria after 21 August 1968. Cf. Jozef Rydlo, "Einige Gedanken zur Geschichte der Slowaken in Österreich," in Emilia Hrabovec - Beata Katrebova-Blehova, (Eds.), Slowakei und Österreich im 20. Jahrhundert, Wien 2008, 41-55, 49.

25 For a more detailed discussion of the activities of the Austrian General Consulate in Bratislava 1968, cf. David Schriffl, "Der „Prager Frühling" 1968 und die österreichisch-slowakischen Beziehungen," in Wolfgang Mueller - Michael Portmann, (Eds.), Osteuropa vom Weltkrieg zur Wende, Wien 2007, 299-311.

The title of this article is well represented by the picture above. It shows Austrian custom officials at the border crossing Berg near the Slovak capital Bratislava on 21 August 1968 observing the developments after the invasion of forces of the Warsaw Pact in Czechoslovakia. In some respects it also illustrates the aim of my work – to have a closer look at the Austrian-Slovak relations.

Conclusion

The Austrian-Slovak relations mirror the political situation determined by Czechoslovakia's road from war to Communism and its relation to the western neighbour. But the relations also comprise many specifics that are subject of my studies. Slovak politics cannot simply be seen as part of Czechoslovak politics. The differences in history and society are both numerous and important for the relations to Austria. For centuries, Slovakia was part of Hungary without a Slovak administration. Nevertheless, Slovaks repeatedly aspired autonomy during the 19th century. Contacts between Bratislava and Vienna often were inspired by this claim. This was the case in 1848, 1938/39 and again after 1945.

The western part of Czechoslovakia has been politically much closer connected to Austria, leading to conflicts and reservations. The contacts with Slovakia were historically less burdened.

After 1948 and especially in 1968, the role of Austria as the only western country with a diplomatic representation has to be kept in mind just as the role of Austrian electronic media as a source for uncensored information. These facts present Slovakia as a specifiable entity that has been influenced by its western neighbour in its modern history. This also explains why the research on the specific Austrian-Slovak relations is a desideratum in historiography.

András Sziklai
(The Hebrew University of Jerusalem)

The Jewish Theme in the Relationship of Sigmund Freud and Sándor Ferenczi, In the mirror of the Garden and the Workshop

Introduction

The following research paper deals with the relationship between two of the most influential intellectuals of the Psychoanalytical movement in its formative decades: Sigmund Freud (1856-1938) and Sándor Ferenczi (1873-1933). The latter, less known to the wider public, was the founder of the Psychoanalytical movement in Hungary, its central figure until his early death, and if not the initiator than at least a fertile source for ideas which constituted the base for advanced tendencies in psychoanalysis.[1]

According to Immanuel Bergman, despite the difference in age, seventeen years, the dialogue between these two emblematical thinkers was conducted as equal colleagues, and established the contours of the present discourse of Psychoanalysis.[2] This personal correspondence, which was first published in the 1990's, deals not only with matters of Psychoanalysis, but also reflects the cultural, social and political developments of the disintegrating Austro-Hungarian Monarchy.

This paper is a work on the nexus between intellectual and sociological history; therefore its emphasis is mainly on the cultural and sociological facets of the Psychoanalyst Movement and of Psychoanalytical theory itself. If the choice upon this theme for a historical investigation of this sort needs explanation, it lies in the historiography of Carl E. Schorske and Péter Hanák whose ideas compose the theoretical foundation of my paper. Though their theories had numerous critics since their appearance in the late 1970's, I found the socio-cultural interpretation of the Garden – Vienna

1 I'd like to thank the Center for Austrian Studies at the Hebrew University of Jerusalem, and personally Mrs. Elisheva Moatti and Prof. Bianca Kühnel for enabling me to present this paper in the conference of the Centers for Austrian Studies in Edmonton, Canada, September 2008. I'd also like to thank Dr. Michael Silber for his devoted guidance.

2 Immanuel Berman, "The other voice: The Contribution of Sándor Ferenczi to Treatment", in: Confusion of Tongues between Adults and Child, Essays 1908-1933, Tel Aviv 2005, 12-13.

- of Schorske and the Workshop – Budapest - of Hanák a very useful theoretical background for my inquiry on the Freud – Ferenczi relationship.

I intend to focus in this paper on the centrality of the Jewish theme in the social and scientific orientation of Sigmund Freud and Sándor Ferenczi. The guiding question is whether there is congruency between the socio-cultural atmosphere depicted by Schorske and Hanák in relation to Vienna and Budapest and the growing importance of the Jewish issue in the context of the Psychoanalytic Movement. On the basis of their theories I try to understand to what extent and in which ways the changing cultural, social and political milieu in Vienna and Budapest influenced Freud and Ferenczi in perceiving their identity vis-à-vis the Viennese and the Hungarian society- in its broadest sense.

The theories of Carl E. Schorske and Péter Hanák

To begin with, I'd like to sketch the theoretical framework of my investigation: the central ideas of Carl E. Schorske and Péter Hanák and their respective critics. In addition, this chapter should give a short overview as well to the reader on the socio – cultural landscape of fin-de-siècle Budapest and Vienna. Schorske's fundamental work Fin-de-siècle Vienna Politics and Culture is Schorske's attempt to analyze as a historian the, according to his view, a-historical Viennese culture of the turn-of-the century. The sharp discontinuity of Viennese modernist culture vis-à-vis its historical precedents brought, according to Schorske, to a flourishing a-historical culture, liberated from the limits posed upon by historical tradition. This a-historical environment deserved a multi-disciplinary research of the different facets of modernist culture. Vienna proved to be appropriate to this sort of research, argues Schorske, due to its coherent context in contrast to London, Berlin or Paris at the time. In Schorske's understanding of Viennese culture, psychoanalysis has a central position, not only as a language in common for the diverse intellectual and artistic branches, but also explaining the revolt of the Modernists against the moral premises of their paternal bourgeois society as an oedipal revolt.[3]

Schorske, in his essay, entitled "Politics and Patricide in Freud's Interpretation of Dreams", defines Freud's revolutionary book the Interpretation of Dreams[4] as a combination of a scientific investigation and a personal

3 Carl E. Schorske, "Introduction", in: Fin-de-Siècle Vienna Politics and Culture, New York 1981, xvii-xxx.

4 The book was intended to be a revolutionary and modern achievement also by Freud himself. Though first edition was published in 1899, Freud asked to have printed 1900 as year of apparition.

confession, a scientific theory combined with an "incomplete but autonomous subplot of personal history."[5] Schorske asserts that there's an attempt by Freud to create an "epoch making interpretation of human experience in which politics could be reduced to an epiphenomenal manifestation of psychic forces."[6]

Schorske claims that Freud's intellectual activity can be seen as a discharge of the tension between the developments of the post-liberal Viennese political system and Freud's social position, which was determined by his Jewish identity. In Schorske's view, the birth of psychoanalysis was inconceivable without Freud's psychological attitude vis-à-vis his father or without his disillusionment from the political environment after the breakdown of the liberal political arrangement of the Monarchy towards the end of the 19th century.

In Schorske's view psychoanalysis was conceived as a result of the interaction of different layers of Freud's own life experience: the personal, the professional and the political. Freud, as a member of the Viennese Bildungsbürgertum, resented very much the atmosphere in the political and in the public sphere. At the end of the 19th century the Christian-socialist Karl Lueger becomes elected as mayor of Vienna, the news of the Dreyfuss affair filled the pages of the Viennese newspapers, and the political mood had a strong influence on the public field. There's no doubt that the professional promotion of Freud and of other Jewish scientist was impeded by this atmosphere. On a practical level Freud retreated to a certain social isolation - his joining of B'nai B'rith in 1897 indicated this social attitude -, whereas on a theoretical level he aimed at creating an intellectual system which enabled him to reduce the political and public reality to "an epiphenomenal status in relation to the primal conflict between father and son."[7] Schorske draw on Freud's dream stories with personal content in order to depict his ambivalent stance towards the Catholic socio-political system of the Habsburg state. His disappointment of the fact that he hadn't, according to Schorske's view, a political career in the hostile Christian society, symbolized by imperial and later Catholic Rome on the level of the manifest dream, fills numerous accounts of dreams, the most significant of all these: the Revolutionary dream. In this dream Freud achieved his victory over the inauspicious political system by patricide, overcoming his aging father symbolizing the prime minister of Austria.[8] In Schorske's opinion

5 Schorske, "Politics and Patricide in Freud's Interpretation of Dreams", Fin-de-Siècle Vienna Politics and Culture, New York, 1981 183.

6 Schorske, "Politics and Patricide", 183.

7 Schorske, "Politics and Patricide", 197.

8 Schorske, „Politics and Patricide", 197.

Freud overcame the unreceptive post-liberal political system by an ahistorical theory of human and social behavior.

Another instance which designates Freud's determination to challenge the Viennese political and social order, argues Schorske, is his citation on the title page of the Interpretation of Dreams from Virgil's Aeneid: "Flectere si nequeo superos, Achronta movebo"- If I cannot bend the higher powers, I shall stir up hell. Freud's message was - believes Schorske - that the unconscious and its sexual forces will overcome the bourgeois political and social system and the science of Psychoanalysis alone will be able to control it.[9] The question arises, whether some of these subversive intentions were connected strictly to the Jewish theme in Freud's social orientation. In addition one may ask to what extent the theoretical basis of psychoanalysis was necessarily conceived, and functioned at least in its first years, in a Jewish socio-cultural environment in the face of the morals of the Christian bourgeois society.

Schorske's Vienna 1900 paradigm of Viennese modernist culture, a paradigm founded around a special relationship between aesthetics and politics was criticized by many. Mary Gluck doubts not the centrality of the psyche to fin-de-siècle culture, rather criticizes two main beliefs of the paradigm. As for the political sphere, she questions the accepted course of the political system in Vienna - a short period of Austrian liberalism and afterwards the collapse of the liberal establishment in the face of irrational mass politics. Instead of accepting the narrative of the short term liberal legacy she points at the dominant elements of the 'dynastic tradition' of the Habsburg state. The latter political tradition was not necessarily opposed to chauvinistic nationalism; it could be even a "prelude" to anti-liberal policies, according to Gluck. Furthermore, she doubts the ahistorical and apolitical nature of Viennese modernism, and asserts that "aesthetic self-fashioning" can be seen as an active political statement and not necessarily as a passive, individualistic act replacing public activity.[10]

Similarly to Mary Gluck, William J. McGrath doesn't doubt the importance of psychological sensitiveness dominating the culture of turn-of-the century Vienna. However he does relates in a different way to the crisis of the liberal political system and sees definitely in a different way the relation between Viennese modernist culture and Viennese politics, two issues closely interrelated in his theory. McGrath considers, primarily in the social sense, the so-called 'anti-liberal mass politics' as a continuation of the Josephinian traditional liberal politics, as a counterculture to the

9 Schorske, "Politics and Patricide", 181-207.

10 Mary Gluck, "Rethinking culture in Central Europe", in: Austrian History Yearbook, vol. 28, 1997, 217-222.

individualist liberal system. Furthermore, he emphasizes the continuity between Austrian modernist culture and its irrational philosophical and artistic sources. As for Freud, McGrath highlights if not the influence than at least the common emotional terms of the psyche between Freudian theories and the philosophical ideals of Schopenhauer and Nietzsche. Through the individual fate of the members of the Pernerstorfer circle, McGrath depicts a different understanding of the relationship between aesthetics and politics in Viennese modernism from that of Schorske, representing, among others, the music of Gustav Mahler and the politics of Victor Adler as public expressions of Wagnerian collectivist emotionalism critical of the impersonal liberal society.[11]

We can find the same critic about the omission of important intellectuals and artists from the range of the subjects in the work of Schorske by Walter Laquer. He too, blames Schorske for his selective policy in choosing the key personages in his theory in order to strengthen its basic premises. Laquer also sees the phenomenon of Vienna 1900 in the framework of the broader European phenomenon of Decadence whose other centers like Paris, Berlin or Moscow were not secondary at any rate to Vienna.[12]

Schorske is often criticized for presenting Vienna as the birthplace of Modernism and disregarding the importance, let alone precedence, of other urban centers of culture in the second part of the 19th century. In this context, Roger Shattuck's theory on avant-garde culture can be very useful to us. Shattuck prefers to designate the artistic figures and tendencies such as Huysmans, Eliot, Mayakovsky, Dada, Picasso, Futurism and Proust as Decadentism instead of the confusing term Modernism. Indeed in Shattuck's view, in the eyes of the above mentioned artistic circles art has still acute political importance and progressive intention, quasi a messianic goal in transforming society according to its own values; and psychology is not a key factor in culture. In this cultural context Vienna - much less important than Paris, Spain or Russia - is far from being a vital center of these artistic tendencies.[13]

On the base of the theory of Shattuck, Steven Beller makes an important differentiation between the artistic tendencies of Modernism mentioned by Shattuck, and Schorske's intellectual and artistic trends depicted in his Fin-de-siècle Vienna. Beller adopts the term Post-Modernism for the intellectual and artistic environment of Vienna, which revolved around the

11 William J. McGrath, Dionysian Art and Populist Politics in Austria, New Haven 1974.
12 Walter Laqueur, "Fin-de-siècle Vienna" review, in: Society, November/December 1980, 89.
13 Steven Beller, "Owls Fly by Night: Recent Literature on Fin de siècle Vienna", in: The Historical Journal, Vol. 31, No. 3, (Sep., 1988), 666.

Psyche and turned its back on the progressive socio-artistic credo of positivism. According to his view Vienna could absolutely be the birthplace of Post-Modernism but not of the Decadence.[14]

William M. Johnson's critic is twofold. On the one hand he claims that Schorske's evident omissions of a long list of artists and intellectuals in his essays are supposed to strengthen his theory i.e. the retreat of the modernist artists and intellectuals from the public realm of Vienna at the end of the 19th century. On the other hand, Johnson does acknowledge the escapist tendency amidst the Viennese upper and middle bourgeoisie even before the last third of the 19th century. Johnson argues that Schorske does not relate in his article to the escapism in the face of the pre-1848 and the post 1848 neo-absolutist political and public atmosphere. Viennese bourgeoisie started first to cultivate its gardens back then because of the reactionary censorship of the neo-absolutist period. Therefore, according to Johnson's critic, turn of the century Vienna lacks its necessary historical background in Schorske's work.[15]

According to the key theory of Péter Hanák's collection The Garden and the Workshop, inspired by Carl Schorske's inquiry on fin-de-siècle Vienna, while we can witness a basically escapist Viennese Modernism (coined the Garden by Schorske), the intellectual and political tendency of the so called "second Hungarian reformist generation" in Budapest- the Workshop - was essentially socially obligated. Hanák's collection of essays is inspired by Schorske's Fin-de-siècle Vienna not only in its understanding of the Viennese cultural environment, but also in adopting Schorske's interdisciplinary approach in his selection of the articles comparing different socio-cultural facets in the two cities. The broad spectrum of themes of the articles in the collection includes urban-architecture, images of minorities, burial customs, literature and music.

Hanák's central essay The Garden and the Workshop compares two allegedly different public approaches of the artistic and intellectual stratum in the two capitals of the Monarchy. As for Vienna, Hanák reflects about the reason of the retreat of Austrian bourgeoisie to its Viennese Gardens. He asserts that while the Viennese middle class was economically and culturally not at all less significant than its counterpart in Budapest, it was bound through a political alliance to "traditional, dynastic state patriotism" and not to modern nationalism as in the case of Western European societies at the end of the 19th century. This bourgeois class was composed essentially of assimilated Slavic, Jewish and to a lesser extent Hungarian and Ital-

14 Beller, "Owls Fly by Night", 666-667.

15 William M. Johnston, „Cultivated Gardeners", in: The American Scholar, 2001, 260-266.

ian immigrants. These immigrants did not internalize German nationalism; they recognized, instead, the Habsburg political system in return for economical and political premises which secured their social and political existence. They preferred a stand of cosmopolitan liberalism to Western style parliamentarism. They favored the liberty of the autonomous individual versus the collective rights of the nation. Towards the fin-de-siècle the Viennese bourgeoisie found itself on the one hand threatened by post-liberal political mass movements of the socialists and of the Christian-Democrats, on the other hand alienated form the technocratic state bureaucracy.[16] As a result of that, it retreated to its Gardens, enjoying the illusion of individualism in harmony- or disharmony- of its avant-garde art. Hanák believes that the Gardens of the Viennese Secession symbolized, in addition to the escape from the crisis of the liberal establishment and public space, artistic endeavor towards "reaching a higher aesthetic level unifying man and nature".

The key notion of the Viennese artistic and intellectual discourse was the dream, which was part and parcel of the psychoanalytical investigations of the time. The relationship between Psychoanalysis and the arts was reciprocal. The investigations of Sigmund Freud nurtured the work of Gustav Klimt, Arthur Schnitzler[17] and Hugo von Hoffmanstahl to the same extent as their artistic creation influenced Freud's understanding of the concepts of the unconscious and of that of the dream.[18]

Though there were similarities between the two capitals of the Monarchy, in Budapest, claims Hanák, the social and political arrangement was different. As in Vienna, the bourgeoisie in Budapest was composed, mainly, of assimilated Jewish and German immigrants threatened by the weakening of the developing but limited liberal system under the attacks of anti-Semitic and post-liberal political forces. In contrast to Austria though, in Hungary the bourgeoisie had never usurped the role of the traditional

16 In this context: Mária Kovács writes about Bertrand Russel's and Friedrich Hayek's concerns at the beginning of the 20th century about the etatist and post-liberal radical tendencies adopted by the state technocrats out of their absolute positivist belief in the possibility of implication of scientific theories on society. Mária, Kovács, Liberalizmus, Radikalizmus, Antiszemitizmus, A Magyar Orvosi, Ügyvédi és Mérnöki Kar Politikája 1867 és 1945 között, [Liberalism, Radicalism, Anti-Semitism, The Policy of the Hungarian Medical, Bar and Engineer Association between 1867 and 1945], Budapest 2001, 12-13.

17 In detail on the parallel traits of Psychoanalysis in the writings of Arthur Schnitzler and those of Sigmund Freud: Kristóf, Nyríri, "A Liberális Antropológia Alkonya", in: A Monarchia szellemi életéről, Filozófiai Történeti Tanulmányok, [„The Twilight of the Liberal Anthropology", in: On the intellectual life of the Monarchy, Philosophical and Historical Treaties], Budapest, Gondolat 1980, 141-142.

18 Péter Hanák, "The Garden and the Workshop", in: The Garden and the Workshop, Essays on the Cultural History of Vienna and Budapest, Princeton 1998, 64-66, 68-74.

political class, the nobility. In this sense, its members could not withdraw from the political scene, they had never fully entered. Furthermore, in contrast to Austria, feudalism was still palpable in the political and social reality of Hungary, not as the impersonal Austrian bureaucratic system: of Kafka's castle. The essential difference between the Garden and the Workshop was the fundamentally different political atmosphere in Hungary, where the intellectuals saw the liberal legislation as emancipatory from the remnants of the feudal system. Therefore the social orientation of the sciences and of the arts was congruent with the progressive air of Hungarian politics- at least until the end of the 19th century. The design of the liberal political and artistic thought took place in the public sphere: in offices of newspapers, clubs and coffeehouses. Though there were exceptions, it can be said, according to Hanák, that political involvement on a social and national level was common to all segments of the intellectual and artistic environment. Modernization of all aspects of the national life was a shared endeavor of the progressive spirit of the 'second reformist generation' whose epicenter was beyond all doubt: Budapest. The orientation of modernist literary styles like Symbolism, adopted in Hungary only from the first decade of the 20th century, or Secession was public. Anti-clericalism, anti-feudalism, belief in progress and their expression in an avant-garde fashion were the core values of the newly established journals, like the Nyugat (West) and the Hét (Week) in literature, Huszadik Század (Twentieth Century) in sociology, and the theatre of the Vígszínház and especially the Thália. Representation of elements from the past in the music of Bartók or Kodály and in architecture by Ödön Lechner was done in modern forms aiming at the regeneration of the national culture. An additional progressive scientific forum was the medical review Gyógyászat (Medicine) edited by Miksa Schächter, and later by Lajos Lévi- Ferenczi's personal physician. Initiated as an alternative to Orvosi Hetilap (Medical Weekly), the established medical journal, Gyógyászat, was more than ready to publish psychoanalytical articles.[19] A complex perception of reality brought closer much of the literary elite to psychoanalysis and a radically new conception of language, which at least until the end of the Great War essentially in the service of the Magyar nation and its rejuvenation. The undertaking of emancipating Hungarian society of its feudal remnants transformed the slogan of Viennese Sezession: "Liberty to art" into: "Liberty to the people".[20]

Concerning Freud's intellectual and social position specifically, Hanák indicates Freud's marginality an important factor in his achievements, and his fundamental position in the history of ideas- as against others in the

19 Michelle Moreau-Ricaud, "The Founding of the Budapest School", in: Ferenczi's Turn in Psychoanalysis, Peter L. Rudnytsky, Antal Bókay, and Patrizia Giampieri-Deutch, eds., New York 1996, 46.

20 Péter Hanák, "The Garden and the Workshop", 66-67, 77-94.

field of Psychology like Krafft-Ebing or Pierre Marie Félix Janet. Freud was a product of bourgeois culture, but at the same time radically criticized its core conceptions, and out of this contradiction Psychoanalysis was born. The incompleteness of the Jewish emancipation, in legislative or in a social sense, granted a special perspective on society specifically for the marginal figure of the Jewish intellectual. In Freud's words: "Because I was a Jew I found myself free from many prejudices which restricted others in the use of their intellect; and as a Jew I was prepared to join the opposition and to do so without agreement with the 'compact majority'." Hanák assumes, to a certain extent, the uniqueness of being a member of the Jewish minority in the post-assimilatory- and post-liberal- European bourgeois society. In this society, Jewish marginality can be considered "as a special case of human marginality, a stage of independence and integrity that offers marginal men a sort of cognitive privilege."[21]

Like Schorske, Hanák is also criticized because of his alleged selectiveness in choosing his intellectual and cultural figures and phenomenon to illustrate his theory. Steven Beller is of the opinion that picking Gustav Mahler and Victor Adler in the case of Vienna- as McGrath does- and the Sunday Circle of Lukács in the case of Budapest could bring Hanák to a completely inverse theory, Vienna as the Forum and Budapest as the Garden.[22]

On the other hand Kristóf Nyíri, examining Sándor Ferenczi's vision on Psychoanalysis, discovers the same socially oriented outlook as the one depicted by Hanák. According to Nyíri, Ferenczi from the very beginning thought about the social implications of Psychoanalysis. In a publication of 1911, he spoke about alcoholism as a symptom of a social neurosis and not as its cause. The healing of the social alcoholism could happen, according to Ferenczi, only by discovering the social reason for it by analysis.[23] During the same year in an article to Szabadgondolat (Free Thought) – periodical of the Galilei Circle - a progressive student organization of fin-de-siècle Budapest – he expressed his opinion about the importance of social awareness and education of psychological matters:

"Impediment of the human passion, diminishing the charge of the soul, prevention of distempers, are not the questions of an abstract science anymore, but the indicators of new and hopeful directions of prosperity and development of humanity in the future...The future will bring a radical

21 Hanák, 161-166.
22 Beller, "Owls fly by night", 672.
23 Nyíri, „A Liberális Antropológia Alkonya", 148.

reform of the psychical education...and this will bring the end of a period of humanity which is characterized by hypocrisy, by the blind worship of dogmas and authorities and by the absence of self-criticism."[24]

Theories about Freud's Jewish identity

I now turn to explore the existing literature on Freud's Jewish identity in the light of the Freud-Ferenczi correspondence. Questions concerning Jewish social and individual identity in the context of the Psychoanalytical society, its members, and Sigmund Freud himself, were raised and examined in length.[25] Different scholars assessed differently the influence of the Jewish factor on the ideological and social activity of Freud and of other members of the Psychoanalytical movement. I would like to outline briefly the theories of those historians whose work I found most fruitful.

Peter Gay, one of the prominent biographers of Freud, very much disclaimed any essential influence not only of the Jewish issue but also of the Viennese cultural environment on Freudian thought. Interestingly enough, Gay arrives at his conclusions when he is well aware, amongst other things, of Freud's pondering about the essence of his Jewish identity, of his involvement and declarations in B'nai B'rith in Vienna or of his thoughts on Jewish marginality in the specific socio-cultural context of fin-de-siècle Vienna.[26]

"Freud, I conclude, was a Jew but not a Jewish scientist. I have no intention of imitating him by trying to take Freud away from his people as he tried to take away Moses. But the decisive distinction between personal identity and scientific allegiance remains intact."[27]

The Jewish theme is much more vital to Yosef Hayim Yerushalmi, who inquired into Freud's intellectual and social attitudes. In his book, Freud's Moses: Judaism Terminable and Interminable, Yerushalmi finds Freud's feelings concerning Judaism crucial to his intellectual work, having its origins in his relationship with his father. Yerushalmi considers Freud's

---

24 Nyíri, "A Liberális Antropológia Alkonya", 145-146. (The translation is mine.)

25 In addition to those analyzed in detail in this paper: David Bakan, Sigmund Freud and the Jewish Mystical Tradition, New York 1969; John Cuddihy, The Ordeal of Civility, New York 1974; Marthe Robert, From Oedipus to Moses: Freud's Jewish identity, New York 1976.

26 Peter Gay, A Godless Jew, Freud, Atheism, and the Making of Psychoanalysis, New Haven 1987, 117-154. See Yerushalmi's critique on Gay's theory on Freud: Yosef Hayim Yerushalmi, Freud's Moses: Judaism Terminable and Interminable, New Haven 1991, 115-116.

27 Gay, A Godless Jew, 148.

intellectual journey from The Future of an Illusion to Moses and Monotheism parallel to the emotional road that Freud accomplishes in relation to the memory of the Jewish identity of his father.

An additional key element in Yerushalmi's analysis of Moses and Monotheism is the question of the historical dimension of Freud's historical novel. Yerushalmi claims that Freud was, more than anything, interested in the way Jewish tradition was passed from generation to generation. The "axis of the book... (is)...the problem of tradition, not merely its origins, but above all its dynamics."[28] According to Yerushalmi's understanding, Freud devised in Moses and Monotheism a radically alternative explanation of history.

"Moses and Monotheism is not merely history, but a countertheology of history in which, the Chain of Tradition is replaced by the chain of unconscious repetition. Indeed, that is perhaps why some will say that Freud has a better claim than Spinoza to be considered the archheretic of Judaism in modern times."[29]

It is the Lamarckian take of Freud (and Ferenczi), that confirms Yerushalmi's claim, that in the expression "godless Jew", used by Freud, "the noun must be taken at least as seriously as the adjective."[30] Freud's very words written to Zweig about the Land of Israel are apposite here: "and we hail from there...our forebears lived there for perhaps a whole millennium... and it is impossible to say what heritage from this land we have taken over into our blood and nerves."[31]

The emphasis, which Dennis B. Klein assigns to the Jewish issue in his volume on the Jewish Origins of the Psychoanalytical Movement, is as strong as that of Yerushalmi. Klein is particularly interested in the social and cultural orientation of Freud and of other members of the Psychoanalytical movement, first and foremost that of Otto Rank. Klein emphasizes the assertion of collective Jewish identity and solidarity amongst the members of the Psychoanalytical movement by emphasizing their close association with B'nai B'rith. Klein highlights the ambivalence of the Jewish collective identity in the post-liberal era, Jacob Katz's analysis of the colliding expectations of non-Jewish society on the one hand, and Jews on the other. According to Klein, the disillusionment in the wake of the breakdown of the liberal political order in Vienna in the last decades of the 19th century caused the development of a positive Jewish self-pride, which

28 Yerushalmi, Freud‘s Moses, 29.
29 Yerushalmi, Freud‘s Moses, 29-33.
30 Yerushalmi, Freud‘s Moses, 116.
31 Yerushalmi, Freud‘s Moses, 35.

raised doubts on part of the non-Jewish society of the credibility of the universalistic arguments of the secular Jewish intelligentsia. Still, asserts Klein, the universal and humanistic efforts of these Jewish intellectuals continued to exist, albeit now conceptualized on the basis strengthened self-pride. In other words, the Zielbewusstsein, the ultimate objective remained the same: social integration, but next to an increased accent on self-dignity and collective identity. The goal of the Psychoanalytical movement, for many of its Jewish members – during the initial years of the movement – was to bring "analytical redemption" to humanity, liberating humanity from depression by curing its crucial disease: neurosis.[32]

Another historian who founds the Jewish issue critical to Freud's theories and to the Psychoanalytical movement was Sander L. Gilman. Gilman's argument concentrates around the question of language. Gilman asserts that, Freud by adopting the scientific language of Psychoanalysis aimed at distancing himself from the anti-Semitic socio-cultural environment of fin-de-siècle Vienna. Freud discovered the sexual origins of neurosis through the sexual discourse of Jewish jokes told by Jews of Eastern European origins – the Ostjuden[33]. But Freud, as a Jew threatened by the anti-Semitic racial discourse of science and of post-liberal politics, did not discuss the language of Jewish Jokes in a feminine language, nor in a Jewish language, neither in the accepted scientific one. He did that in a new scientific language: that of psychoanalysis, which aims at becoming a universal language, the language of the unconscious, present in every human being.[34]

"The exercise of collecting and retelling the Jewish jokes, of removing them from the daily world in which Freud must live to the higher plane of the new scientific discourse, that of psychoanalysis enables Freud to purge himself of the insecurity felt by his status as a Jew in fin-de-siècle Vienna."[35]

Indeed, Freud's scientific discourse has to be seen in the context of the scientific discourse of his time. Gilman criticizes Frank J. Sulloway[36] and Peter Gay because, he argues, they did not appreciate the importance of

32 Dennis B. Klein, Jewish Origins of the Psychoanalytical Movement, Chicago 1985, 138-154.

33 The theme of the Ostjuden is crucial to the understanding of the Jewish question in turn of the century Central Europe. On its origins and formulations: Steven E. Aschheim, Brothers and Strangers, Madison, 1982.

34 Sander L. Gilman, "Freud and the Hidden Language of the Jews", in: Psychoanalysis and Contemporary Thought, 1984, Vol. 7, No. 4, 591-614; Sander L. Gilman, Jewish Self-Hatred, Anti-Semitism, and the Hidden Language of the Jews, Baltimore 1990, 259-270.

35 Sander L. Gilman, „Freud and the Hidden Language of the Jews", 611.

36 Frank J. Sulloway, Freud, Biologist of the Mind, Beyond the Psychoanalytic Legend, New York, 1979.

the racial element of the scientific discourse of the end of the 19th century. He mentions Cesare Lombroso and Rafael Becker, two Jewish scientist, who themselves wrote in this tone. Masculinity became connected with the Aryan race, while the Jewish male was characterized with feminine and sickly attributes like nervosa and other such diseases. For a Jew, to become a man of science could be his emancipator ticket to masculinity.[37] The constant critic of the values of the bourgeois society 'form inside' by Freud gets its confirmation from Gilman as well: "It is necessary to understand that Freud on one level of his self-definition as Jew and scientist accepted the centrality of race as an epistemological category while constantly needing to draw it into question."[38]

Discussion

The Freud Ferenczi correspondence, which began in 1908 and came to its end only in 1933 with the early death of Ferenczi, is an enormous intellectual but also socio-cultural documentation of the disintegrating Monarchy, much beyond the specific personal context of the two authors. According to Ferenc Erős, the correspondence can also be seen as an identity project of psychoanalysis in the turn of the century. Alluding to Paul Ricoeur and Robert Musil he argues, that the identity of the 'individual without qualities' becomes a personal narrative in a liberal society without clear categories. The mutual nature of the correspondence, he asserts, enables Ferenczi and Freud to construct a common narrative.[39]

I would like to add a note on the biographical traits of the two thinkers. The biographies of Freud and Ferenczi have much more in common than one may assume. Ferenczi's father, Baruch Frankel, was born in Galicia, in the same socio-cultural environment where Freud's father was born. Being children of second generation Jewish emigrants had far reaching consequences both on Freud and on Ferenczi in terms of their linguistic awareness. Eva Brabant mentions that the fathers of Ferenczi and Freud grew up in a Yiddish speaking environment and she tells that they had difficulties in adapting themselves to the German and the Hungarian lingual environment. She also mentions Ferenczi's sensitivity during his childhood of his

37 Sander L. Gilman, Freud, Race, and Gender, Princeton N.J. 1993, 3-11.

38 Gilman, Freud, Race, and Gender, 10.

39 Ferenc Erős, „Az Osztrák-Magyar Monarchia felbomlásának képei a Freud-Ferenczi levelezés tükrében“, in: Kultuszok a pszichoanalízis történetében, Egy Ferenczi-Monográfia vázlata, [The Pictures of the Disintegration of the Austro-Hungarian Monarchy in the Mirror of the Freud-Ferenczi Correspondence, in: Cults in the History of Psychoanalysism, A Draft for a Ferenczi Monograph], Budapest 2004. 128-129.

father's accent.[40] It may be assumed that, in this context, a lot more was said and heard than what was or could actually be put on paper.[41]

Baruch Frankel immigrated to Hungary and actively participated in the 1848 revolution; thereafter he took over a most important bookshop and publishing house in the city of Miskolc, in the North-Eastern parts of Hungary. The contribution of the Ferenczi family to Hungarian literary life was important, and came to its end only in 1944 when Ferenczi's brother Károly was murdered in Auschwitz. Ferenczi himself was part of Freud's socio-cultural milieu during his years as a student. He chose to be a doctor; a profession much cherished by the children of families from an Eastern European Jewish background, and completed his medical studies in Vienna. Some 30% of the medical students in Vienna at the turn of the century were indeed from a similar social background as Ferenczi.[42]

In the Freud - Ferenczi correspondence one can sense that the prominence of the medical career for Jews could be thought of as a crucial "emancipatory path"[43], but Jewish intellectuals, like Ferenczi, nevertheless remained somewhat distanced from it, or at least critical about it. Ferenczi sent a letter to Freud on December 7, 1909, in which he thanks Freud for writing an introduction to his book. Ferenczi tells Freud that he is very satisfied with his introduction; however he made a minor change.

"I have added a word... (Instead of) the man of education in his own country," I want to have printed "the doctors and the men of education in his own country." I don't want this book to be described as "popular science." Probably no one will notice that in doing so, the doctors will be

40 Eva Brabant, "Má nistanö, avagy mi marad meg?", in: A megtalált nyelv, ["Ma nishtana, or what remains?", in: The found language], Ritter Andrea, Ferenc Erős, eds., Budapest 2001, 150-151.

41 Just to illustrate, how much the question of the theme of the 'Ostjuden' was central to the Viennese political discourse of the time, Eva Brabant mentions the reaction of Victor Adler to the proposal of Numerus Clausus against Jews in the 1880's. The future Jewish figure of Austrian socialism proposed as a reaction: the distinction between the already assimilated Jews and the newly immigrated ones, the Ostjuden, Brabant, "Má nistanö", 152-153.

42 Ferenc Erős, "Egy vásott kölyök az ismeretlen tartományból", in: Kultuszok a Pszichoanalízis Történetében, Egy Ferenczi-Monográfia Vázlata, ["A pickle from the unknown province", in: Cults from the History of Psychoanalysis, Draft for a Ferenczi- Monography], Budapest 2004. 81-83.

43 The phrase is borrowed from: Pierre Birnbaum and Ira Katznelson eds., "Introduction", in: Paths of emancipation: Jews, states and citizenship, Princton N.J. 1995, 3-36.

removed from the circle of the educated (even though this ironic conception would not be inappropriate)."[44]

Later, one of the grounds for the disagreement between Freud and Ferenczi was the authority of the analyst over the patient, and Ferenczi's desire to institute a more democratic set up in the relations between the patient and the analyst. Similar criticism to that of Ferenczi will be formulated later in the conception of Gilman and Foucault about the bourgeois institution of the medical doctor.

Psychoanalysis between the state and the private sector

After returning to Hungary, Ferenczi began to work as a psychiatrist in the public health service, in the St. Rókus Hospital in the department of prostitutes with sexual diseases. Afterwards from 1900 he worked in the Erzsébet Poor-House and Hospital in the department of neurology and psychiatry. From 1904 till 1910 he was the responsible for the neurological outpatient treatment of the Healthcare Institution in Budapest. From 1905 till after the end of the Great War he worked as a neurological expert in the Budapest Court of Justice.[45]

At this point, I'd like to investigate the relationship between the state and Psychoanalytical Movement in Hungary. Results of this sort of investigation could shed light on the viability of Péter Hanák's theory about the socially obligated intellectual approach in Budapest. I base my investigation on the research of Mária Kovács who explored the policies of the associations of the doctors, the engineers and the bar association vis-à-vis the state and vis-à-vis the minorities in Hungary, mainly the Jews. Kovács's conclusion regarding the medical branches is equally relevant to the psychoanalysts of the time. Though Freud and Ferenczi were in favor of lay-analysis – one of the main debates of the formative years of the Psychoanalytical Movement -, at the time there were nearly no analysts who were not graduates of medical faculties. Therefore the results of the investigations of Kovács regarding Jewish medical doctors and the Hungarian state are identical to the relations between the psychoanalysts and professional associations of state organs.

44 Sándor Ferenczi to Sigmund Freud, December 7th, 1909, in: The Correspondence of Sigmund Freud and Sándor Ferenczi, vol. 1, 1908-1914, Eva Brabant, Ernst Falzeder and Patrizia Giampieri- Deutsch, eds., under the supervision of André Haynal, Cambridge, Massachusetts 1994, 111.

45 Pál Harmat, Freud, Ferenczi és a magyarországi Pszichoanalízis, 33.

Kovács surveys the story of the free-professions in Hungary from 1867 – the year of the so-called Compromise between Austria and Hungary – till the end of World War Two. Regarding the period from 1867 until the end of the Communist Republic in 1919, Kovács argues as follows: The Hungarian state implemented a policy aiming to create more liberal market conditions than even in Western Europe – Kovács's main counter example in this sense is England. In Western Europe the associations of the free-professions succeeded in preserving most of their privileges achieved in the Middle Ages. In contrast, in Hungary, associational life was very limited during the different absolutist periods that Hungary passed under Habsburg rule, and after 1867 there was no associational infrastructure of the free-professions. The relations between associations – like the Magyar Orvosi Kör (Hungarian Medical Circle) - which were established in the post 1867 period - and the state, remained till 1920 on a liberal theoretical base. The main intention of the Hungarian Medical Circle was the establishment of a General Medical Association – on the model of the medieval guilds - which would unite the doctors in their struggle against the Healthcare Institutions representing more and more out of the market of the patients giving them a favorable position of bargaining vis-à-vis the doctors. Regarding the Jewish question, the official policy was liberal, but the question of the high percentage of Jewish free-professionals was a sensitive issue. The percentage of Jewish medical students at the turn of the century was close to half of the overall number of students. This was especially delicate, when the free-professions, at least according to the 1848 reform ideas of the nobility, were supposed to be filled by the young generation of the gentry. Practically, they began to enter into these professions only a generation after the Jewish youth did. The issue of regulating the number of professionals became even more acute after the Peace Treaty of 1920, when their percentage vis-à-vis the population was even higher than it was before the war. There were also additional professionals who immigrated to the territory of Hungary from the territories that were adjudged to the countries around. Though there were avant-garde neo-conservative groups amongst the free-professionals who criticized the dominant liberal ideology, their influence was limited – for example József Madzsar who was amongst the first scientists propagating eugenics in Hungary. The issue of numerus clausus in the field of the medical professions – and those of engineering and law –, was proposed before 1914 out of pure professional considerations, in order to regulate the quantity of professionals in each field and not out of ethnical or racial considerations.[46]

The situation changed dramatically after the communist revolution of 1919. With the establishment of the neo-conservative Horthy regime the

46 Kovács Mária, Liberalizmus, Radikalizmus, Antiszemitizmus, 21-37, 45-66.

first Numerus Clausus Law in Europe was legislated which was designed according to racial and ethnic considerations. The law had substantial support from race-defending organizations which were established already in an underground form during the 133 days of the Kun Béla regime. One of the prominent organizations of this sort was the MONE (Magyar Orvosok Nemzeti Egyesülete- The National Association of Hungarian Doctors), at its head András Csilléry, which already during the communist regime began to prepare "lists of physicians with a sure Hungarian pedigree". With the establishment of the Bethlen administration, Csilléry got the medical portfolio. Next to actively backing the legislation of the Numerus Clausus, MONE was willing to banish Jewish physicians from the state sector, leaving the sector of the Healthcare Institutions only to non-Jewish doctors. Ironically enough, this move was, in a sense, beneficial to the Jewish physicians after the 1929 economical crisis, when the private sector was no doubt preferable in the economic sense than the bankrupted state sector. The general association of physicians was established only in 1932, in the spirit of the corporatist state-reforms of the Gömbös administration. It should not surprise us that it was András Csilléry in March 1938 who submitted the proposal for the First Jewish Law in Hungary, aimed at depriving the Jewish citizens of Hungary from their citizenship on a racial basis.[47]

Indeed, if we examine the Hungarian Psychoanalytical Movement's or individual analysts' relation to the Hungarian state, Kovács's analysis is confirmed. The climax in the relations of the Hungarian Psychoanalytical Movement and the Hungarian state was, no doubt, at the end of the First World War. On September 28-29th 1918 the 5th international congress of Psychoanalysis took place in Budapest. The central theme of the conference was war neurosis (PTSD) and next to the central figures of the Psychoanalytical Movement, high ranking officials from the Imperial, the Hungarian and the Prussian Ministry of Defense took part. Abraham, Simmel and others presented their papers in uniform. Partly as consequence of the conference, the Imperial Ministry of Defense published a regulation, Building additional stations of neurology and treatment of crippled war veterans, and the regulation made allusion to Psychoanalytical treatment for war veterans in cases when the patient expressed resistance in more than one station of neurological treatment.[48]

In the context of the Psychoanalytical Movement and the state it should be mentioned also that the first ever university department of Psychoanalysis was established, surprisingly enough, during the 1919 Soviet Republic in Hungary. In March 1919 Ernő Jendrassik was asked to write an opinion about a proposal submitted by students to the University of

47 Kovács Mária, Liberalizmus, Radikalizmus, Antiszemitizmus, 62- 66, 73-92, 108-118.

48 Harmat Pál, 85-88.

Medical Studies in Budapest on the issue of establishing of a department of psychoanalysis. Jendrassik, in his opinion, emphasized that half of the undersigned were women, and argued, that nowhere in any university in the world the "so-called" Psychoanalysis is taught which is practically "pornography and dream-interpretation"[49]. He was against the teaching of Psychoanalysis "whose main theoretical subject is the young hysterical woman, with whom they endlessly discuss sexual things, though its known that these are highly suggestible individuals, and their analysts take their suggested memories as proving data."[50] Amongst the many perversities of the analysts Jendrassik objected specifically to the interpretation of the church towers in the dream as phallic symbols. Despite the negative opinion of the department of medical studies, the council of education decided to set up a department of psychoanalytical studies. The signature on the letter of appointment of Ferenczi and the dean of the Medical Faculty was that of György Lukács, the deputy commissar of the education council, and of Tódor Kármán, responsible for academic issues, the future world known scientist of aerodynamics. The only demand from Ferenczi, who indeed accepted the appointment as head of the department, was that he renounce his private practicum. The establishment of this faculty, to a great extent, was due to the warm personal and professional relationship between Ferenczi and prominent members of Béla Kun's regime.

This tendency changed dramatically after the Communist Revolution of 1919. Similar to the Viennese model of the pre-war period, the analysts in Budapest retreated into their private clinics – constrained by the state to leave their positions in the public sphere. The biographical data of the members of the Hungarian association, their occupational patterns are in accordance confirm the premises of Kovács. István Hollós, the successor of Ferenczi as the president of the Hungarian Psychoanalytical Movement after his death, was maybe the only one who remained for a short time in the public sphere after 1919. Before the war he worked in the National Psychiatric Institution of Lipótmező and as director of a hospital in Nagyszeben in Transylvania, then, after the war for a short time in the Psychiatric Hospital in Angyalföld. Hollós was amongst the first analysts who used psychoanalysis in the treatment of psychotics. The methods used by Hollós in the treatment of the psychotics resounded the principals developed by Ferenczi: active attitude on the part of the analysts and a special emphasis on empathy. Lilly Hajdu and her husband Miklós Gimes were central figures in the Hungarian movement. Two of them left the public sector after the war; Hajdu Lilly took over the Frimm Institution and until 1934 she administered it as the 'Hajdu Lilly Institute for Special Education and

49 Harmat Pál, 95.
50 Harmat Pál, 96.

Children Camp. Lajos Lévy, the famous internal physician of Ferenczi - who married the cousin of Rabbi Lipót Lőw – worked in the Mária Valéria Hospital and in the Zita Hospital and after the war he was employed in the private Jewish Hospital.[51] Correspondingly to the pattern of Hungarian analysts, Imre Hermann also opened a private clinic after serving in the army till 1918, and working as the academic assistant of Géza Révész during the Soviet Republic in 1919. The public clinic of the Psychoanalyst Movement was inaugurated on December 18th 1931 in Mészáros Street 12 in the Kovács Residence. The clinic was financed though by Vilma Kovács, and other members of the movement, the Hungarian state bureaucracy still tried to impede the establishment of the clinic.[52]

In august 1919 the neo-conservative regime of Horthy and the anti-Semitic White terror put an end to the brief renaissance of Psychoanalysis in Hungary. Not only the department of Psychoanalysis was closed, but Ferenczi was even excluded after 20 years of membership from the Physicians' Association of Budapest. The initiative to exclude doctors who participated in the Communist revolution came from the MONE - mentioned before. The same Jendrassik lobbied for the exclusion of Ferenczi. The establishment of the Horthy regime brought to the first wave of emigrations of the members of the Psychoanalytical society, Hárnik and Radó, which was only the first in a series of emigration waves from Hungary.[53]

In accordance with the above said, Hanák's theory is certainly valid, judging on the basis of the occupational patterns of Ferenczi and other members of the Psychoanalytical Movement, at least, until 1920. The figure of Ferenczi in Budapest's coffeehouses spending his time together with the progressive writers and artists of his age very much confirms this picture. Ferenczi from the very beginning was very sensitive to the possible social implications of Psychoanalysis.[54] Later, especially after the Great War, Ferenczi's attitude became more and more similar to the pre-war escapist Freudian stance. He wrote as follows to Freud on March 22nd 1910 approximately a year and a half after they first met.

"I would like to recommend to you another point for consideration (in case you haven't come upon it yourself). That is the sociological significance of our analyses in the sense that in our analyses we investigate the

51 Harmat Pál, 148-157.

52 Harmat Pál, 217-230.

53 Harmat Pál, 95-107; Ferenc Erős, "Az Osztrák-Magyar Monarchia Felbomlásának Képei a Freud-Ferenczi Levelezés Tükrében", 138-143. Further on the waves of emigration of psychoanalysts from Hungary and their worldwide influence: Judit Mészáros, "The Tragic Success of European Psychoanalysis: "The Budapest School"", Int Forum Psychoanal, 1998; 7:207-214. Stokholm ISSN 0803-706x.

54 Erős Ferenc, 44.

real conditions in the various levels of society, cleansed of all hypocrisy and conventionalism, just as they are mirrored in the individual."[55]

An additional instance which demonstrates the connectedness of the Psychoanalytic Movement of Hungary with the literary-public field of Budapest: are the opening sessions of the association. The association was established on May 19th 1913. Ernest Jones, who participated in the second session, recounts that Hugó Ignótus, lay-member of the association and the editor in chief of the progressive literary review Nyugat, was cast in the role of the public.[56]

Indeed, Budapest did not cease even after the war to be adoptive of the new science. Its main ground was in Lipótváros, one of the main concentrations of the Jewish population in Budapest from the forth quarter of the 19th century on. István Vas speaks about a subculture in Lipótváros, in which this "secret discovery, doctrine, ceremony" in somewhat a snobbish way was constantly mentioned, not necessarily read about."[57] Without this environment, Psychoanalysis, and other branches of progressive culture, could simply not have been adopted in Hungary for decades. Psychoanalysis became the target of anti-Semitic, conservative, nationalistic political and public forces. Sexual conservatives projected on the Jews even "the perception of sexuality as sin". The critics against Psychoanalysis had an anti-Semitic subtext, or used anti-Semitic symbolism even when it was explicit. Sándor Solymossy criticized in the following way Géza Róheim – one of the prominent psychoanalysts in Budapest.

"The way, in which [Róheim] represents before us the son of the earth is, none other, than the (how is the Freudian expression?) »projection« of the antsy mental life of the man of the coffeehouse of the capital on the Hungarian farmer, an all together different type."[58]

The disintegration of the Monarchy

The years 1918 -1920 brought to the disintegration of the Austro-Hungarian Monarchy, and especially for Ferenczi, to the collapse of the socio-cultural premises of the world before the Great War. Freud's post-liberal Vienna has disillusioned him from early on about his chances of being part of German or Austrian nationalism- if it existed at all. The Hungarian po-

55 Ferenczi to Sigmund Freud on March 22th, 1910", *The Correspondence of Sigmund Freud and Sándor Ferenczi*, vol. 1, 153.

56 Ernest Jones, The Life and Work of Sigmund Freud, New York 1961, 130.

57 Harmat Pál, 111.

58 Harmat Pál, 109-113.

litical atmosphere, however, was different till 1918. The post-liberal tendencies came to the forefront of the political arena not before the end of the Communist Revolution of 1919. Because of the limited suffrage, the liberal forces dominated the Hungarian parliament and the Hungarian political discourse during the period between 1867 and 1918. The political ideologies and forces which in Vienna after the expansion of the franchise made Karl Lueger the mayor of Vienna around 1900, also existed in Hungary, but they had to wait till the establishment of the Horthy regime to take control over Hungary. At the time, when Karl Lueger and the Christian-Socialists came to power in Vienna, there was a Jewish mayor in Budapest. The bourgeois revolution of Count Károlyi and the dictatorship of Béla Kun still had to come to their end before anti-Semitism could become a dominant political pattern in Hungary. It's understandable in this atmosphere that Hungarian Jewry was still eager to promote emancipation and integration to the Hungarian society. It's not until he moved to Vienna, and afterwards, to Paris, that Herzl became a Zionist- until then he wrote patriotic poetry in Hungary, like Ferenczi. To a certain extent the above said can explain the social involvement of the progressive artistic milieu of Budapest in Hanák's argument if we take into consideration the high percentage of Jews in these circles.[59] Because of his bitter experience in Vienna, Freud understood better than Ferenczi the developments in Hungary and tried to bring him to a 'reconsideration' of his stance on his emotional commitment to Hungary. Freud urged him to withdraw into the circle of psychoanalysis where there was no danger of disappointment for him because of his identity. Freud wrote to Ferenczi on October 27th 1919 as follows.

I know that you are a Hungarian patriot, and you have to except some painful experiences in that regard. It seems that the Hungarians are submitting to the deception that they alone could evade the threatened diminution because they are especially loved or respected in the world outside, in a word, that they are "exceptions."...Disappointment will not be absent and will bring bad times along with it...Withdraw your libido from your fatherland in a timely fashion and shelter it in Psychoanalysis, or else you will have to feel uncomfortable.[60]

If not Freud's urges, than the aftermath of the Great War and the establishment of the anti-Semitic Horthy regime in Hungary in 1919 naturally intensified Ferenczi's awareness about the implications of his Jewish identity. The following letter to Freud shows just how much the "awakening

59 Ervin Junger, Bartók és a zsidó diaszpora, Adatok Bartók Béla művészi és társadalmi kapcsolataihoz, [Bartók and the Jewish Diaspora, Data on the artistic and social connections of Béla Bartók, Budapest 1997, 7-50.

60 Freud to Ferenczi on October 27th, 1919", The Correspondence of Sigmund Freud and Sándor Ferenczi, vol. 2, 304.

from the illusion of the Era of Emancipation" was cruel. Ferenczi's position as a psychoanalyst, a Jew and as a former professor in the Bolshevist era became unbearable under the White Terror. The students, who tried to obstruct the progressive Gyula Pikler's lectures in the university around 1900[61], achieved their will by means of legislation – the Numerus Clausus Law – and through terror in the public space. Ferenczi writes to Freud on August 28, 1919:

After the unbearable "Red terror," which lay heavy on one's spirit like a nightmare, we now have the White one. For a short time it seemed as if they would succeed in moderating the parties toward a just compromise, but in the end the ruthless clerical-anti-Semitic spirit seems to have eked out a victory. If everything does not deceive, we Hungarian Jews are now facing a period of brutal persecution of Jews. They will, I think, have cured us in a very short time of the illusion with which we were brought up, namely, that we are "Hungarians of Jewish faith." I picture Hungarian anti-Semitism – commensurate with the national character – to be more brutal than the petty-hateful type of the Austrians.

It will very soon become evident how one can live and work here. It is naturally the best thing for Psychoanalysis, to continue working in complete withdrawal and without noise. Personally, one will have to take this trauma as an occasion to abandon certain prejudices brought along from the nursery and to come to terms with the bitter truth of being, as a Jew, really, without a country...The police jails are full of anonymously reported "Bolshevists," who are being mistreated there. The blackest reaction prevails at the university. All Jewish assistants were fired, the Jewish students were thrown out and beaten. From these few data you may get a picture of the situation that prevails here![62]

These lines are important mostly as testimonies to the turbulent times of the beginning of the 20th century viewed by Jews in the disintegrated Monarchy. Fourteen years later, two month before the passing away of Ferenczi, it was he who urged Freud to leave Austria. His premonition about the years to come in Vienna was no less valid than Freud's forewarning about post-war Hungary. Ferenczi writes to Freud as follows on March 29th 1933 under the influence of political developments in Germany.

I advise you to make use of the time of the not yet immediately dangerously threatening situation and, with a few patients and your daughter

61 On the Pikler affair and the Galilei circle: Zsigmond Kende, A Galilei Kör Meglakulàsa, [The formulation of the Galilei Circle], Budapest 1974, 67-70.

62 Ferenczi to Freud on August 28th, 1919", The Correspondence of Sigmund Freud and Sándor Ferenczi, vol. 2, 365-366.

Anna, to go to a more secure country, perhaps England...I, myself, am harboring the idea, in the event that the political danger gets closer to Budapest, of, at the proper time, going to Switzerland, where some patients who are still capable of paying will accompany me...Please take my warning seriously...[63]

The question of identity became more and more relevant for Freud and Ferenczi as the post-liberal political trends came to threaten the Jews of Central Europe. After the collapse of the pre-war political reality, Ferenczi was retreating to his Jewish identity from his Hungarian one, which was denied him by anti-Semitic Hungarian nationalism. In the following lines written by Ferenczi to Freud on October 4th 1919, Ferenczi discerns along with his Jewish ego a psychoanalytic one. Similarly to the professional identity of a physician, this psychoanalytic ego served as well to grant a social respectability, though this one was not anymore accepted by the society.

The beginning of the breakdown of our old political world, among other things also of the Glubus Hungaricus, is deeply injuring our narcissism. It is a good thing that one has a Jewish and a psychoanalytic ego along with the Hungarian, which remain untouched by these events.[64]

There is a more subtle feature discernable throughout the literature on the history of the Psychoanalytical Movement in Central Europe. Ferenc Erős claims that the Psychoanalytical Movement in Hungary owes its underground survival during the fascist and the communist regime to the inspiration of the teachings of Ferenczi. Erős indicates the emphasis of Ferenczi on primordial feelings as love, connection and relationship as deriving from the early connection between the mother and the child. These mother type feelings, says Erős, connected together the members of the Psychoanalytical Movement in their resistance against the father type collective authoritative state.[65]

The same "family" motive is detectable in Michelle Moreau-Ricaud's article about the foundation of the Budapest School and its difficult history in the interwar period. She writes about the "extended-family" type gatherings of the 24 members of the movement in Hungary, amusingly enough, on the occasion of Christmas in the 1920's at Ferenczi's home.[66] In the

63 Ferenczi to Freud on March 29th, 1933", The Correspondence of Sigmund Freud and Sándor Ferenczi, vol. 3, 447-448.

64 Ferenczi to Freud on October 4th, 1919", The Correspondence of Sigmund Freud and Sándor Ferenczi, vol. 2, 297.

65 Erős, 50-51.

66 Michelle Moreau-Ricaud, "The Founding of the Budapest School", in: Ferenczi's Turn in Psychoanalysis, Peter L. Rudnytsky, Antal Bókay, and Patrizia Giampieri-Deutch,

same spirit, Freud characterized his relationship with Ferenczi in 1933, just months before Ferenczi's early passing away, as "an intimate community of life, feeling, and interest."[67]

In the face of the disintegrating Austro-Hungarian Monarchy and the threats that the post-liberal political and social environment signified, the Jewish self-consciousness of Freud and Ferenczi grew stronger. This assertion may be confirmed both by Freud's intimate discourse on his Jewish identity through his inquiry on Moses, as by Ferenczi's understanding of the crude Hungarian political conditions till the point of considering emigration to the US. Their friendship inside the Psychoanalytical movement throughout the turbulent years of the 1920's and the 1930's, constituted for them a bulwark in the face of the menacing political and socio-cultural reality.

Conclusion

The Freud-Ferenczi correspondence is a fundamental document of the socio-cultural milieu of the beginning of the twentieth century in Central Europe. The young science of Psychoanalysis and its pioneers reflected their very society to the same extent as they were critical about it. Freud and Ferenczi, children of Eastern European Jewish immigrants had to face the collapse of the illusion of emancipation in the liberal-bourgeois society. However they themselves were at the same time the outcome of the same Bildungsbürgertum surroundings. Their faith in the feasibility of scientific investigation of culture and healing of the illnesses of mass-society had no limits.

Amid general decay, they envisioned abiding structures that promised to lay new foundations of self-understanding, and expected these structures, whether of art or of the psyche, to outlast the flux of styles that had concealed them. They cherished the hope that at last the bedrock of artistic and psychic experience had been stuck. They had unearthed, they believed, the secrets of the ages, the very foundations of cultural experience.[68]

The Jewish issue in the context of the Psychoanalytic movement was researched in depth. However, the incorporation of the Jewish issue into the historical scheme of Schorske, Hanák and Kovács did produce results in terms of our understanding of the rule that the state and the public sphere

eds., New York 1996, 55.

67 Ferenczi to Freud on January 11th, 1933", The Correspondence of Sigmund Freud and Sándor Ferenczi, vol. 3, 446.

68 William M. Johnston, "Cultivated Gardeners", in: The American Scholar, 2001, 260.

played in shaping the consciousness of Freud and Ferenczi of their Jewish identity. Indeed, there are interesting parallels between social phenomena and intellectual trends. István Hollósi, mentioned above, wrote in his autobiography that being a Jew, an outsider in the Christian public, brought about his occupation with mentally handicapped people, the outsiders of the society.[69]

Although Ferenczi did not write any work in the field of social psychology specifically; in contrast to Freud he considered the social implications of psychoanalysis from the very beginning of his acquaintance with the new science. His social interest corresponds to Hanák's theory on the social engagement of the progressive intellectual and artistic environment in Budapest around 1900. However this tendency came to its end, at least for the Psychoanalytic Movement in Hungary after the Great War. The change of this tendency was a direct result of the change in the state policies which came about upon in response to the demands made in the public sphere- especially by free-professionals. In contrast to Ferenczi, Freud moved from an escapist intellectual stance towards exploring the social repercussions of psychoanalysis.[70]

As we learn from the literature and from the primary sources examined, Ferenczi's and Freud's choices of social and professional orientation very much reflected the cultural-political setting which surrounded them in the capitals of the disintegrating Monarchy. 1919 constitutes a watershed only in the case of Ferenczi, because of the post-liberal tendencies coming to power in Budapest with the establishment of the Horthy-regime, which were already dominant in the Viennese political arena from the last years of the 19th century. The long century could only prolong Ferenczi's illusion about Jewish emancipation in Hungary, and Ferenczi's understanding of the condition of Jews and of the Psychoanalytic movement in Central Europe became similar to that of Freud, after 1919. Against their own will, the socio-political situation of Freud and Ferenczi reflected to a great extent the changing reality of the society they lived in.

69 Harmat, 150-151.
70 Harmat, 132-133.

Anat Varon
(The Hebrew University of Jerusalem)

Franz Werfel and the Search for Identity in the First Austrian Republic[1]

The First Republic and the Crisis of the Austrian Identity

Austria post World War I was a "state that no one wanted", as put in the words of Hellmut Andics.[2] Most political groups, from the pan-Germans (Deutschnationale) on the right to the Social-Democrats (especially them) on the left, were looking for union (Anschluss) with Germany.[3] In that spirit, the newly founded Staatsrat (state-council)[4] led by the Social Democrat Karl Renner, declared on November 12, 1918 the establishment of the Republic of German Austria (Republik Deutschösterreich), which, according to the second article of its charter, was to be seen as a part of the German Republic. It seemed that in postwar-Austria no one believed in the ability of the small republic to survive, and no one believed that the former German-speaking Habsburg citizens could be seen as an independent "Austrian Nation". After hundreds of years living under Habsburg rule in a multi-national Monarchy (Vielvölkerstaat), what would be the basis for a national Austrian identity?

The Austrians thought they did not need to answer this question since they would be united with Germany and thus become a part of the German nation, where they believed to belong. However, the Treaty of Saint-Germain (10 September 1919) put an end to the Anschluss dream; not only was Austria forbidden any form of unification with Germany, even the name

1 I would like to thank the academic and administrative staff of the Center for Austrian Studies and the European Forum at the Hebrew University of Jerusalem for giving me the opportunity to present this paper in the Conference of the Centers for Austrian Studies in Edmonton , Canada 2008. A special thanks is due to Mrs. Elisheva Moatti for all of her support and Prof. Bianca Kühnel. Another special thanks is due to Prof. Robert S. Wistrich from the Hebrew University, my instructor, and to Dr. Christian Gerbel from Vienna for their support in my work.

2 Hellmut Andics. Der Staat, den keiner wollte: Österreich von der Gründung der Republik bis zur Moskauer Deklaration, Wien/München/Zürich 1968.

3 Andics, Staat, 15ff.

4 The improvised national assembly elected the state-council for government of the 'German-Austria' Republic in its meeting on October 30, 1918. On the problems and meaning of this decision see Andics, Staat, 16-23.

of the republic had to be changed from 'German-Austria' to 'Republic of Austria' (Repbulik Österreich).[5] But what did it mean to be an 'Austrian'?

It took the Austrians another World War and a newly founded Second Republic to answer this question. At the time of the First Austrian Republic, from 1919 till 1934, the Austrians were struggling with one another over the question of their identity and the nature of Austrian society and politics. As long as democracy stood, fragile as it may have been during the First Republic, this question remained an open one, with different answers coming from different political and cultural groups in Austrian society. A good example for this is the reestablishment of the Salzburg Festival in 1920, an attempt of the conservative Catholic elite in Austria to return to the age of Baroque-Catholic Austria, and to present an Austrian identity vis-à-vis Germany, namely, the Austrians as the better «Germans», as Michael Steinberg's research showed.[6]

The rise of the Austrian Ständestaat (corporate-state) left no more room for exploring the question of Austrian identity as an open issue; and the coming of Hitler in 1938 made it disappear into thin air. At the end, the First Austrian Republic failed to present a valid Austrian identity.[7]

The Crisis of the Jewish-Austrian Intellectuals

While the Austrians were struggling with their own crisis of identity, it seems that the situation was even more complicated for the Jewish citizens. After the fall of the Monarchy there were about 200,000 Jews living in Austria, 180,000 in Vienna alone. The rising Anti-Semitism in post First World War Austria left no room for great optimism about the situation and the status of Jews in the new Republic. Already from the early days of the Republic of German Austria the political Anti-Semitism, rooted deep in Austria ever since the end of the 19th century when it came to its peak with the rise of Karl Lueger, the Anti-Semite Mayor of Vienna, prevailed.[8] The loss of the war and the hard economical crisis due to the loss of the old Habsburg's territories[9] were seen in part as the fault of the Jews, just as in neighboring Germany. The Jews were seen

5 The name was officially changed on October 21, 1919..

6 For the meaning and close connection between the Salzburg Festival and the attempt to construct an independent Austrian cultural identity see: Michael P. Steinberg, Austria as Theater and Ideology: The Meaning of the Salzburg Festival, Ithaca/London 2000.

7 Steven Beller, A Concise History of Austria, Cambridge 2006, 197.

8 For a clear picture of the Austrian political Anti-Semitism during the First Republic see Kurt Schubert, Die Geschichte des österreichischen Judentums, Wien 2008, 103-115.

9 Especially crucial was the stop of food and coal supplies from the former crown-lands of Hungary and Czechoslovakia. In the winter of 1918-1919 this meant a humanitarian

both as the war-profiteers and as the radical Bolshevik revolutionary element. In light of the fear from an upcoming revolution, as it happened in Germany and Hungary,[10] this played a crucial role in the fight against the Jews during the 1920's.

Another aspect was the question of the Jewish war refuges from Galicia (southern Poland), who had arrived in Vienna during the First World War. These former Habsburg citizens stood in the middle of Austrian political Anti-Semitism, from right to left,[11] which called for their expulsion back to where they had come from, namely Poland. The poor Jewish immigrants were seen as an "economical and social burden" for the struggling Austrian republic. And after the Treaty of Saint Germain the Austrians feared that many Jews would use their right as former Habsburg citizens and ask for an Austrian citizenship, as article 80 in the treaty granted.[12] Few, however, actually did so.

One of the testimonies for the Jewish insecurity in Austria after the war, in light of the growing Anti-Semitism and the unstable political and economical climate, was without a doubt Hugo Bettauer's Zeitroman (Contemporary-novel) entitled The City without Jews (Die Stadt ohne Juden) published in 1922 and filmed in 1924. The 'Utopian' story tells in a satirical way how after the war the government in Vienna decides to pass an anti-Jewish law and has all of the Jews expelled from the city. Since the Jews are responsible for the entirety of Austria's political and economic problems, it is decided that, once the Jews are evicted, it will be possible to reestablish the Bodenständige Gesellschaft (rooted to the soil society) in Vienna.

It is easy to take the Jews out of Vienna but it later turns out it is not as easy to replace them. In a short time the city of Vienna becomes deserted. The cafés, the elegant shops, the banks, the opera and theaters are all missing the "Jewish Touch", missing the Jews. In the (happy) end the Austrians have no choice but to recognize their mistake and ask the Jews to return to Vienna. (Indeed utopia, if not total fantasy! After the Second World War, there were not too many Austrians who were looking for the "return of the Jews".)

---

disaster at the Austrian capital. For more on the economical hardships of the first years of the First Republic, see Beller, History, 202ff.

10 Schubert, Geschichte, 103.

11 For the use of Anti-Semitic propaganda in service of the political right and the Social Democrats, especially during the elections of 1923, see Schubert, Geschichte, 104ff.

12 Schubert, Geschichte, 106.

Although Bettauer's novel became a bestseller (it sold about 250,000 copies!) it did not change the political situation or help fight the ever growing Austrian Anti-Semitism. It did not even help prevent Bettauer's murder in 1925 by an Austrian Nazi (who shortly after his trial was set free, having been declared "unfit to stand trial"). Bettauer's murder may be the ultimate example of Austria's betrayal of its Jewish intellectuals in the period of the interwar years. It seems that the "Age of Security" was long gone even before the coming of Hitler.

Some of the most prominent Jewish intellectuals felt this even before the First World War ended. Karl Kraus wrote his great drama, The Last Days of Mankind, and prophesied the decay of the late imperial Habsburg society; the same generation which brought the catastrophe that was to be remembered as the First World War. But Kraus did not choose to leave Austria, not even Vienna. Others actually chose to do so, and the first name that comes to mind is of course Stefan Zweig. This most famous, loyal son of Vienna, decided already in 1917 to move to Salzburg, closer to the German border. In 1934 he decided to leave Austria for good. He returned to Vienna one last time in 1937, and he was no more optimistic about the future of the city, as he wrote in a letter to Arnold Zweig: "...I was in Vienna (and visited Freud) and looked on that city just as if the enemy were already at the gates."[13]

It seemed that the economical and political crisis of the first years of the Austrian Republic took its toll on the cultural life in Vienna. Not only did it lose some of its past glamour to other Austrian towns like Salzburg, the old rivalry between Vienna and Berlin surfaced again, and in many cases when asked Wien oder Berlin? (Vienna or Berlin?), Berlin won. It was even noticeable outside of Austria, as Willy Haas wrote in a letter from 1919 to Hugo von Hofmannsthal: "Vienna will become a (spiritless) [geistlos] periphery of Berlin".[14]

Vienna did lose some of its great Jewish intellectuals,[15] who preferred the Weimar Republic to the Austrian Republic; among them the composer

---

13 Cited by Robert S. Wistrich, Stefan Zweig and the > >World of Yesterday< <, in: Mark H. Gelber (ed.). Stefan Zweig Reconsidered: New Perspectives on his Literary and Biographical Writings, Tübingen 2007, 59-77, 74.

14 Willy Haas to Hugo von Hofmannsthal, 21.6.1919. in: Hugo von Hofmannsthal. Hugo von Hofmannsthal/Willy Haas. Ein Briefwechsel, Berlin 1968, 40.

15 Hilde Spiel in her book also describes this period as a time of flight for major intellectuals. See and compare: Hilde Spiel. *Vienna's Golden Autumn, 1866-1938*, London 1987, 214:"Some of the greatest talents in those years avoided the hopelessness of the capital by either moving to the country, staying in the provinces if they were born there, or seeking out the more vital intellectual and artistic centers of Frankfurt, Dresden and Berlin."

Arnold Schoenberg, who, after an Anti-Semitic incident that took place in Mattsee, a spa resort near Salzburg, in the summer of 1921 when he was asked to prove he was an "Aryan" and then told to leave because Jews were no longer welcome, concluded that Austria was unfähig, has no ability to survive. He left for Berlin the first chance he got, in 1926. Next we may mention the name of Joseph Roth, who came from the little town of Brody (today in the Ukraine) and dreamed like so many Ostjuden (eastern-Jews) about Vienna. He actually managed to arrive there in 1913, and after the war used his right according to the aforementioned article 80 in the Saint Germain Treaty, and got the Austrian citizenship. He soon found out that "to be an Ostjude may be hard everywhere but it is hardest in Vienna". He too left for Berlin in 1920 and stayed till Hitler came to power in 1933.

The case of Arnold Schoenberg illustrates that the rising Anti-Semitism in Austria of the First Republic affected not only the poor Ostjuden living in crowded apartments at the second quarter of Vienna, the Leopoldstadt, but touched the most assimilated, even converted Jewish intellectuals! The rising Anti-Semitism proved that no one was immune, and contributed to the general identity crisis of Austrian Jews that stemmed from the loss of the monarchy, and brought about a feeling of insecurity.

Many Jewish intellectuals were forced by the crisis to deal with an aspect of their identity that they didn't even think existed: their Jewish identity, or at least their Jewishness. A good example for this is the growing interest in the bible during the 1920's and 1930's, seen in many works; from Zweig's early play Jeremiah (1916) to Freud's Moses and Monotheism (1939). We can also mention Schoenberg's opera Moses and Aaron (1930), Joseph Roth's Hiob (1930) and Werfel's Hearken unto the Voice (1937). Unsurprisingly we find that the most representative Jewish authors of the so called 'Habsburg-Myth' in the Austrian literature post First World War were also representative in what can be called the "Bible-Myth" or the "Myth of the Diaspora" in the Austrian literature. Both represent, to some extent, different, yet connected aspects of identity crisis among some of the prominent Jewish intellectuals, from Zweig to Werfel, that of the Austrian-Jewish identity post First World War.

Finally, I want to return to Stefan Zweig and his reaction to yet another example of the change that was evident in Austria during the First Republic towards the Jewish intellectuals. That is the death of one of the greatest Jewish Austrian writers, Arthur Schnitzler (1862-1931), the man whose most famous works stood in the middle of the Austrian Kulturpolitik and controversy. We can mention his novella Lieutenant Gustl (1900) and the play from the same year, Reigen. The play was re-performed in the theaters of Vienna and Berlin during the early 1920's and stood in the middle of Anti-Semitic personal attacks against Schnitzler.

When Schnitzler died in October 1931, the First Republic was close to its democratic end. It was already ruled as far back as 1922 by the conservative right Christian Social Party, now headed by the Chancellor Karl Buresch, the last Chancellor before the rise of the "Dollfuss and Schuschnigg Era".

In an article that Zweig wrote in 22 October 1931 for the Neue Freie Presse he describes how the Austrian Republic said her farewell to one of its most important Jewish-Austrian intellectuals: "Neither the Old Austria nor the new, the imperial Austria nor the Republic, have weighed him [Schnitzler] with medals or decorations for his free will to stay unattached, Nulla crux, nulla corona, neither Cross, nor Crown decorated the dear casket".[16] And in a letter that he wrote in November 1931 to Felix Salten, in order to explain why he doesn't want to have his 50's birthday celebrated in Vienna, Zweig elaborated upon which conclusion should be the drawn from the Schnitzler case: "abroad we Jews are still considered [to represent] Austria but not in the eyes of Herr Czermak [Cultural minister] and Miklas [Austrian President]. Let's leave this small inland, this poor, provincial and rural remain of the true Austria to these men and their followers".[17]

With the death of Schnitzler the early generation of Jewish Viennese intellectuals of the Fin de Siecle, and the early generation of the Young-Vienna movement of the pre First World War came to an end. It was the time of the new generation of intellectuals in Vienna. Among them we can mention those who came from Prague, names like Leo Perutz, Egon Erwin Kisch, and of course Franz Werfel. Next to them were new young intellectuals that came from outside the former Austro-Hungarian Monarchy, namely Elias Canetti, who came from a Sephardic Jewish family in Bulgaria or Jura Soyfer, who came from a Russian Jewish family.

Vienna of the First Republic did lose some of its great intellectuals, who either left it or passed away,[18] but it did not in the end become the "periphery of Berlin" as was prophesized. Donald Daviau reminds us that: "Despite the many difficulties and uncertainties that had to be faced and overcome during this stressful, exciting period, these two decades from 1918 to 1938

16 Cited by Gert Kerschbaumer, Stefan Zweigs Ekel vor jeglicher Politik, in: Gelber (ed.). Stefan, 79-90, 82, n.11.

17 Cited by Kerschbaumer, Stefan, 84.

18 Among the intellectuals that passed away we can mention Peter Altenberg who died in 1916, Gustav Klimt and Egon Schiele who died from the Spanish Influenza in 1918, Hugo von Hofmannsthal died in 1929. See, Donald D. Daviau (ed.), Major Figures of Austrian Literature: The Interwar Years, 1918-1938, Albany 1990, 9.

must be recognized – perhaps surprisingly – as the most fertile and productive epoch of Austrian cultural history to date".[19] We ought to remember, also, that most of what today is known as Austrian literature about the so called Welt von Gestern, was written not at the end of the 19th century but at the time of the First Republic.

Franz Werfel was among those who voted for Vienna and contributed to this "fertile and productive epoch". It is time to present him and his work on the background of the First Austrian Republic.

Der Weltfreund chose Vienna

Franz Werfel (1890-1945) was born in Prague in 1890, then a part of the Austro-Hungarian Monarchy, to a wealthy assimilated Jewish family. Most Jewish families in Prague at the time had assimilated into the German-Austrian culture,[20] thus being perceived by the general Czech population as collaborators with the Habsburg rule and the forefront of the ruling culture. Due to this image, they suffered both hostility and estrangement. Werfel himself felt that burden, not so much as a Jew but as a „German" (according to him) and already in his early 20's decided to leave Prague (he actually left in 1912) because he felt that, „this City has no reality [keine Wirklichkeit] for a non-Czech person...". He continues to explain that: „it is a daydream for him which does not render him any experience; a paralyzing ghetto without having even the poor relations of the ghetto, a musty world from which no or only false activity emanates. You can bear Prague only as intoxication, as a fata morgana of life, and that is the reason why so many artists did not flee". The fact that Werfel did leave Prague does not mean he left it behind him. He himself explained that "the Homeless person has a better understanding of the secret of the city at home [daheim] and even better when he is abroad [in der Fremde]".[21] This understanding of Prague expresses itself in many of Werfel's works, such as Class Reunion (1928), which tells the story of his Gymnasium days in Prague or The Pure in Heart (1929), which is also a tribute to his beloved Czech-Catholic Nanny, Babi.[22] Also Werfel's first success in the lyrical world started with a poem that he wrote, The Gardens of the City (Die Gärten der Stadt), about Prague's gardens;

19 Daviau, Figures, 9.

20 Werfel once claimed that in Prague "Germans and Jewis are identical", see: Franz Werfel, Erguß und Beichte, in: Franz Werfel, Zwischen Oben und Unten (ZOU), München/Wien 1975, 690-700, 692.

21 Cited by Hans Wagener, Understanding Franz Werfel, University of South Carolina 1993, 4.

22 Wagener, Franz, 5.

ironically it was published (1908) in Vienna, in the Sunday edition of the Viennese daily Die Zeit.

After leaving Prague "for good" as he put it, Werfel needed to find a new home. It took him some time but, after a stint in the Austro-Hungarian army during the First World War, and a previous sojourn in Germany, he finally made it to Vienna in 1917, shortly before the monarchy was lost for good. He still had some time to serve at the place that was a safe haven for many intellectuals from across the monarchy – from Roda-Roda to Rilke, from Stefan Zweig to Leo Perutz – the Austrian War and Royal Archives, at the Press Bureau (KPQ).[23] There, the intellectuals were occupied working for Austrian war propaganda, work that was criticized by Karl Kraus as an „intellectual betrayal".[24] It is worth noting that this post allowed the young intellectuals not only to take a closer look at the war zones such as Galicia or the Ukraine, but also enabled them to reach Switzerland, where they switched from pro- to counter-war propaganda.[25] Here we can mention Werfel's Speech to the Workers of Davos, given in early 1918. The Speech marks not only his anti-War stand but corresponds with the short flirt Werfel had, right after the war, with the Austrian anarchist Communist group, Die Rote Garde (The Red Guard), led by Egon Erwin Kisch (Werfel's childhood friend from Prague). At the end of the war, therefore, one finds the young Werfel on the barricades in Vienna calling to loot the Banks in the name of the revolution against Capitalism. But this period ended soon. Werfel realized very quickly that political activism was not his task. From that time on, like many other Austrian intellectuals of his era, he would stay out of politics and concentrate more on his literary work.

Though Werfel's first days in Vienna started with a call for revolution, his last days there were at the very peak of his success under the regime of the Austro-Fascist government, having received the highest honor of the government, the Verdienstkreuz für Kunst und Wissenschaft (Order of Merit for Art and Science) in 1937, personally bestowed upon him from the hands of Chancellor Kurt von Schuschnigg, the head of the Austrian Ständestaat (Corporate State), and a close friend of Werfel's wife, Alma Mahler-Werfel.

23 KPQ stands for "k.u.k. Kriegspressequartier".

24 See Edward Timms, Poetry, Politics and Personalities: The Kraus-Werfel Controversy, in: Joseph Strelka (Hg.). Unser Fahrplan geht von Stern zu Stern: Franz Werfels Stellung und Werk, Bern 1992, 111-138, 113-114.

25 Stefan Zweig in his Die Welt von Gestern gives a description of this time in Switzerland during the end of the First World War, he also mentions Werfel among the people he met there. See Stefan Zweig, Die Welt von Gestern, Frankfurt am Main 1982, 287, 298ff, 312.

Werfel lived in Vienna for twenty years, and it seems that it was the closest he ever got to have a Heimat. Vienna was where Werfel wrote some of his most important works, from his early expressionist Play Der Spiegelmensch (The Mirror-Man, 1920), through his biography on his idol composer, Verdi – Roman der Oper and till his Höret die Stimme (Hearken unto the Voice, 1937). The work best remembered of Werfel today is his 40 Days of Musa Dagh, which he wrote in 1933 to recount the story of the Armenian genocide.

Perhaps the best evidence of his success during the 20 years that he spent in Austria is the simple fact that in the 1920's and 1930's Werfel became one of the most acclaimed writers of German language.[26] Testimony of that are the many awards he received; among them, the Grillparzer Preis (1926) and the Schiller Preis (1927). Werfel also had some international success and was known in the US even before he emigrated there in 1940. Some of his works were translated into English and adapted to the American stages. For Example, his novel The Eternal Road was adapted into a play (1935) in cooperation with the composer Kurt Weill and the famous Austrian director Max Reinhardt. Werfel's cooperation with Max Reinhardt is another evidence of his importance and success at that time.[27]

Werfel himself carried a sense of gratitude and loyalty to Vienna and to the home it offered him. In a diary entry from the day of the Anschluss, 13 March 1938, he expressed his feelings about Austria and the fact that he was now losing his home: „Today, Sunday, the 13 of March, my heart wants to break from suffering, since Austria is no longer my home. Oh, my house in Breitenstein, where I worked for 20 years, must I never see you again? It is better to keep silent!".[28]

But Werfel did not remain silent, and the events of the Anschluss will appear not only in two major literary works he wrote: A Pale-Blue Woman's Handwriting (1941) and Cella, or, The Survivors (published post mortem), but also in Poems about the events in Austria after the Anschluss. One of these poems was entitled The Good Place in Vienna

26 Wagener, Franz, 8.

27 Max Reinhardt, the famous Austrian theater director collaborated with Hugo von Hofmannsthal on the Salzburg Festival during the 20's. After Hofmannsthal's death in 1929, Reinhardt hoped for a closer collaboration with Werfel. But, although they had a close friendship that lasted into their exile in the US it never came to be a close collaboration as Reinhardt hoped for, mainly because of the "artistic differences" between the two men. See, Georgina Clark, The Eternal Road: Werfel's Theatrical Collaboration with Max Reinhardt, in: Lothar Huber (ed.). Franz Werfel: An Austrian Writer Reassessed, Oxford/New-York/Munich 1989, 211-224, 213ff.

28 Franz Werfel, dairy entry from 13.3.1938, in: Werfel, ZOU, 743.

(Der gute Ort zu Wien). The good place is the Jewish part of the Zentralfriedhof (Central Cemetery) in the Viennese district Simmering, the last public garden still open to the Jews after the Anschluss. The poem included the following lines: "Volksgarten, Stadt-and Rathauspark, never was your spring so strong. For the Jews of Vienna it is forbidden. For them the only Green is growing by the Dead." [29]

In the end Werfel fled Europe via France, Spain and Portugal and reached the USA in 1940, but the home that he lost in 1938 would not leave him. In his last novel, The Star of the Unborn (Stern der Ungeborn), published post mortem in 1946, the mysterious traveler, F.W (Franz Werfel) keeps wearing the cross of the Austrian Order of Merit for Art and Science close to his heart, [30] a constant reminder of the author's loyalty to his only home, Austria.

Franz Werfel, an Attempt to Mirror-Time or the Forgotten Biography of Richard Specht

In 1926 Richard Specht (1870-1932), an Austrian lyricist, dramatist and musicologist, published a contemporary (now much outdated) quasi-biography that looks into Werfel's creative work and tries to define the connection between it and his cultural background as an intellectual of the Austrian republic. The work is entitled Franz Werfel – an attempt to Mirror Time (Franz Werfel – Versuch einer Zeitspiegelung).[31] In the introduction Specht provides a clear definition of Werfel as a prominent contemporary Austrian intellectual, and writes: "Once in more years than I care to count comes a poet who appears to me to be great. A poet who has a mission. A poet who possesses not only the creative talents to produce literary works, but also to become a speaker for the times. ... Franz Werfel is that kind of a Poet....then it is not about him alone, it is not only about that that he is clearly the "voice of God". It is also about time itself, that he is its exponent and result".[32]

Specht's biography made its impression on Werfel's contemporaries, and some of them even mention it in their autobiography (Max Brod) or letters (Egon Erwin Kisch, Stefan Zweig).

29 Franz Werfel, Der gute Ort zu Wien, in: Gerhard C, Krischker (Hg.). Wien im Gedicht, Leipzig 1993, 153-155, 153.

30 Wagener, Franz, 161.

31 Richard Specht, Franz Werfel – Versuch einer Zeitspiegelung, Berlin/Wien/Leipzig 1926.

32 Specht, Franz, 10-11.

Werfel, who was involved in many cultural circles, from his youth days in the Café Arco in Prague to his days in the Café Central and then the Café Herrenhof in Vienna, collected many friends and rivals. In some cases the friends became rivals (like Karl Kraus). Others, like Egon Erwin Kisch lost touch. But they all found their place in Specht's biography.

As we already mentioned, for a short time in his early days in Vienna Werfel did have connection to Kisch's anarchist Communist group, The Red Guard. When Specht is writing about that time in Werfel's life he tries to minimized Werfel's involvement in the group as he writes: "Kisch was the one who drew Werfel to Communism and wanted Werfel to play a part in the establishment of a 'Soviet Republic' (Räterrepublik) in Austria. It was Werfel's luck that he only ever played the part of an observer and not of a participant."[33] It is incorrect to claim that Werfel was a mere bystander in the Red Guard. A testimony by the Viennese journalist Richard A. Bermann in his autobiography shows Werfel's involvement in the Red Guard was a bit more "active" than Specht would like us to believe: "I could mention a few other Viennese literati (among them one who is world renowned) [Werfel], who at that time acted in a much more revolutionary way than Kisch; they called in the Cafés and in the streets for looting the capital banks, and soon I have come to know them as brave followers of the Clerical-Fascist Corporate state of Mr. Schuschnigg".[34]

It seems that Specht's description was somewhat anachronistic and corresponded with Werfel's turn to a more conservative world-view during the mid 20's.

Another friend and rival of Werfel from his Prague days was the Zionist writer Max Brod. Brod is actually connected with Werfel's early career as he was the one who got Werfel's first book of poems, Der Weltfreund (Friend to the World) (1911), published.[35] The book sold-out and made Werfel instantly known and admired in the German speaking world.[36] Brod also dedicated a relatively big portion of his autobiography to his memories of Werfel. Yet another evidence of his importance! Already at the introduction Brod mentions Werfel: "One of the biggest

33 Specht, Franz, 46.

34 Richard A. Bermann, Die Fahrt aus dem Katarakt: Eine Autobiographie ohne einen Helden, Wien 1998, 231-232. For more about Werfel's involvement in the Red Guard, see and compare Peter Stephan Jungk, Franz Werfel, London 1990, 71-72.

35 Brod was very insistent with the German publisher Axel Junker, who was not in favor of publishing Werfel's poems. Brod threatened that if the book will not be published, he himself will take his businesses elsewhere. See Jungk, Franz, 25ff.

36 Jungk, Franz, 27.

disappointments of my life is the case of Werfel. With Franz Werfel there was never a hearty friendship [as with Kafka] ....and yet there were signs for it, and our friendship, and mutual understanding, seemed fresh and strong and quite deep. And due to all that love was the disappointment twice bitter....and I would be lying if I said that I ever got over that disappointment".[37]

The big disappointment that Brod is referring to is the fact that already during the First World War Werfel published an "Open Letter" entitled "The Christian Mission" (Die christlische Sendung, 1916). In it he declared himself a "Christian Author" and spoke about the supreme morality of Christianity. Brod from his end tried for some time to convince Werfel to turn to Zionism and even answered Werfel's "Open Letter". That same issue stood as a disagreement between Brod and Martin Buber during the First World War.

The other disappointment Brod had is related to Specht's biography: "And then appeared Specht's biography of Werfel, in it (as far as I can remember), there was no mention of my early efforts on behalf of Werfel's first successes. I cannot assume that Werfel did not see the manuscript before it was published. I never asked him about it. And so it remains to me, although it is a thing of very little importance, a riddle".[38]

Surprisingly enough Specht's biography did not find its rightful place in modern research.

It is true that it is panegyric and outdated and, as we saw, not so accurate and dependable but its importance lays in the fact that it was the first attempt to represent Werfel as a prominent intellectual of Austria in the First Republic.

The great attention it received by Werfel's contemporaries is a good testimony to his relevance to the cultural milieu in Austria at that time, a fact that seemed to be obvious to Werfel's contemporaries but is much overlooked in modern research.

Franz Werfel and the Search for Identity in the First Austrian Republic: Jewish, Catholic and Austrian

Specht's biography was already completed by 1925 so it covered Werfel's oeuvre only up till his play *Paul among the Jews*, which at that time

37 Max Brod, Streitbares Leben: Autobiographie, München 1960, 9.
38 Brod, Leben, 63.

was not even published (Specht had only the manuscript, it was published in 1926). And yet, already then Specht concluded that the one theme that characterized Werfel's works, from his poems to his dramas and short stories, was the representation of the "dualism of the self" as he called it. We may call it the search for identity.

It seemed that much like Austria at the time Werfel as well was caught between the two worlds of Old and New Austria, and in multiple identities of which we may count at least three: Jewish, Catholic and Austrian. The search for them is reflected in Werfel's vast and diverse opus from 1918 till 1938: From early plays and up to his last written novel in Austria, *Hearken unto the Voice*, including his most famous work, *The 40 Days of Musa Dagh*, the question of identity is always evident though it is not always the same identity that Werfel is looking for.

It was not a mere coincidence that Werfel's search for identity found its expression in Austria. It seems that Werfel's image of old-Austria played a major role in his attraction to Vienna (apart from his love affair with Alma Mahler that kept him there), but the fact remains that, by the time he had arrived there, Old Austria has disappeared in favor of New Austria.

Whereas for some Jewish intellectuals Vienna no longer offered a suitable cultural and political climate, for Werfel it seemed to be just the right place: "I live in Vienna since autumn of 1917. In Vienna I unconsciously found the great happiness which I was always looking for."[39]

Could it be that the "great happiness" to which Werfel refers was his belief that in Austria all of his identities could co-exist without being caught in a conflict? And if so, which Austria was it that offered him such a safe home? Was it Old-Austria or was it the New one? Was it the Austria of the Habsburgs or was it the Austria of the democratic republic and the "golden-days" of 'Red Vienna', or was it the Austria of Chancellor Schuschnigg and his *Ständestaat*, which kept him wearing the merit they awarded him in 1937 in his final utopian novel?

The answer to this question may not be clearly evident when we notice that, in the late 1930's, Werfel returns to write in two parallel literary genres indicative of the Old Austria; the one of the 'Habsburg Myth' (as Claudio Magris noted long ago in his classical work on the subject) and the other of the 'Bible Myth' – the myth of the Jewish Diaspora through the biography and historical background of the Jewish prophet Jeremiah.

---

39 Franz Werfel, Autobiographische Skizze, in: ZOU, 701-705, 703.

It seems that from the perspective of the political and cultural elite of the *Ständestaat* Werfel served as an example for the kind of Austrian intellectual who represented the values of the regime, and without going into the question of what these values actually were, I wonder whether Werfel himself saw it that way. Did the Austrian Clerical-Fascist state with its model of conservative-catholic Austrian identity serve in some way as a solution for Werfel's search for identity? Did it only touch the aspect of his Catholic or Austrian identity? And if so, where did it leave the Jew Werfel? Could he too find his place in this model of Austrian identity? I wish to be very careful but I think that he did not. The mere fact that Werfel returned to Old-Austria especially during the time of the *Ständestaat* should reopen the question of his relation towards it.

Another problem that should be addressed is: which identity was dominant in Werfel's life and when? This question, I believe, is especially important if we consider Werfel's search for his Jewish identity during the First Republic. The close connection between the atmosphere in Vienna after the First World War with its rising Anti-Semitism and Werfel's awakening of his Jewish identity is evident by Werfel's own testimony that it was not until he moved to Vienna that he was consciously aware of the "conflict with his Jewishness".[40]

Werfel's conflict with Judaism is maybe the most stimulating and interesting thing to follow in his works from the period of the First Republic. Although he did not approach political events directly, he did touch on the most fundamental challenges in the new chapter of Austrian Jews during the time from 1918 till 1938: from the encounters of different groups of Jews with one another during the service in the Austro-Hungarian army in the First World War (*Pogrom*) to the question of the relationship between Jews and non-Jews in post World War Austria (*Hearken unto the Voice*), from the problems of Anti-Semitism to the theological questions about the relation between Judaism and Christianity (*Paul among the Jews*) and up to his criticism of Zionism and assimilation. We must also not forget his two visits in Palestine in the 1920's and 1930's and his close connections to two of the most prominent Zionists intellectuals, Max Brod and Martin Buber.

It is no wonder that in another contemporary work from 1933, written about the history of Austrian Jews from the beginning till post First World War, entitled *Die Juden Wiens: Geschichte, Wirtschaft, Kultur* (The Jews of Vienna: History, Economy, Culture), a book that may serve as the "academic" parallel to Hugo Bettauer's satirical novel from 1922, the author, the Jewish Art historian Hans Tietze, who devoted only 8 pages to the entire period after 1918, still mentions Werfel's two most relevant works

40 See Werfel, Erguß, 693, and compare, Jungk, Franz, 36.

(*Paul among the Jews* (1926) and *The Pure in Heart* (1929)) as a resource for understanding the situation of the Jews in Austria: this is yet another indication to the kind of attention Werfel received from the intellectual milieu in Vienna during the time of the First Austrian Republic. Again we encounter the discrepancy between Werfel's perception by his contemporaries and modern research: few would turn to Werfel as a resource for the history of the Austrian Jews during the First Republic.

Finally, we are left with Werfel's Austrian identity, which could be regarded as the sum of his Jewish and Catholic identities, as the metaphysical identity which holds the two opposites together. But it goes further than Werfel's own personal identity, since his success was seen by some of the other intellectuals as a threat to the nature of Austrian cultural identity. Therefore, the controversies and rivalries Werfel had with people like Robert Musil and especially Karl Kraus should also be looked at from the angle of a search for identity. In this case, they represent the struggle to define Austria's cultural identity as a whole at the time of the First Republic. We are left with the question of the connection between Werfel's works and his Austrian background, first as a Habsburg citizen and then as a citizen of the First Republic and the Ständestaat, and, in all cases, as an Austrian-Jew.

Conclusion: Franz Werfel and the First Republic: Some problems of definitions

We began our presentation with the historical background of Austria's identity crisis during the time of the First Republic. The period of the First Austrian republic was used here in its broad meaning, taking as its reference the period of Austrian independence that lasted from 1918 till the Anschluss in 1938. Methodologically speaking it remains to be seen if this kind of periodization will serve this research best. From the perspective of the identity search it can be argued that this search had ended with the final end of the Austrian Democratic Republic and the establishment of the Austro-Fascist Ständestaat after the civil war of February 1934. It is true that some of the open questions were no longer relevant (mostly on the political sphere), but I suspect that Werfel's search did not end even under this regime with which he shared common views and values at least as regards the image of Conservative Catholic Austria. To which degree was he in agreement with them is still unclear.

Another problem regarding this period is that often, seen by cultural historians, it is dealt with from the perspective of Fin de Siècle Vienna – the golden age of Jewish creativity in the city. Steven Beller's cultural history, Vienna and the Jews, 1867-1938, serves as a good example. The period is seen here both from the perspective of the Jewish emancipation and creativity since its beginning with the constitution of 1867 till its historical end with the Anschluss, and from the perspective of the golden age of Fin de Siècle Vienna. So the names of the "new intellectuals" like Jura Soyfer or Elias Canetti (even Leo Perutz) do not appear even once in the whole book!

It is true that cultural history is not always parallel to the immediate political events and some cultural movements or phenomena outlast the political changes, but during the transformation from Monarchy to republic to Ständestaat some changes did take place and somewhere along the way the Fin de Siècle Vienna did come to its end, but it is not clear when that happened and what replaced it.

Also if we recognize that next to the "old generation" of intellectuals, who shared the same social, political and cultural background, we witness the establishment of the "new generation" of intellectuals, who do not share the same common background. We need to find a theoretical frame that would enable us to include both groups into the cultural mosaic of the period. Also, we need to carefully think of how we define these abstract terms of "old" and "new" intellectuals. Some of the names we can mention might fit into both categories, creating yet another methodological and theoretical problem.

For now I think that the abstract term of the "Interwar years", 1918-1938, that was offered by Donald Daviau[41] serves as a good starting point for this research. One problem with this definition, in my opinion, is that political events become neutralized and disappear altogether into an almost too-abstract timeframe.

Finally I wish to conclude with one last definition, that of Werfel, as he saw Old Austria and himself as an Austrian writer at the time of the Austrian Ständestaat. In his prolog to the American anthology, Twilight of a World (written in April 1936), he explains to the reader what kind of a writer he really is: "...to belong not only to the two epochs but to the two worlds – that, I should think, is the lot of those alone who are the children of that dead world of which I write".[42] And then at the end of his

41 See Daviau, Figures, 8ff.

42 Franz Werfel, Twilight of a World, translated by H.T. Lowe—Porter, New-York 1937, 4. Werfel's prolog is an essay that deals with the Old imperial Austria and Werfel's image of it. The essay shows Werfel as a representative of yet another literary genre in the Austrian literature of the post First World War period, the so called Habsburg Myth literature. Werfel, with Joseph Roth and Stefan Zweig are the most representative Jewish authors of this kind of literature. More on Werfel as Habsburg Myth writer see Claudio Magris, Der Habsburgische Mythos in der österreichischen Literatur, Wien 2000, 314ff.

prolog Werfel returns back to his Austria, not that of the First Republic or that of the Ständestaat, but that of the Old imperial Austria: "Austria Was a wonderful home, a home of humanity without regard to blood or confession, to the origin or goal of its children. The Austrian born in old Austria has no longer a home. Or, does man's securest possessions abide in that which he no longer has?".[43] Werfel wrote all this about a year before he reached his peak in Austria and before receiving the highest honor from Schuschnigg's regime in 1937.

43 Werfel, Twilight, 10.

Börris Kuzmany
(University of Vienna)

The Town of Brody in the Course of the Long 19th Century.

A History of Failure?

Brody, a town today lying in Western Ukraine, became part of the Habsburg Empire following the First Partition of Poland in 1772. Until Austria-Hungary's collapse at the end of the First World War the town was right on the border with Poland (1772-1795) and later with Russia (1795-1918). This paper embraces a time span of almost 150 years, excluding the First World War and examines Brody's economic and social history. The most important material, which serves as the basis for this research are archival sources, mainly holdings in Lviv, Vienna, Paris and Krakow as well as published sources such as statistics, administrative handbooks and travel reports.[1]

Economic rise and fall of the city of Brody

Since the second half of the 17th century Brody had progressively developed into a trade junction far beyond the local dimension. The city owed its growth mostly to the strong support of several noble families who possessed the town in the course of centuries.[2] After the middle of the 18th century Brody must be considered as an economic transfer zone between Eastern and Western Europe and vice versa. It fits thus well into Schmale's definition of a historical region in the transeuropean networks of economic, cultural, religious, intellectual and political communication.[3]

1 This article is a synopsis of my thesis defended in December 2008 (Börries Kuzmany, Die Stadt Brody im langen 19. Jahrhundert - Eine Misserfolgsgeschichte? PhD Wien/Paris 2008) and was supported by the Austrian Science Fund (FWF).

2 Sadok Barącz, Wolne miasto handlowe Brody, Lwów 1865, 100, 120; Ivan Sozans'kyj, Z mynuvšyny mista Brodiv. Pryčynky do istoriji mista v XVII v., Brody 2003 [L'viv 1911], 3-5.

3 Wolfgang Schmale, Historische Komparatistik und Kulturtransfer. Europageschichtliche Perspektiven für die Landesgeschichte; eine Einführung unter besonderer Berücksichtigung der sächsischen Landesgeschichte, Bochum 1998, 1-34.

Brody's partner cities (with important fairs) were mainly Leipzig in the West and Berdychiv in the East. Brody thus became a hub for the exchange of primary wares like wax, flax, honey, hemp or fur from Poland and Russia with manufactured goods like textiles, British cotton, Styrian scythes, so called Nuremberg wares or French silk.[4]

The First Partition of the Polish-Lithuanian Commonwealth established a new border just ten kilometres eastwards of Brody, which threatened to cut through ancient trading lines. The newly established Austrian bureaucracy quickly understood Brody's importance, as the city's trade volume exceeded that of the regional capital Lviv by eight times and accounted for more than the half of Galicia's commercial exchange.[5] In 1779 an imperial decree declared Brody a free zone that allowed transit trade to continue without any nuisance.[6]

This free trade privilege was something new per se. Free cities had been existing in the Habsburg Empire already since 1719 (Trieste and Rijeka) [7], but with Brody for the first time a landlocked town was declared a free zone. Squeezed between Austria and Poland – after 1795 between Austria and Russia – Brody could serf as a trading hub only as long as both neighbouring states consented.

At the end of the 18th century Brody became a model for other Galician towns that received similar privileges to stimulate trade and thereby increase the province's prosperity in general. This was the case in Podgórze

---

4 Katharina Middell, Brody, Leipzig, Lyon: europäische Handelsbeziehungen und ihre Träger (1770-1820), in: Hartmut Zwahr - Uwe Schrimer - Henning Steinführer (Eds.), Leipzig, Mitteldeutschland und Europa. Festgabe für Manfred Straube und Manfred Unger zum 70. Geburtstag, Beucha 2000; Ernst Hasse, Geschichte der Leipziger Messe, Preisschriften der Fürstlich-Jablonowskischen Gesellschaft der Wissenschaften 25, Leipzig 1885, 352; Josef Reinhold, Polen-Litauen auf den Leipziger Messen des 18. Jahrhunderts, Abhandlungen zur Handels- und Sozialgeschichte 10, Wien 1971; Barącz, Wolne miasto, 121.

5 Tadeusz Lutman, Studja nad dziejami handlu Brodów w latach 1773-1880, Badania z dziejów społecznych i gospodarczych 26, Lwów 1937, 57; Henryk Grossmann, Österreichs Handelspolitik mit Bezug auf Galizien in der Reformperiode 1772-1790, Studien zur Sozial-, Wirtschafts- und Verwaltungsgeschichte X, Wien 1914, 81.

6 For the discussions on the free trade privilege see: Österreichisches Staatsarchiv / Hofkammerarchiv [abbrev. ÖStA/HKA], Cammerale, Nr. 210, Fasc. 7, 40 ex dec. 1777, ÖStA/HKA, Cammerale, Nr. 211, Fasc. 7 Gal., 183 ex aug. 1778 and ÖStA/HKA, Cammerale, Nr. 211, Fasc. 7 Gal., 205 ex Octobri 1778; Grossmann, Österreichs Handelspolitik, 267-274. For the text of the privilege see: Continuatio edictorum et mandatorum universalium in Regnis Galiciae et Lodomeriae a die 1. januar. ad ultimam decemb. anno 1776 emanatorum, Leopolis 1779, 52-57.

7 Tadeusz Lutman, Wolne miasta handlowe, in: Roczniki Dziejów społecznych i Gospodarczych 1, Lwów 1931, 89-98, here 89-91.

(1784) and Biała (1789).[8] The case of Pogórze is particularly interesting: It was a former suburb of Kraków lying south of the Vistula river and was thus part of Austrian Galicia since 1772 whereas Krakow remained Polish. Owing to the new border between the two towns Podgórze could dare to compete with its far more powerful neighbour. This case reminds us of the relationship between Brody and its neighbour on the other side of the border, though under inverse conditions. Radyvyliv also gained importance due to fact of being separated from overwhelming Brody by an international boundary. The supporters of Brody's free trade privilege constantly argued its necessity with the need to minimise Radyvyliv's potential rivalry.[9]

Brody also set a precedent for other countries. After the Duchy of Warsaw annexed new territories in 1809 the Polish government accorded Terespol, a city on the border with the Russian Empire, a free trade privilege in 1810. This decision immediately caused concern among the Austrian administration, fearing Terespol could replace Brody as the major trade junction between Central Europe and Russia.[10] These worries were though unfounded. During the age of the Napoleonic Wars no other town in East Central Europe could compete with Brody. The Habsburg Empire heavily depended on colonial goods imported legally or illegally via Brody especially after Austria had to cede all costal provinces after the Treaty of Vienna in 1809. The French government knew about Brody's importance as well. The daily bulletins Napoleon received from his secret police repeatedly indicate the considerable smuggling activities in this border town.[11] The French consul in Leipzig mentions several times the contraband routes

---

8 Tomasz Kargol, Wirtschaftliche Beziehungen zwischen Galizien und den Ländern der österreichisch-ungarischen Monarchie in der ersten Hälfte des 19. Jahrhunderts, in: Christoph Augustynowicz - Andreas Kappeler (Eds.), Die Galizische Grenze. Kommunikation oder Isolation, Europa Orientalis 3, Wien 2007, here 38-42; Grossmann, Österreichs Handelspolitik, 404; Ewa Danowska, "Nowe miasteczko zaraz za mostem cesarscy stawiają". O początkach Podgórza, in: Podgórze w dziejach wielkiego Krakowa. Materiały sesji naukowej odbytej 17 kwietnia 1999 roku, Kraków 2000, 7-28, here 14, 18-19.

9 On the anxiety concerning the rivalry see: ÖStA/HKA, Cammerale, Nr. 211, Fasc. 7 Gal., 183 ex aug. 1778. For the general relations between the two towns see: Börries Kuzmany - Laurie Cohen - Paulus Adelsgruber, Kleinstädte entlang der galizisch-wolhynische/podolischen Grenze. Ein Vergleich, in: Jahrbücher für Geschichte Osteuropas 55, Nr. 2, München/Regensburg 2007, 232-263.

10 Österreichisches Staatsarchiv / Allgemeines Verwaltungsarchiv [abbrev. ÖStA/AVA], Hofkanzlei, Ktnr. 947, IV J, Gal. Brody, 163 ex feb. 1811; Österreichisches Staatsarchiv / Polizeihofstelle [abbrev. ÖStA/PHSt], Ktnr. 319, Zl. 914/1810.

11 Nicole Gotteri, La Police secrète du Premier Empire. Bulletins quotidiens adressés par Savary à l'Empereur de juin à décembre 1810, Paris 1997, Vol. 1-4 (1997-2000). For remarks on Brody see e.g.: Vol. 1, Bulletin 15.11.1810, 572; Vol. 2, Bulletins 21.2.1811, 150; 16.3.1811, 222; 2.4.1811, p.272; Vol. 4, Bulletins 12.3.1812, 164; 16.5.1812, 358.

passing from Odessa or Riga to Central and Western Europe via Brody.[12] On the other hand France also benefited from Brody's role as a commercial hub. For a secure importation of desperately needed colonial goods, alternatives to transport by ship had to be found. Especially Ottoman cotton was shipped from Constantinople to Odessa and then further to Brody.[13] In a certain way France even profited from Brody's involvement in illegal trade. When Russia switched to a prohibitive tariff system in 1811 silk fabric from Lyon could be most easily smuggled into the Tsarist Empire by merchants from Brody, who were known for having good contacts to local corrupt customs officers.[14]

Until the end of the Napoleonic Wars Brody did very well, but on the long run Russia's (as well as Austria's) protectionist economic policy caused a long stagnation of the city's wealth as it suffered from its location in the borderzone. Nevertheless, for four more decades almost all goods in transit coming to Russia via Austria passed by Brody.[15] Only in the second half of the 19th century, in the age of industrialisation, the city lost its international importance. Symbolically we can take the fire of 1859 that devastated two thirds of the town as the beginning of Brody's decline. For the reconstruction works the local authorities took a loan from the National Bank. Already in the 1870s the municipality had difficulties to pay the interests and finally in 1883 Brody went bankrupt and was put under sequestration of the National Bank until 1888.[16]

12 Lettre du consul à Leipzig, le 26.7.1812, Archives Nationales [abbrev. AN], F12 1853, Doc. Nr. 2513; Lettre de Bignon à Duc de Bassano, Varsovie le 21.8.1811, Archives du ministère des affaires étrangères [abbrev. AMAE], CP Pologne, Vol. 328, 50; Lettre de Bignon à Duc de Bassano, Varsovie le 21.9.1811, AMAE, CP Pologne, Vol. 328, 172; Lettre du consul à Leipzig, Thérémin le 14.4.1812, AMAE, CCC Leipzig, Tome 1, 45.

13 Mure, au Ministère des Relation extérieures, Nr. 1, Odessa, le 1.8.1808 [rather 31.10.1808], AMAE, CCC, Odessa Vol. 1, 166-169; Extrait du registre des certificats d'origine des marchandises, délivrées par M. Mure, Consul général de France à Odessa, AMAE, CCC, Odessa Vol. 1, 277-315.

14 Lettre du consul à Leipzig le 15.4.1812, AN, F12 1853, Doc. Nr. 374; Lettre du consul à Leipzig, Thérémin le 5.3.1812, AMAE, CCC Leipzig, Tome 1, 30; Middell, Brody, 37-39.

15 Tafeln zur Statistik der österreichischen Monarchie, Wien 1843-1848 as well as Ausweise über den Handel von Oesterreich im Verkehr mit dem Auslande und über den Zwischenverkehr von Ungern, der Woiwodschaft Serbien sammt dem Temeser Banate, dann von Kroatien, Slawonien, Siebenbürgen und der Militärgrenze mit den anderen österreichischen Kronländern im Jahr 1840, Wien 1849-1855: See categories: „Eintrittsdurchfuhr" and „Austrittsdurchfuhr".

16 Sitzung des Generalrats vom 3.11.1882, Protokoll, Archiv der Oesterreichischen Nationalbank [abbrev. OeNBArchiv]; Sitzung des Generalrats vom 25.10.1883, Protokoll, OeNBArchiv; Sitzung des Generalrats vom 8.11.1883, Protokoll, OeNBArchiv; Misto Brody pid sekvestorom, in: Dilo, L'viv, 8.11.1883, 1.

There are several reasons for Brody's failure. One was the increasing rivalry with other towns in the region. The case of Radyvyliv was already mentioned before; owing to its less peripheral geographic location Ternopil replaced Brody more and more as Eastern Galicia's regional centre, especially because it was on the main railway line to the most important Odessa harbour.[17] The railroad connecting Brody was only secondary and the first bilateral railway junction with the Tsarist Empire was opened on the trunk line in Pidvolochysk (Austria) and Volochysk (Russia) in 1871. Brody-Radyvyliv followed only two years later.[18]

Most contemporaries argued that the removal of the free trade status in 1880 was the main reason for the city's decline. Nevertheless we have to take into account that in a modern economic system Brody's former role in international trade became more and more obsolete. For centuries its task was not to sell goods but to offer services as a middleman between the wares' provenance and the wares' destination. However, in the age of railways intermediary cities are hardly needed on the passage in between. At the border goods still had to be reloaded from railcars of different gauges but these wares in transit weren't traded anymore in Brody.

Another reason for the city's downfall might be the almost exclusive orientation of Brody's economic elites on trade, neglecting any investment into industrial undertakings. With very few exceptions Brody totally missed the industrialisation of the second half of the 19th century. Although maybe even with a stronger dedication of local entrepreneurs to the development of industry the lack of capital in the region would have caused severe troubles anyway. Except some savings banks there were no serious credit institutions in Brody, until a tiny Bohemian bank opened a

17 Sprawy miejskie, in: Gazeta Brodzka. Dwutygodnik poświęcony sprawom społeczno-ekonomicznym i przemysłowym powiatów brodzkiego i złoczowskiego. Organ brodzkiej Rady powiatowej, Brody, 15.1.1897, 2-3.

18 For the railroad to Brody and Pidvolochysk see: Ihor Žaloba, Infrastrukturna polityka avstrijs'koho urjadu na pivničnomu schodi monarchiji v ostannij čerti XVIII – 60-ch rokach XIX st. (na prykladi šljachiv spolučennja), Černivci 2004, 354-369; Ignaz Konta (Ed.), Geschichte der Eisenbahnen Oesterreich-Ungarns. Vom Jahre 1867 bis zur Gegenwart, Geschichte der Eisenbahnen der oesterreichisch-ungarischen Monarchie, 8 vol., Wien [Wien/Teschen/Leipzig] 1999 [1908], vol. 4, 31. Copy of the "Übereinkommen welches durch die internationale Kommission in Betreff des Anschlußes des Flügels Dubno-Radziwilow der Kiew-Brester Bahn, an den Flügel Krasne Brody der Carl-Ludwig Bahn geschlossen wurde", Deržavnyj archive L'vivs'koji oblasti, F. 350, op. 1, spr. 2313, 57-58; Central'nyj deržavnyj istoryčnyj archive Ukrajiny u Kyjevi, F. 442, op. 44, spr. 667, 28-38, 70-72.

branch office in 1906.[19] For five decades the city had demanded the establishment of an agency of the National Bank but achieved it solely in 1912[20]

Only during the last ten years preceding the First World War Brody's modernisation gained momentum. Several small industrial enterprises were founded, health care was improved and the municipality introduced a sewer system in 1903 and built an electric power station in 1911.[21] In consequence after to decades of population decline Brody starts to grow again and reached the number of 18,055 inhabitants in 1910 (see table 1). However, from its formerly ranking among Galicia's three largest towns (after Lviv and Krakow) it had dropped to the 11th position.[22]

Table 1: Demographic development of selected Galician towns 1778-1910.[23]

19 Geschäftsbericht pro 1910, Central'nyj deržavnyj istoryčnyj archive Ukrajiny u L'vovi [abbrev. CDIAL], F. 146, op. 25, spr. 3667, no page indicated.

20 Bericht der Handels- und Gewerbekammer in Brody an das hohe k.k. Ministerium für Handel, Gewerbe und öffentliche Bauten, Lemberg 1850-51, 27-28; CDIAL, F. 146, op. 55, spr. 49, 1-8; Sitzung der Bankdirektion vom 15.4.1875, Protokoll, OeNBArchiv; Sitzung des Generalrats vom 27.10.1880, Protokoll, OeNBArchiv; CDIAL, F. 146, op. 4, spr. 5220, 50-85; Clemens Jobst, Gouverner une banque centrale décentralisée: l'exemple austro-hongrois 1847-1914, in: Olivier Feiertag - Michel Margairaz (Eds.), Gouverner une banque centrale du XVIIIe siècle à nos jours, Paris voraussichtlich 2010.

21 Vasyl Ščurat, Cerkvy hr.-kat. parochyji v Brodach, in: Svit (1.-15. März), 24.2.1907, L'viv, 1907, 80; Pavlo Dubas, Bridščyna. Vyjimky z archivu, in: Jaroslav Čumak (Ed.), Brody i Bridščyna. Istoryčno-memuarnyj zbirnyk, Ukrajins'kyj archiv XLVII, Toronto 1988, 621-649, here 642-643.

22 Statistisches Jahrbuch der österreichischen Monarchie, Wien 1910.

23 **For Brody**: *1778*, *1783*: ÖStA/HKA, Cammerale, Nr. 218, Fasc. 7 Gal., 169 ex jan. 1785, Produktnr. 7; *1786*: CDIAL, F. 146, op. 88, spr. 188, 36; *1805*: Georg Hassel, Statistischer Umriss der sämtlichen Europäischen Staaten in Hinsicht ihrer Grösse, Bevölkerung, Kulturverhältnisse, Handlung, Finanz- und Militärverfassung und ihrer aussereuropäischen Besitzungen, vol. 1, Braunschweig 1805, 45; *1810*: Classification der vorzüglicheren Städte und Marktflecken des österreichischen Kaiserstaates in Ansehung ihrer Häuserzahl und Volksmenge, in: Vaterländische Blätter für den österreichischen Kaiserstaat, 24.7.1810, 230; 1820: Majer Bałaban, Dzieje Żydów w Galicyi i w Rzeczypospolitej Krakowskiej 1772-1868, Kraków [Lwów 1914] 1988, 94; *1830-1857*: Tafeln; *1869*: Orts-Repertorium des Königreiches Galizien und Lodomerien mit dem Grossherzogthume Krakau. Auf Grundlage der Volkszählung vom Jahre 1869, Wien 1874, 20; *1880*: Special Orts-Repertorium der im oesterreichischen Reichsrathe vertretenen Königreiche und Länder, Vol. 12 Galizien, Wien 1886; *1890-1910*: Statistisches Jahrbuch.

For Ternopil, Przemyśl, Kolomyya et Drohobych: *1830-1857*: Tafeln; *1869-1910*: Statistisches Jahrbuch.

For Lviv (Lemberg): *1772-1819*: Isabel Röskau-Rydel, Kultur an der Peripherie des Habsburger Reiches. Die Geschichte des Bildungswesens und der kulturellen Einrichtungen in Lemberg von 1772 bis 1848, Studien der Forschungsstelle Ostmitteleuropa an der

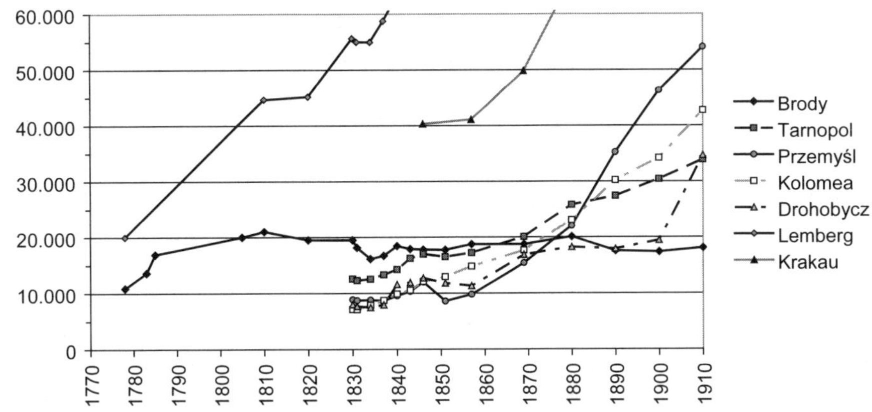

An extraordinary Galician town

Despite its continuous loss of interregional economic importance during the second half of the 19th century, Brody was not just a small Galician town like others. Only in the very last years before the outbreak of the First World War Brody became a truly peripheral town on the North-Eastern fringes of the Habsburg Empire.

For centuries Brody was playing a crucial role in the Jewish world. Since the beginning of the 18th century the city was one of the religious and cultural centres of East Central European Jewry, especially in the domain of rabbinic and Talmudic scholarship. Rabbis having received their education in Brody later lead important Jewish communities all over Europe, like for instance Moses Ehrenreich in Rome or Elijah Rokach (also Rokeach) in Amsterdam.[24] When the Haskalah, the Jewish Enlightenment, started to spread beyond the narrow circle around the Berlin philosopher Moses Mendelssohn (1729-1786) merchants from Brody who stayed in Prussia or Saxony were among the first ones to adopt these new ideas. Besides Lviv and Ternopil Brody became one of the very few centres of the Haskalah in Galicia and had a key position in the dissemination of the Jewish Enlightenment in Russia. Closely connected with the propagation of these new ideas was the adoption of German as the main language of communication

Universität Dortmund 15, Wiesbaden 1993, 352; *1830-1857*: Tafeln; *1869-1910*: Statistisches Jahrbuch.

For Krakow (Krakau): *1847*: Ludwik Mroczka, Krakowianie. Szkice do portretu zbiorowego w dobie industrialnej transformacji 1890-1939, Kraków 1999, S. 12; *1857*: Tafeln; *1869-1910*: Statistisches Jahrbuch.

24 Encyclopaedia Judaica. Das Judentum in Geschichte und Gegenwart, Berlin 1929, vol. 4, 451-452.

among the local elite.[25] Although the Austrian government wanted to ingrain the Haskalah among all its Jewish subjects, the lower classes continued to adhere to the Hassidic movement. This repeatedly caused conflicts within the Jewish community. However, the lines separating the partisans of the Haskalah from the supporters of classical Rabbinism or Hassidism weren't always that sharp, especially between the first two groups. Some wealthy merchants supported the Enlightenment as well as the Talmudists; and everybody continued to be part of the same congregation – a reform synagogue was never installed in Brody[26]

Characteristic for Brody was its ethno-confessional composition. It was the Austrian Empire's most Jewish town: Two thirds to three quarters of the total population were Jews; fifteen to twenty percent were mostly Polish speaking Roman Catholics, and five to ten percent were Ukrainian speaking Greek Catholics (sometimes also called Uniates).[27] The authorities had to accommodate this Jewish dominance by accepting or at least by tolerating exceptional political and administrative regulations for Brody. In no other town of the Empire Jews could participate so widely in the local representation institutions and in the municipality's administration. Since 1798 half of the deputies elected to the municipal diet (Stadtausschuss) had been Jewish dignitaries, which would be unthinkable in any other place in Austria before the full emancipation of Austrian Jewry in 1867. What might be even more astonishing is the fact that the Christian deputies declared themselves explicitly in favour of this representation system. On the

25 Jerzy Holzer, Enlightment, Assimilation, and Modern Identity: The Jewish Élite in Galicia, in: Israel Bartal - Antony Polonsky (Eds.), Polin. Studies in Polish Jewry, Vol. 12, Focusing on Aspects and Experiences of Religion, London/Portland 1999; Péter Varga, Die drei Mendelssohns. Wirkungen der deutsch-jüdischen Aufklärung in Osteuropa, Asteriskos 2, Budapest 2001; Josef Meisl, Haskalah. Geschichte der Aufklärungsbewegung unter den Juden in Rußland, Berlin 1919.

26 Raphael Mahler, The Social and Political Aspects of the Haskalah in Galicia, in: YIVO, Annual of Jewish Social Science 1, New York 1946, 64-85; Raphael Mahler, Hasidism and the Jewish Enlightment. Their Confrontation in Galicia and Poland in the First Half of the Nineteenth Century, Philadelphia/New York/Jerusalem 1985, 32-29 Haim Gertner, Rabanut wedajanut beGalicia bemachcit harišona šel hamea hatša-esre: Tipologia šel hanehaga mesortit bemešber, Jerušalajim 2004, 111-169; Dov Sadan, Broder gasn. A shpatsir iber a gevezener shtot, in: Nekhemie Tsuker - Nokhem Lindman (Eds.), Yerlekher gedenk-bukh, 1, Buenos Ayres 1961, 71-81, here 76-77.

27 Encyclopaedia Judaica, vol. 4, 1094; Nathan Michael Gelber, Toldot jehudej Brodi 1584-1943, Arim wemahot beJisrael 6, Jerušalajim 1955, 258; Statistische Mitteilungen über die Verhältnisse Galiziens, 24/2, Lwów 1912; Lutman, Studja, 125; Bohdan Wasiutyński, Ludność żydowska w Polsce w wiekach XIX i XX. Studjum statystyczne, Warszawa 1930, 119; Max Rosenfeld, Die jüdische Bevölkerung in den Städten Galiziens 1881-1910, in: Zeitschrift für Demographie und Statistik der Juden 9/2 (Februar), Berlin 1913, 17-24.

local level the interconfessional relations were thus marked by a pragmatic concord.[28]

Only towards the end of the 19th century, when national identities started to win over religious identifications, the ethno-confessional relations got more complicated. The more and more self confident Polish elites nevertheless pushed Jews to abandon their supranational Austro-Habsburgian identity and to accept the Polish-Galician reality.[29] Still, unlike the rest of Galicia the Jews of Brody weren't caught so heavily in the crossfire of the Polish, Ukrainian or Zionist national movements.

The Brody Jews' orientation towards the central government and towards a network of several Central and Eastern European cities as well as the minor importance of the Crownland of Galicia had a long tradition in the conscience of the city's Jewish population. Firstly, because on Jewish mental maps administrative subdivisions of a state didn't have much importance; secondly, the free trade privilege had forced Brody's merchants to engage in a good understanding with the central government and with other commercial centres outside the country; and thirdly, the close economic relationship with German states had led to the introduction of the Haskalah and the German language in Brody.

The Austrian authorities supported the implantation of the Haskalah in Galicia mainly by founding German-Jewish schools (deutsch-jüdische Schulen) where Jewish children should study secular subjects like German language, mathematics or geography in addition to their religious education. Orthodox and Hassidic Jews severely opposed these modern schools and obtained their closure in the whole province in 1806.[30] Brody's elites on the other hand regretted this decision and encouraged the installation of a renewed German-Jewish commercial school. After years of negotiation

28 Archiwum Państwowe w Krakowie na Wawelu [abbrev. APKW], Teki Schneidera, 199, 64-79; APKW, Teki Schneidera, 189; ÖStA/AVA, Hofkanzlei, Ktnr. 947, IV J, Gal. Brody, 30 ex dec. 1826; Filip Friedmann, Die galizischen Juden im Kampfe um ihre Gleichberechtigung. 1848-1868, Frankfurt Main 1929, 121-125.

29 Harald Binder, Galizien in Wien. Parteien, Wahlen, Fraktionen und Abgeordnete im Übergang zur Massenpolitik, Studien zur Geschichte der österreichisch-ungarischen Monarchie 29, Wien 2005, 237, 261-262, 290-291, 623-670; Leila Everett, The Rise of Jewish National Politics in Galicia, 1905 – 1907, in: Andrei S. Markovits - Frank E. Sysyn (Eds.), Nationbuilding and the Politics of Nationalism. Essays on Austrian Galicia, Cambridge MA 1982, 151-177, here 173-174; Yehoshu'a-Shiko Mandel - Aviv Meltzer - Josef Parvari-Leiner - Sarah-Samith Shmuszkin-Rubinstein (Eds.), Ner tamid. Jizkor liBrodi: sefer zikaron liqehilat Brodi usevivata, Jerušalajim 1994, 35.

30 Röskau-Rydel, Kultur an der Peripherie, 71-72, 94-104, 107-117; Mieczyslaw-Jerzy Adamczyk, L'éducation et les transformations de la société juive dans la Monarchie des Habsbourg 1774 à 1914, Paris 1999, 55.

such an Israelitische Realschule (Jewish secondary school) with German as language of instruction opened in 1818.[31]

Although it was called a Jewish school and was financed entirely by the Jewish community, from the very beginning Christians made up about twenty percent of all pupils.[32] This institution was turned into a publicly maintained school in 1853 and became the k.k. vollständige Unterrealschule (imperial and royal complete secondary school) – two thirds of the expenses being covered furthermore by the province and one third by the municipality of Brody.[33] In the 1860s and 1870s it was gradually expanded to a complete Gymnasium (high school). Whereas in all other parts of Galicia high schools were polonized, the community of Brody insisted on a German language education. Only around the turn of the century the city's elites increasingly approved schooling in Polish. Finally in 1907 this high school progressively changed its language of instruction.[34]

This gymnasium was the region's most important educational institution. Especially for the rural Ukrainian population on the town's outskirts the school became a place where new elites could be formed. Their share among the students increased from less than ten percent in the 1870s to a quarter of all pupils in 1910 (see table 2). Even if ethno-confessionel tensions intensified at the end of the 19th century, the every day school life with students from different ethnic background continued flowing rather smoothly. To a certain extent this can be explained by the choice of German as language of instruction, because in Galicia's Polish-Ukrainian antagonism, Austria's dominant lingua franca had a rather neutral status and was a pragmatic need.[35]

---

31 For the discussion see: Neue Schule für Israeliten, zu Tarnopol in Galizien, in: Sulamith, eine Zeitschrift zur Beförderung der Kultur und Humanität unter den Israeliten, IV, Vol. 2; Reden bei der feierlichen Eröffnung der Israelitischen Realschule zu Brody in Gallizien, gehalten am 8ten Februar 1818, in: Sulamith, eine Zeitschrift zur Beförderung der Kultur und Humanität unter den Israeliten, V, Vol. 2; CDIAL, F. 146, op. 66, spr. 32, 32-33, 39, 42-44; CDIAL, F. 146, op. 66, spr. 33, 55-67.

32 CDIAL, F. 146, op. 66, spr. 40, 34-36.

33 Rudolf Kustynowicz, Entstehungsgeschichte des k.k. Rudolfs-Gymnasium in Brody (1. Teil), in: Jahresbericht des k. k. Rudolf-Gymnasiums in Brody, Nr. 26, Brody 1904, 3-26, here 3-7.

34 CDIAL, F. 178, op. 3, spr. 936, 20, 26-27, 32-39, 49; CDIAL, F. 146, op. 8, spr. 602, 2-10.

35 Jahresbericht des k. k. Real und Ober-Gymnasiums in Brody [since 1908 in Polish: Sprawozdanie c. k. Gimnazyum im. Rudolfa w Brodach), Brody 1879-1914; Svjatoslav Pacholkiv, Emanzipation durch Bildung. Entwicklung und gesellschaftliche Rolle der ukrainischen Intelligenz im habsburgischen Galizien (1890-1914), Schriftenreihe des Österreichischen Ost- und Südosteuropa-Instituts 27, Wien/München 2002, especially 122-129.

Table 2: Number of pupils in Brody's Gymnasium (and its predecessors) by confessional adherence 1851-1914.[36]

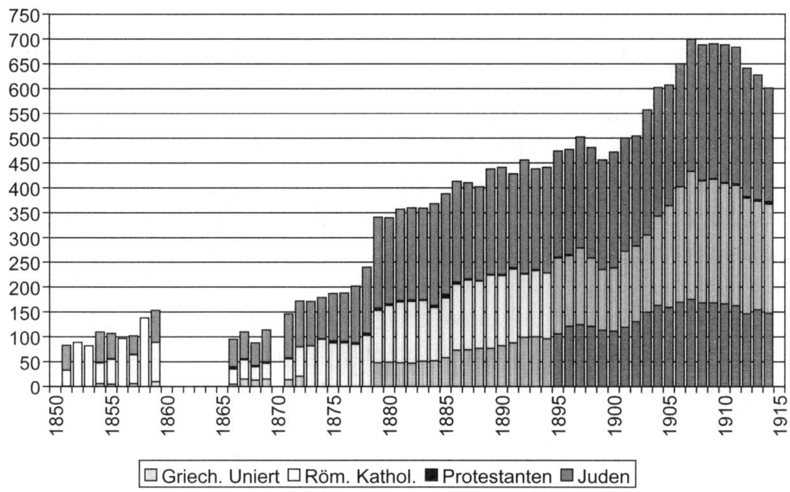

Another feature making Brody an exceptional Galician town results from its position on the border. It did not only have the reputation of a hub for legal trade and the exchange of ideas but also for smuggling, espionage and other illegal communication. Especially during the Napoleonic era trade, contraband and intelligence were closely interlinked.[37]

Due to its vicinity to Russia, Brody often was the first stopover for deserters avoiding military service and refugees fleeing persecution in the Tsarist Empire. This was the case for instance in 1863 when Polish insurgents sought asylum in Galicia. After Russian forces had won the Battle of

---

36 It is easier to distinguish the three ethno-confessional groups according to their religious adherence. Greek Catholics [griech. uniert] can be largely identified with the Ukrainian speakers, Roman Catholics [röm. kathol.] with Polish speakers. The mother tongue of Jews [Juden] can be very difficultly deduced from language or nationality statistics, as multilingualism (Yiddish, German and Polish) was as common as were multiple national identities. Sources for the table: **1851-1864**: Tafeln; **1865-1878**: Statistisches Jahrbuch; **1879-1914**: Jahresbericht Gymnasium.

37 See e.g.: Lettre d'Aubernon, Lemberg 9.8.1812, 342, AMAE, CP Pologne, Vol. 331; Extrait d'un rapport d'un officier envoyé en Volhinie et Podolie, 19.11.1811, AMAE, CP Pologne, Vol. 328, 332; Vadym Adadurov, "Napoleonida" na schodi Jevropy. Ujavlennja, proekty ta dijal'nist' urjadu Franciji ščodo pivdenno-zachidnych okrajin Rosijs'koji Imperiji na počatku XIX stolittja, L'viv 2007, 387-390.

Radyvyliv approximately 400 Polish combatants and several local civilians crossed the border into Austria.[38]

Another example for Brody's role as a save haven was during the pogroms in 1881 and 1882. When the first refugees arrived several Jewish dignitaries of the city launched a special committee. Thanks to their close contacts with the Alliance Israélite Universelle they could instigate a worldwide solidarity and relief movement unseen until then. The local committee assisted by collaborators from the Paris and Vienna sections of the Alliance Israélite managed the registration and emergency supply of the newcomers.[39] They gathered in Brody before they continued their emigration towards America. The Austrian authorities clearly encouraged the city's role as a huge refugee camp, and often escorted Jews who had illegally crossed the border elsewhere to Brody. By concentrating the refugees in one town the Austrian administration hoped to keep a better eye on the steady influx of foreign citizens into Galicia.[40]

It is almost impossible to reconstruct the exact number of Russian Jews that passed through Brody in the course of these two years. Among the approximately 24,000 to 25,000 refugees who had come to Austria about 20,000 might have sought asylum in Brody. Howsoever, in June and July 1882 almost 15,000 refugees are documented to have stayed in Brody contemporaneously – an enormous number if we consider the city's total permanent population of approximately 20,000 inhabitants. To establish a precise number of those refugees who continued their flight to America is even more difficult. In 1881 Jewish organisations in the United States were still quite willing to accept able emigrants, but in the following years they were much more restrictive. As the European Jewish communities were extremely hostile to any immigration into their countries, about two thirds of the refugees returned to Russia after the political situation had calmed down.

38 Brody, in: Gazeta Lwowska, Lwów, 2.7.1863, 601; Brody, in: Gazeta Lwowska, Lwów, 3.7.1863, 605; Brody, in: Gazeta Lwowska, Lwów, 4.7.1863, 610.

39 See the extensive correspondence between the local committee and the Alliance Israélite in Paris: Archives de l'Alliance Israélite Universelle [abbrev. AIU], URSS I B; AIU, URSS I C; Moritz Friedländer, Fünf Wochen in Brody unter jüdisch-russischen Emigranten, Wien 1882; Leo Goldenstein, Brody und die russisch-jüdische Emigration. Nach eigener Beobachtung erzählt, Frankfurt Main 1882.

40 Benyamin Lukin - Olga Shraberman, Documents on the Emigration of Russian Jews via Galicia, 1881-82, in the Central Archives for the History of the Jewish People in Jerusalem, in: Gal-Ed. On the history of the Jews in Poland 21, Tel Aviv 2007, 101-117, here 105-108.

None of the described phenomenon are uniquely linked with Brody, but e. g. the fact that smuggling was so widespread in this town underlines the city's crucial commercial role in general. The same is true for espionage. Intelligence services engaged so many spies in this town because its inhabitants had an extraordinary good knowledge of Eastern Europe due to their multiple commercial contacts in the region. The concentration of Jewish refugees in Brody had its logic as well. From the emigrants point of view the city was easily joinable by train or carriage; furthermore they knew Brody as a Jewish place, which strengthened their confidence to find appropriate help. For the Austrian authorities on the other side the concentration in Brody was also advantageous, not only because there was a huge Jewish community that could not have refused to assist their brethren from Russia, but also because of Brody's excellent contacts with other Jewish centres that could activate an international relief operation.

Conclusion

At first glance, Brody's performance throughout the long nineteenth century definitely would not qualify as a success story: The city transformed from a centre of international trade and cultural importance into a peripheral town at the Galician-Russian border. Brody lost its position as major commercial hub in East Central Europe and failed to embrace an urbanisation and modernisation that was so characteristic for cities in this period. When we think of the urban space in the second half of the nineteenth century we imagine growing cities, urbanisation and industrialisation. If these developments arrived in Brody at all, it was much later than in other Galician towns.

From the Galician perspective on the other hand, the economical transformation of Brody was desirable, because the city's former international orientation had led to a certain self isolation from its Galician surroundings. From a regional point of view Brody's shrinking proved the city's successful integration into the social and political realities of the Crownland. At the end of this decades long process Lviv had become Brody's focus and replaced Vienna and international commercial cities such as Leipzig, Berdychiv or Odessa as Brody's point of reference. Successfully "galicianised" by the outbreak of the First World War, Brody was everything a Galician city could be: It was a regional commercial centre with a branch line railway station and a branch office of the Austro-Hungarian National Bank like several other Galician middle-sized towns; it was one of the more important border-crossing towns such as Pidvolochys'k or Husyatyn; and it was a local educational centre such as Ternopil, Ivano-Frankivsk or Kolomyya. Put simply, the difference between 1800 and 1900 was the indefinite article replacing the definite: Until the mid-nineteenth century Brody was the centre of trade between eastern and western Europe, the border city between the Austrian and the Russian Empires and the Galician educational centre with a clear supraregional orientation.

Nevertheless, several features distinguished Brody from other Galician towns even at the beginning of the twentieth century, some of which were vestiges of Brody's former economic importance. Brody continued to be the seat of one of the three Galician chambers of commerce and thus ranked in the same category as Lviv and Krakow. The town's ethno-confessional composition also continued to be an important exception. No other Austro-Hungarian town was so predominantly Jewish, with Roman-Catholic Poles and Greek-Catholic Ukrainians never accounting for more than a third of the total population. Moreover Brody continued to play a certain role in Jewish thinking, in Rabbinic-Talmudic scholarship as well as in the spread of the Haskalah in East Central Europe. In close connection with the strong support of Brody's Jewish elites for the Enlightenment, the German language kept its importance many decades longer than in other Galician cities. However, by the outbreak of the First World War Brody's Jewish elites had switched from an orientation towards the German-speaking centre of the Empire to a certain degree of auto-polonisation. Special to Brody was also the strong commitment of the city and its environs to Russophile currents, whereas in the rest of Galicia the Ukrainian national movement rapidly gained popularity at the turn of the century. The local gymnasium also deserves special attention, as not until 1907 did Polish replace German as the language of instruction, and even then the shift occurred only gradually. Coincidentally, the last Matura (A-levels, high school diploma) to be held in German was in June 1914. Among the pupils graduating in 1913 was Joseph Roth, who in his later literary works often referred to his hometown, thus highlighting the importance of Brody in the German speaking world.

Marion Wieser
(University of New Orleans)

Selected Observations on the Influence of Religion on the 2006 Midterm Elections

Introduction

After the election of George W. Bush as President of the United States in November 2000, the question about the influence of religious groups in politics became (again) of topical interest. Not since the years of the "Moral Majority" has there been so much discussion about the role of religion in politics.

The 2000 and 2004 presidential elections were not only extremely close, but the campaigns were also fully loaded with moral and religious issues. Various religious interest groups tried to influence the elections, especially groups representing the so called "Religious Right".

Such groups like "Focus on the Family" or the "Family Research Council" use different methods and strategies to influence the political landscape, the decision making process, and elections in the U.S., including nominating candidates directly from their group, promoting these candidates, mobilizing voters, and influence the media and public opinion. They organize protests, boycotts and demonstrations, hire professional lobbyists to work on drafting bills and build coalitions in Washington, D.C., employ attorneys to argue cases before courts, engage in voter registration efforts, invite candidates to hold speeches, and provide financial aid to candidates.[1]

All these efforts by religious groups, mostly from the "Religious Right", helped the Republicans and George W. Bush gain power in 2000 and helped re-elect him in 2004. The most common strategy was targeting key states by mobilizing as many members and supporters as possible and bring them to the polls.

In 2006 the picture was somewhat different. The "Religious Right" was not really satisfied with the Republican effort in promoting their agenda

1 For a detailed analysis of different methods and strategies used by the "Religious Right" cf. Kenneth D. Wald, Der Einfluss der Religion auf die amerikanische Politik, in: Manfred Brocker (Ed.), God Bless Amerika. Politik und Religion in den USA, Darmstadt 2005, 187-207.

during the previous years and the overall approval rating for the President – also within the members of the "Religious Right" - was not even closely as high as in 2004. George W. Bush's approval rating in the fall of 2006 was the lowest of any president since Harry Truman in 1950. [2] All in all the 2006 midterm elections were a clear referendum on the performance of the Bush administration and the Republican majority in Congress.

The war in Iraq, various scandals like the one involving lobbyist Jack Abramoff and a general dissatisfaction with the Republican lawmakers in D.C. were the main reasons for the Republicans to lose the majority in both houses of Congress.

The Republicans answered to these challenges with a very well prepared "get-out-the-vote" campaign, targeting especially conservative voters. This includes the base of the so called "Values Voters" who supported George W. Bush in large numbers in 2000 and helped him get re-elected in 2004. The Republican Party was hoping to out-mobilize the Democrats[3], especially through this voter base. As during the 2004 campaign, Republican candidates reached out to Evangelical voters by including certain "moral issues" to their agenda, like abortion, same-sex marriage, and stem cell research. Republicans were very confident that bringing these voters to the polls will help them keep the majority in Congress. But the strategy didn't work out as planned and the Republicans lost the majority in both houses. This loss of the majority did not result from so called "Values Voters" staying away from the polls or giving their votes to the Democrats, but from Republicans losing votes within other voter groups whereas Democrats gained votes within the Evangelical churches.

In this paper I will discuss some of the major observations that can be made by analyzing some of these "religious" or "moral" issues and what role they played for the outcome of the 2006 midterm elections. Generalized observations about the influence of religious groups on the midterm elections and about some major new trends in the relationship between "Religion and Politics", the "Religious Right", the Republicans and the American voters will be analyzed as well.

The „God Gap" and the "Values Voters" in 2006

First, I would like to track the so called "God Gap" and how the 2006 midterm election outcome influenced this hypothesis. The hypothesis

2 Gary C. Jacobson, Referendum: The 2006 Midterm Congressional Elections, Political Science Quarterly, Vol. 122, Number 1, Spring 2007, 1.

3 Ibid., 16.

about a „God Gap“ in the United States emerged right after the 2000 presidential election, when George W. Bush got a lot of votes from people who attend church regularly (which means at least once a week). Since then the so called „Faith Gap“, „Religion Gap“, „God Gap“ or also „Church Attendance Gap“ has been widely described in political analysis.[4] White Evangelicals and those who attend church frequently support Republicans by large margins, while secular voters and voters who go to church only once in a while are more likely to vote Democratic. In 2004, 75 percent of the people identifying themselves as "Evangelicals" voted for George W. Bush and the Republican Party.[5] In 2006 the percentage stayed nearly the same. At the same time it got harder for the Republican Party to attract voters outside the traditionally religious base. The Democrats on the other hand, could attract votes from the "non religious" and from "not frequent" church goers.[6]

These facts draw to the conclusion that the "God Gap" has actually widened in the 2006 elections.[7] Both parties made religious voters key targets in the election campaigns. And despite predictions that the Republican Party could lose some Evangelical votes due to dissatisfaction with the Bush administration´s performance, this did not happen.[8] The percentage point of Evangelical voters fell only slightly from 75 percent in 2004 to 72 percent in 2006.[9]

On the other hand, Democrats reached out more to voters that are religious, but don´t go to church regularly and who follow a more liberal stand on issues like abortion, the environment or poverty. 59 percent of occasional churchgoers voted for the Democrats in 2006. In 2002 this number was only 51 percent.

The "Religious Right" proudly declared the so called "Values Voters" as their backbone in the last campaigns. The term „Values Voter“ is a rather new phrase[10], that appeared especially during the 2004 campaigns, when it was first used by social conservatives and later adopted by the media.

4 Cf. John C. Green, Mark J. Rozell, Clyde Wilcox (Ed.), The Values Campaign? The Christian Right and the 2004 Elections, Washington, D.C. 2006; David E. Campbell (Ed.), A Matter of Faith. Religion in the 2004 Presidential Election, Washington, D.C. 2007.

5 The Annenberg Public Policy Center 2005, http://www.annenbergpublicpolicycenter.org, October 14, 2008.

6 Scott Keeter, Elections ´06: Big Chances in Some Key Groups, Pew Research Center Publications, November 16, 2006.

7 Greg Smith, Scott Keeter and John Green, Religious Groups React to the 2006 Election, Pew Research Center Publications, November 27, 2006.

8 Scott Keeter, Elections ´06.

9 Ibid.

10 George F. Will, Who Isn´t a "Values Voter"?, in: The Washington Post, May 18, 2006, A23.

The term is used for voters who claim to defend traditional family values, oppose same-sex marriage as well as abortion and want to distinguish themselves from others, by claiming that they are the only ones concerned about "the real values". "Values Voters" were the voters that helped George W. Bush to be re-elected in 2004.[11] The term drew a lot of criticism from all different sides. People with other issue priorities or a more liberal attitude toward certain topics criticized that they too would be voting for "their values". The term however would imply that only the social conservative would be "values voters".[12] The media accommodated to this term as well and is since referring to "Values Voters" as social conservatives, Evangelical-fundamentalists or "Religious Right" voters.

In 2006 the term was often used by "Religious Right" groups. In March 2006 "Vision America" hosted a conference in Washington, D.C. called the "War on Christmas and Values Voters 2006 Conference". Another conference organized by the "Family Research Council Action" ("FRCA") followed in September 2006: The Values Voter Summit 2006", which will be discussed in the next section of this paper.

The "Religious Right" saw in the 2006 midterm election a key battle in their "War against Secularism" and therefore saw political activism during the campaign as vital to their interests. According to Tony Perkins, director of "FRCA", "it's important for Christians to vote because that's how we register our opinions by who we vote into office. People who either reflect our values, or people who abhor our values." James Dobson from "Focus on the Family" invited Christians to the "Values Voter Summit 2006" stating that the main issues for 2006 would BE preserving the family, protecting children and pursuing peace through strength. "We're here to do something about the dangers and threats that are out there." Dobson openly criticized the Republicans and even President George W. Bush to not have done enough since taking office in 2000 to implement the agenda of the Religious Right. "I'm disappointed in Republicans and about what they have done with the power we gave them. We have no choice but winning, because the alternative is terrible."[13]

11 John C. Green and Mark Silk, Why Moral Values Did Count, Religion in the News, Spring 2005, http://www.trincoll.edu/depts/csrpl/RINVol8No1/WhyMoral%20ValuesDidCount.htm, December 14, 2008.

12 George F. Will, Who, A23.

13 James Dobson at the "Values Voter Summit 2006". Transcript by the author, September 22, 2006.

The „Values Voter Summit 2006“ as an example for voter mobilization by the “Religious Right”

The “Values Voter Summit 2006” was held in Washington, D.C. from September 22 till September 24, 2006. It was organized by the “Family Research Council Action” and cosponsored by “Focus on the Family Action”, “Americans United to Preserve Marriage” and the “American Family Association Action”. The event was defined as “call to action for voter participation, education and training and a rallying event for patriotic Americans who want to transform the political landscape on issues such as the sanctity of life and marriage, immigration reform, religious freedom, health care, radical Islam, judicial activism, geopolitics, the media and much more.”[14] Tony Perkins, the President of “FRCA”, called the event “the most important event in the [FRC´s] history – and potentially one of the most important events in the history of the pro-family movement.”[15]

The event was similar organized and carried out as the “Road to Victory” conferences of the “Christian Coalition” in the 1990s. The “Christian Coalition” used the strategy of targeted voter mobilization in key states already during the 1990s. By convincing a small but decisive number of voters to vote for their issues and candidates, they were able to tip some key races in local and national elections. This was called the “15 percent” solution, since that is generally the number of votes needed to change an election outcome.[16]

To participate in the event, interested people needed to register with “FRCA”, paying the conference fee of $100 (with additional fees for certain optional speeches, breakfasts and dinners). About 1700 people from 48 states, mostly grass root activists attended the summit. Some of the most prominent speakers at the event were: Jerry Falwell, Mike Pence (R-IN), Gov. Mitt Romney (R-MA), James Dobson, Marilyn Musgrave (R-CO), Sen. Sam Brownback (R-KS), Gov. Mike Huckabee (R-AR), Sen. George Allen (R-VA), Gary Bauer, Ann Coulter, Sean Hannity, Bill Bennett, Sen. Rick Santorum (R-PA), Paul Weyrich, and Newt Gingrich.

The audience was primarily conservative Evangelicals with lots of grass root Republican activists actively involved in their local churches. Many pastors were present as well. The majority of the attendees were white with only a very small portion of African-American and Hispanics attending.

---

14 Family Research Council Action, http://www.fraction.org/index.cfm?i=WX06C06 , April 8, 2008.

15 Ibid.

16 Greg Goldin, How the Christian Right is Building from Below to Take Over Above, in: The Village Voice, April 6, 1993.

Although the audience was composed of about 50 percent women, only very few women were on stage or gave speeches. [17]

The summit opened with a common prayer, the presentation of the flag by members of the Armed Forces, the Pledge of Allegiance and the National Anthem. The room was decorated with American flags and two mega screens ensured a good view from every corner of the large room. The whole stage area looked very attractive and high tech. Media representatives were only allowed inside the conference room if they registered beforehand. It was not allowed to take pictures or record inside the room. A sign urged people attending the event to report if anyone approaches them and asks questions or if they see anyone recording or taking pictures. A "Radio Row" sent live broadcasting of reports and interviews to some Christian radio stations. There was also an exhibition from different interest groups, e .g. "Americas for Tax Reform", "Freedom Alliance", "Priests for Life", "Bible Literacy Project", Alliance Defense Fund", "Restore America", "The Heritage Foundation", "Christian Educators Association International" and many others.

The main strategy promoted at the "Values Voter Summit 2006" was to contact as many potential voters in the Evangelical community and among "Values Voters" as possible and mobilize them to actually go to the polls. The "Religious Right" hoped once more that they could make the difference by micro-targeting constituencies in specific key states. "Twenty million Christians did not vote in 2004. Voting is important. Mobilizing is everything", James Dobson told the audience at the beginning of the event. And Tony Perkins added: "We use the power of numbers, but we have to explain this to the public, which is not easy. It´s a negative job because the media is not reporting right about us." Senator Sam Brownback (R-KS) even tried to mobilize attendees by recalling Mother Teresa: "We need to do it like Mother Teresa did: Go from door to door before elections." Gov. Mike Huckabee (R-AR) called for "an Evangelical shock and all".[18]

Attendees could sign up for a special workshop on September 23, 2006, led by Connie Marshner, one of the first members of the pro-family movement during the years of the "Christian Coalition". The workshop was based on applying the strategy of micro-targeting to local churches. Marshner presented a 17 page long paper on how she helped getting Rick Santorum (R-PA) re-elected in 2000 by mobilizing local church members. The title of the paper was "Voter Identification and Turnout: A Church Plan". "The purpose of this manual is to give ordinary, church-going citizens a

17 All observations and conclusions about the summit are drawn from personal observations of the author.

18 All transcripts by the author.

means to make a difference in an election", she wrote in the introduction to the paper. "The church plan is designed to work in any church or parish. The more geographically compact the area in which members of the church reside, the more efficient will be the operation of the plan. As such, it can make a critical difference when directly applied to local elections."[19] What sounded like a general's plan for an important military operation, turned out to be a very detailed voter mobilization strategy.

During the workshop, Marshner urged people to "motivate and activate" other voters and to do so even without the consent of the church's pastor. "There is no need for the pastor to be informed about your efforts, especially if he doesn't necessarily approve your efforts."

The church plan relies on only a minimum of resources: volunteers, a church directory, index cards, telephones and prearranged scripts. The voter mobilization operation first starts with anonymous calls to members of the church ("phase one"). Callers should find out what the church members voting preferences were. The caller should identify himself/herself as working for a polling company and the paper provided by Marshner gives an exact script of what people should say and what not. Voters that respond favorable to the "Religious Right" agenda and candidates will be identified and contacted again later during the campaign. Answering a question from the audience what to do if people asked where the caller had gotten their name from, Marshner told the audience to lie and to never reveal where the names and phone numbers came from. These remarks draw some criticism from the audience.

After the initial call, people should send out voter registration forms to non-registered voters and make sure they get registered. Follow-up calls should be made one week after the first contact, ideally in late September of any election year ("phase two: follow-up voter contact"). During this phase advocacy phone calls are made, with callers identifying themselves either during a "personal visit" or by a "accidentally contact at the grocery store".[20] "Uncommitted voters" should get several phone calls, committed voters only one in early October.[21] The "Church Captain" who is coordinating all the mobilization efforts should hand over all the information volunteers had gotten to the individual campaigns.

"Phase Three" consists of clear instruction how to proceed on Election Day. "Think of the campaign as a retail business: the candidate is the prod-

19 Connie Marshner, Voter Identification and Turnout: A Church Plan, workshop handout, "Values Voter Summit".

20 Ibid., 13.

21 Ibid., 14.

uct to sell, the voters are the public who will buy: the campaign is the advertising program. One slight difference: this retail store is open only one day, Election Day"[22], writes Marshner in her paper. On the evening before Election Day, people should put "door hangers" on every door of targeted voters' houses, stating "Don't forget to vote for XY!" For the Election Day, Marshner suggests having volunteer poll watcher at every precinct. At 2pm the volunteers should sit down and call every person on their list: "Now is when having those phone numbers and e-mail addresses really matters. On Election Day you have to contact every identified voter, and you need every means available to do that."[23] Marshner also told the audience at the workshop to leave messages on answering machines. She wrote in her paper: "Don't be shy about interrupting them at work – you can honestly say it won't happen again." Volunteers should ask about other family members and the time the person plans on going to vote. They are urged to call them again half an hour after that time. Volunteers should also provide potential voters with baby sitters or a ride to the polling station, if needed.

Altogether such an aggressive mobilization campaign can jeopardize the tax exempt status of many churches. Marshner recommends the audience to skirt this problem by shifting the action from the church pastor to members of the church and maybe not even let pastors and church leaders know about the campaign. This includes getting the church directory without the pastor's approval!

It's not the Religion, Stupid! - How important religious issues really were during the 2006 campaign

In the 2006 midterm election religious issues played a major rule at the beginning of the campaign, mainly between the fall of 2005 and the spring of 2006. Abortion, same-sex marriage, traditional family values, intelligent design, school prayer, the phrase "under God" in the Pledge of Allegiance – all these issues were discussed in national media, in church publications, speeches, and during worships. But over time and especially during the summer of 2006 religious issues lost attraction to the different campaigns. The media stopped promoting religious issues during the summer of 2006 as well because other, non-moral or non-religious, issues drew a lot more attention to voters at that time, namely the Iraq War, National Security and - once more – the economy.

22 Ibid., 16.
23 Ibid., 17.

Nevertheless, Evangelical voters still put "moral issues" like same-sex marriage, stem cell research or abortion high up on their priority list of topics they think are most important for the election. For 59 percent of these voters, these issues were "extremely important" to their vote. Only 29 percent of other voters listed "moral issues" as "extremely important" to them.[24]

There was also the trend for more mainline Protestants and liberal Catholics to put more emphasis on issues like poverty, health care and education when deciding who they are going to vote for in the elections. This trend helped to enforce the movement of the so called "Religious Left", discussed later in this paper.

But at the same time it could be observed that on a local level, within the single communities, moral issues still played a big rule. They just didn´t get the same attention in the media and the national public as other issues. When people were asked, what the most important issue was for them they rarely named „moral values" as number one, but if asked whether moral values were important to them they mostly affirmed. This can especially be said for white Evangelicals, were issues like gay marriage, abortion, family values etc. were still highly discussed and candidates judged according to their stands on these issues. 59 percent of white Evangelicals stated that moral issues were "extremely important" to their vote, whereas only 29 percent of other voters affirmed the same question.[25]

Overall the main topic of interest to voters in general was the Iraq War with 53 percent naming it as the most important issue, followed by 37 percent naming the economy and 27 percent values issues.[26] So moral issues ranked just behind the war and the economy and therefore still ahead of terrorism, national security or health care. In general still 90 percent of voters believe in God and 70 percent are affiliated with organized religion. Numbers that are higher than in any other industrialized nation.[27]

It Was All About Gay Marriage

Since the late 1970s two main issues have dominated the agenda of the "Religious Right": anti-abortion and anti-gay. During Ronald Reagan´s

---

24 Scott Keeter, Elections ´06.

25 Ibid.

26 Ibid.

27 For a detailed analysis about this fact see The Pew Global Attitudes Project, U.S. Stands Alone in its Embrace of Religion, http://pewglobal.org/reports/pdf/167.pdf, November 7, 2007.

campaign 1980 abortion was the central issue for the “Christian Right”. Rose vs. Wade still heated up the feelings of many and contributed to the wider cultural divide between conservatives and liberals.

The “Religious Right” was very active in promoting the same-sex marriage issue, making it a priority on their agenda. The so called “Defense of Marriage” campaign became the defining moral issue of the 2006 midterm elections. President George W. Bush supported the campaign and pushed for a constitutional ban on same-sex marriage in Congress in the spring of 2006. The ban called for a definition of “marriage” as only being between a man and a woman. Despite the proposal didn′t get a valuable majority in the House or the Senate[28], it helped the “Religious Right” in getting additional media attention and “helped the voters identify who is and is not supportive of the family”, as “Focus on the Family” founder James Dobson acknowledged.[29] “Focus on the Family” was running ads against politicians that did not support the ban, especially in states were Senate or House seats were highly contested. “Family Research Council” proposed to lawmakers to take a “Marriage Protection Pledge” and would then tell voters who signed it and who didn′t.

So far 29 states passed constitutional amendments barring same-sex marriages. Only three states offer the possibility for civil unions. Massachusetts recognizes same-sex marriages. In 2004 a ban on same-sex marriage was on 13 state ballots and drew a lot of “Values Voters” to the polls, which definitely benefited the Republicans in these states. The same tactic should be used in 2006, but the outcome was only half a victory for the “Religious Right”. Mainly because voters were paying more attention toward other issues and some “Values Voters” were just not satisfied enough with the Republican agenda since 2004 and therefore didn′t vote for all the Republican candidates as faithfully as in 2004.

In 2006 eight states had a ban on same-sex marriage on their ballots: Arizona, Colorado, Idaho, South Carolina, South Dakota, Tennessee, Virginia and Wisconsin. The amendments passed in all but one state, Arizona[30], defining a “marriage” as between a man and a woman. This was a triumph for the “Religious Right”. But at the same time, voters did not support Republican candidates as loyally as they did in 2004, which led to the loss of seats and ultimately the Republican defeat in Congress.

28 The voting fell short of 18 votes of the two-thirds majority in the Senate that would have been required to pass the constitutional “Marriage Protection Amendment”.

29 Jim Rutenberg, Conservatives Watching Senate Debate on Gay Marriage, in: The New York Times, June 6, 2006.

30 Arizona pasted a proposition banning same-sex marriage in November 2008. Alabama passed an amendment about the “Sanctity of Marriage” in June 2006.

Despite the successful efforts by the "Religious Right" to block the recognition of same-sex marriages through court decisions and constitutional amendments, they still argue that their religious freedom was in danger - especially if same sex couples should be allowed to marry. Several cases to overturn the constitutional amendments are in front of judges, will be decided soon or will sooner or later be discussed in courts, as it was the case in California in 2008. Many from the "Religious Right" call this "judicial arrogance" and fear that this might lead to the same situation as in Roe vs. Wade. They accuse and criticize the courts for deciding against the "democratic will" of the majority of the people and call for a stop on "legislating from the bench", as Senator George Allen (R-VA) called for in his speech at the "Values Voter Summit" in 2006. Princeton University Prof. Robert George, who is also a member of President George W. Bush´s Council on Bioethics, was invited to the "Values Voter Summit" in 2006 as expert to discuss the topic of "The Preservation of Traditional Marriage". He explained to the audience that "the Supreme Court is not a fully pro marriage Supreme Court yet. But one more solid nomination and it will be. Until then the Supreme Court is a continuing threat and danger."[31] Tony Perkins from "FRC Action" stated: "The opposition is working aggressively to stop the vote on the marriage amendment. They want to silence the church!".[32]

For the "Religious Right" allowing same-sex marriages would be an "assault on marriage", as James Dobson called it in 2004. "With the gay marriage our religious liberties are gone", warned Marily Musgrave (R-CO) at the "Values Voter Summit" in September 2006. "To win this battle is the most important thing. The future is grim. We need to fight for our children."[33] Gov. Mitt Romney (R-MA), Presidential candidate for the Republican Party in 2008, said that "Our culture is under attack. (...) Every child has the right to have a mom and a dad. (...) Religious liberty is affected by the gay issue."[34] Connie Mackey, senior Vice President of "Family Research Council" and powerful lobbyist on Capitol Hill is convinced that "putting a child in a gay partnership is child abuse."[35]

Such comments are clearly aimed at polarizing the country and promoting the thesis of a "Culture War" going on within American society. The same-sex marriage issue was the "hot button issue" in 2006 to further increase this cultural divide between conservatives and liberals. It was also

31 Robert George at the "Values Voter Summit". Transcript by the author.

32 Sppech giveb by Tony Perkins at the "Values Voter Summit". Transcript by the author.

33 Speech given by Marilyn Musgrave at the "Values Voter Summit". Transcript by the author.

34 Speech given by Mitt Romney at the "Values Voter Summit". Transcript by the author.

35 Remarks by Connie Mackey at the "Values Voter Summit". Transcript y the author.

the perfect issue for the "Religious Right" to mobilize it's voter base without having to deal with the frustration and anger of some conservative members over the Bush administration's overall performance. It served as a perfect distraction from problems within the movement and the Republican party.

A War At Home and Abroad

An interesting observation of the 2006 midterm election campaign was the constant blending of domestic and foreign policy issues by groups of the "Religious Right". The "Religious Right" tried as often as possible to connect the "War on Terrorism" with the "War against Liberalism" that they lanced nation wide. In nearly every publication and nearly every newsletter there was the attempt to connect the "enemy from outside", in the form of Islamic Terrorism, with the "enemy from the inside", namely Liberalism. This approach seems to have been very effective within certain voter groups. Especially people that see themselves, their families and their country threatened by both "enemies". This effort by the "Religious Right" to mobilize voters clearly appeals to people's emotions. Examples for such an approach could be observed once again during the "Values Voter Summit" in Washington, D.C., where pictures of the collapsing World Trade Center Towers on September 11, 2001 were shown on mega screens next to pictures of an aborted fetus, captioning both pictures as "murder". Such pictures obviously upset the audience and let emotions run high.

Prominent leaders of the "Religious Right" like Gary Bauer or Ann Coulter used this emotional, but illogical approach to heat up the audience at the "Values Voter Summit". The audience was applauding and giving standing ovations for the speeches of these two icons of the "Religious Right" movement. "We are engaged in two different wars", stated Gary Bauer, "first against the Islamic fascists and second in a battle over our values".[36] Ann Coulter named two evils to blame for the "current situation": "There are twin evils: Islamic fascists and the Supreme Court." This is a clear attempt to connect the very real threat by terrorists with the liberal agenda of the Democrats during the campaign. The statement "Another Supreme Court nomination would mean World War III for the Liberals" made by Ann Coulter, was another attempt to shatter conservative voters and mobilize them to the polls. The directed use of horrifying images and pictures in people's minds like the terrorist attacks of 9/11 had certainly an effect on "Value Voters". This could clearly be seen in the affirmative reaction throughout the audience. With paying with the fear of the people

36 Statement by Gary Bauer at the "Values Voter Summit". Transcript by the author.

for their own personal safety, the "Religious Right" tried to get people to vote for their candidates.

Speakers at the "Values Voter Summit" tried to make this "connection" between foreign and domestic policy issues by using humor through exaggeration: "The five judges who found the gay marriage in the Massachusetts constitution should go to find Osama Bin Laden, since they seem to find everything."[37]. "We will find the stock of WMDs in Iraq before liberals will find the right to sodomy in the Constitution."[38] Radio talk shower and Fox News prominent Sean Hannity first declared in his speech that "the debate should be about right vs. wrong, good vs. evil, not conservative vs. liberal", just to state moments later that "first we should fight the liberals, than terrorists".[39]

Religious Groups and the Clergy - A new Alliance?

Another new development that could clearly be observed during the 2006 campaigns was the attempt by the "Religious Right" to get the clergy more involved in active politics. According to "Religious Right" leaders like James Dobson, Paul Weyrich and Gary Bauer not only church members should engage more in political campaigning, but also pastors and the official clergy. This puts many churches on the edge of acting illegally according to Internal Revenue Service rules posed on them as non-profit organizations. [40]

There are different ways on how religious groups try to get the clergy involved. Some organizations and their leaders do so openly by reaching out to pastors in speeches, newsletters and organized events like workshops etc. others do it by reaching out to church members who then should try to get their church officials involved. At the "Values Voter Summit in Washington, D.C" on September 24, 2006, Tony Perkins from the "FRCA" told the audience clearly: "We need to reach out to pastors! Do not fear the I.R.S., this is not a campaign of fear!" He continued by assuring the clergy the help of his organization in case they should get in trouble with the I.R.S: "We defend all pastors who get sued by the I.R.S. No pastor will stand alone!" Religious advocacy groups offered the clergy judicial help if

37 All statements from transcripts made by the author during the "Values Voter Summit" 2006. In this case made by Ann Coulter.

38 Statement by Ann Coulter.

39 Statement by Sean Hannity.

40 The I.R.S. has the authority and control over all tax-exempt organizations under 26 U.S. C. $501(c), which bans such organizations to engage in political activities. The ban was passed by Congress in 1954.

they should get problems with the I.R.S. or "secular interest groups" like the "ACLU" or "American United for Separation of Church and State".

The Internal Revenue Service grants non-profit organizations such as schools, charities or churches exemptions from paying the income tax as provided by 26 U.S.C. §501(c). With this exemption the government wants to help promote non-profit work. At the same time the I.R.S. sets clear rules about what rules and limits need to be followed by such groups to gain and keep this tax-exempt status. The I.R.S. started paying special attention to whether churches infringed their tax-exempt status by actively getting involved in campaigning during and after the 2004 campaigns. Reports by the I.R.S. suggested that there was a sharp increase in prohibited political activity by charities and churches.[41] According to this report the I.R.S. got many complaints about churches distributing materials to encourage people to vote for a certain candidate or directly giving money to candidates.

The I.R.S. rules state clearly that charities and churches can only take stand on issues and topics, but not on single candidates or political parties. Many non-profit groups praised the I.R.S. guidelines for the election 2006 as very clear and straightforward. "Americans United for Separation of Church and State" filed complaints about different churches they believe are not following the I.R.S. rules. These complains included the group of Jerry Falwell and his homepage www.falwell.com. "Americans United for Separation of Church and State" accused "Jerry Falwell Ministries" to have endorse George W. Bush in 2004 and to have urged readers to donate for the Republicans.

But not only the "Religious Right" was trying to get churches involved in political activities. The I.R.S. also looked into the church of Rev. Rick Warren in California. The mega church attracts more than 20,000 people any given week and was suspected to openly campaign for the Democrats.

For many churches being exempt from income tax is important for their financial survival. Therefore they need to pay special attention to the issue. During the 2006 campaign at least two large churches in Ohio were accused of being illegally engaged in political activity: "Fairfield Christian Church" and "World Harvest Church".[42] Both churches openly supported the Republican candidate for governor, J. Kenneth Blackwell in a highly contested race. These two churches were already involved in "getting-out-

41 Stephanie Strom, I.R.S. Finds Sharp Increase in Illegal Political Activity, in: The New York Times, February 25, 2006.

42 Stephanie Strom, Group Seeks I.R.S. Inquiry of Two Ohio Churches, in: The New York Times, January 16, 2006.

the-vote" efforts for George W. Bush in Ohio in 2004. Both churches argued that they had formed groups to increase political participation among Christians and that they encouraged people to vote, bot say, everything was happening in line with the I.R.S. rules.[43] The churches were also accused of sponsoring several political events without asking the regular market rent as provided by the I.R.S. rules.

As for inviting candidates to speak at a tax-exempt church, the I.R.S. allows such invitations, but only if all candidates are invited. This rule was updated in 2002 by adding that "an organization that invites two opposing candidates to speak at its events with the knowledge and expectation that one will not accept the invitation because of well-known opposing viewpoints may not be considered to have provided equal opportunity to all candidates."

There are many gray areas in the field of the political activities of tax-exempt churches. For example the I.R.S. states clearly that a pastor of a certain church cannot endorse a candidate during his salmons or from the pulpit. But what if this pastor visits another church and talks to people there? Or what about the I.R.S. rule that says a pastor cannot endorse a candidate during regular worships? Some pastors may just organize a "special, non-regular worship" and talk about candidates.[44]

How successful the efforts of the "Religious Right" in getting the clergy more involved is still an open question. The Pew Forum conducted a survey on the 2006 elections, asking people if they got information about parties or candidates from their churches. Nearly 3 in 10 (27 percent) affirmed. In 2000 only 14 percent gave the same answer.[45] What data also showed was, that these numbers are not so high for Catholics and mainline Protestants which leads to the conclusion that Evangelical churches are more involved in political action and voter information than other churches. A look on which candidates and party church members were encouraged to vote for, reveals, that 4 percent acknowledged to have been urged to vote for the Republican candidates and only one percent were urged to vote Democratic. About 7 percent affirmed that they were clearly and openly encouraged to vote for a particular party or candidate, which is a clear violation of the I.R.S. rules for the tax exempt status of churches.[46]

---

43 Ibid.

44 The author witnessed such tactics during the 2006 campaign in Georgia.

45 The Pew Forum on Religion and Public Life, Religion and the 2006 Elections, http://pewforum.org/docs/index.php?DocID=174, December 15, 2008.

46 Ibid.

A „New Religious Left"?

Despite the wide ranging attention the "Religious Right" gets in the public through media and their own activism, we should not forget about the significant number of Americans who are religious, but consider themselves "liberal" and more attracted to the Democratic political agenda. Numerically this so called "Religious Left" might even be as substantial as the "Religious Right" but they lack attention in the public. There are two main reasons for this lack of attention: First of all, members of the "Religious Right" believe in the strict separation of church and state and therefore don´t engage in political activism and voter mobilization as intense and committed as the "Religious Right". Secondly, members of the "Religious Left" are usually members of denominations that are declining in numbers and where the clergy is very reluctant to engage in political activity.[47]

Since the 2004 elections, a „New Religious Left" - more active and organized - is forming in the U.S. The media presence of this new social movement is not so strong yet, but is getting more and more obvious. New national organizations were formed, like "Faithful Democrats" or "Third Way". The later released a statement ("Come Let Us Reason Together") in October 2007 to bridge the "Culture War" between liberals and conservatives. Also some powerful church leaders like Joel Hunter in Florida or Rick Warren in California started to promote a new agenda that includes poverty, international aid and environmental issues as well. Prior to these efforts, mostly local and statewide organizations promoted the progressive agenda of the „Religious Left". Rev. Joel Hunter from the "Northland Church" in Longwood, Florida, declares himself as pro-life. He said he would be excited if Roe vs. Wade would be overturned but that he would also like to help pregnant low-income women who want to carry their babies to term. "They really don´t have a choice. The old ways of encouraging the reduction of abortion, the strident ways, aren´t productive".[48] Hunter also opposes same-sex marriage but believes that "honoring human dignity and protecting committed relationships requires recognition of the basic human rights of gay and lesbian couples."[49] He is therefore looking for ways to work together with political leaders and religious groups from all sites and parties.

---

47 Laura R. Olson, Whither the Religious Left? Religiopolitical Progressivism in Twenty-First-Century America, in: J. Matthew Wilson (Ed.), From Pews to Polling Places. Faith and Politics in the American Religious Mosaic, Washington, D.C. 2007, 53-79.

48 E.J. Dionne Jr., A Culture War Treaty, in: The Washington Post, October 9, 2007, A17.

49 Ibid.

The new movement advertises its agenda mostly through e-mails, newsletters, blogs and websites. Also because of this kind of "public presence" mainly through the world wide web and not through traditional media, rallies and open events, so far attempts to promote their agenda and to organize a consolidated base was not as successful. In contrast to the "Religious Right", these groups mostly see religion as a private issue that should be kept out of politics as much as possible.

But not only does the new social movement consist of people already politically leaning to the left. Some Evangelicals that until recently favored the Republicans started rethinking some of their stands on "moral issues". The old rivalry between environmental activists and Evangelicals starts to pave the way for new common grounds. This new movement within Evangelical churches started out in Great Britain around the year 2001, when church leaders called on their American colleagues to reconsider their mostly negligent stands on environmental issues like greenhouse gas reduction, trash recycling, etc[50].

Parts of the American scientific community reached out to right-wing Christian Evangelicals, which they thought would be the only group with enough influence on the Republican Party to really be able to make a difference.[51] In the summer of 2006 – in the middle of the midterm elections campaign – the first open statements from Evangelicals about this issue could be seen on national TV or read about in newspapers and heard in salmons in different mega churches. But these efforts are clearly only at the beginning at best. The majority of the "Religious Right" is still not putting any urgency on environmental questions. Abortion and same-sex marriage are still higher up on their priority list. Some have even left their Evangelical church because the pastor got too involved in environmental concerns, that they think are not the fault of mankind, but God′s will only. IT will highly interesting to follow the new developments over the next years and over the next election cycles.

Conclusions

It is still a little early in the year to have all necessary and reliable data to make a substantial comparison between the 2006 and 2008 elections. But some statements can already be made. The 2008 Presidential elections were different from previous elections for many reasons, starting with the Democratic candidate for the Presidency, Sen. Barack Obama. But con-

50 Juliet Eilperin, Warming Draws Evangelicals Into Environmentalist Fold, in: The Washington Post, August 8, 2007, A01.

51 Ibid.

centrating on "Religion and Politics" we can say, that religious issues and questions of personal faith – again - played a much more prominent role at the very beginning of the campaign, namely during the fall of 2008, when the public asked statements from candidates about their personal relation to their faith and their religious believes, than during the fall of 2008. After a forum on religion hosted by Rick Warren in August 2008, and especially with the outbreak of the economic crisis, religious issues moved way in the background. Even more so as was the case in the fall of 2006. This is once again a sign that religious issues – while still important to a lot of voters – are never as important as the economy or national security. With gas prices around $4 per gallon it was really hard for both, the "Religious Right" and the "Religious Left" to mobilize their voter base by promoting "moral issues" like abortion, stem cell research or same-sex marriage.

Looking at some numbers, exit polls showed that Obama could close the "God Gap" a little better than John Kerry in 2004, getting 24 percent of the votes of Evangelicals, compared to the 21 percent John Kerry got.[52]

Both sites - the "Religious Right" and the "Religious Left" - used the same tactics as in previous years, but were lacking public attention to be widely noticed. This was also the case because the "Religious Right" did not support either candidate, not Barack Obama and not even the Republican candidate John McCain.

How the "Religious Right" will react now that they don´t have such a great advocate in the White House anymore as they did with George W. Bush, remains to be seen. For now we can expect that they will try to bring more religious issues in front of courts and maybe concentrate more on local and state initiatives to promote their agenda.

What the recognition of same-sex marriage is concerned, President Barack Obama already favored a repeal of the „Defense of Marriage Act" passed by Congress in 1996, in which marriage was defined as a union between a man and a woman. Nevertheless this will be one of these issues that will most likely be decided in every single state legislature and in front of courts.

The number of progressivists among the Evangelicals is growing and is pressuring beyond the traditional agenda of the "Religious Right", focusing more and more on social and economic justice. How well such groups can organize their interests and how involved they want to get in politics also remains to be seen. So far they are not nearly as organized and active as the

52 Suzanne Goldenberg, Democratic converts narrow "God Gap", in: The Guardian, November 7, 2008.

"Religious Right" even though they are trying to adopt strategies and methods from the "Religious Right", especially regarding sensitize the public and mobilize a voter base. But with Barack Obama in the White House and a solid majority in Congress they should feel more energized and motivated than ever before to promote their agenda, especially in regard to environmental issues, stem cell research and health care. President Obama is also already favoring taking back some measures by the Bush-administration about abortion, stem cell research and civil liberties – issues that are of great interest for both sides..

The current economic crises gives religious groups and church communities many new pastoral challenges. More people will rely on their charity activities. How churches and religious groups can deal with these new challenges and how they approach issues like poverty, unemployment, minimal wage, AIDS etc. will give some clue in which direction both, the "Religious Right" and the "Religious Left" will move.

Even though it looks like the "Religious Right" seems to be somewhat in defense now, that ca also main new fresh ideas coming up for the next election cycle. The "Religious Right" proofed over and over again that they come back strong after they have already been written off. New leaders and maybe a new agenda, which also includes environmental issues together with new tactics could easily put them back into the spotlight. A lot will depend on how the "Religious Left" will be doing and if they can meet the expectations that many faithful Christians put in them now.

Susanne Cohen-Weisz
(The Hebrew University of Jerusalem)

The suitcases are unpacked: From Liquidationsgemeinde to the Development of an Austrian-Jewish identity

Since the 1950s, the so-called Western European, i.e. the non-communist, and since 1989 also former communist countries gradually engaged in the process of Europeanization – the most important trend and development of the second half of the 20th century in Europe. Europeanization denotes the emergence and development at the European level of distinct structures of governance, with the aim to establish an effective cooperation among the member states. It also stands for a diffusion of European pluralistic democratic norms and ideas, and the idea of Europe being a community of values, with the aim to, at a later stage, increase the feeling of European identity among the various populations.

With the European Union (EU) becoming an arena of institutionalized international policy cooperation in which cooperation and networking among various groups became common and necessary to set agendas and influence policy processes, and the increased acceptance of a multiple identity, ethnic and religious communities are gaining importance in national and European decision-making and politics. It is, therefore, significant for the various communities to strengthen their group identity and self-confidence; and for the nation states in general it is important that each group also possesses a strong national identity, meaning that the members of the group feel part of the national society, part of the country in which they live and see their future in the country. The development of the country's groups' group identity, national-group identity and European-group identity, thus play an important role for a country's unity and strength. Analysis of the influence of national politics and other relevant factors – which might vary from group to group – on group identity are thus essential for effective policy-making.

Jewish communities in Europe present a well-suited case study due to their presence in every EU member state, their stabilized population and the role some of their representatives play in the national, or even international, development of their respective field of action, academia, economy, and sometimes also politics. The Austrian Jewish Communities, in particular, provide an interesting analysis, since the period between March 1938 (the Anschluss, the integration of Austria into Nazi Germany) and the end of World War II (WWII) was an important benchmark in the history of Austria, as well as for the Jews living within it. For both, the post-War period was characterized by the necessity of political, economic and social reconstruction. The common point of departure and the fact that the Jewish communities are developing within the Austrian nation state raises the question of whether, how and to what extend the political and social processes in Austria have influenced the reconstruction and development of the Jewish communities.

During the Nazi occupation the 770 Jewish communities existing in Austria in 1938 with a population of some two hundred thousand Jews (of whom about 90 percent lived in Vienna) were almost completely annihilated and at its end less than five thousand Jews remained in the country. Up to the early 1950s there was a large consensus among Jews and non-Jews alike that there was no way that Jewish communal life in Austria could be revived. In May 1948 the Jewish Telegraphic Agency (JTA) issued a special report that began: "For Jews there is no life in Austria, no future"[1].

Today, despite the gloomy prediction, the six re-established Jewish communities (Baden, Graz, Innsbruck, Linz, Salzburg and Vienna), though still small in size, present themselves as self-confident, culturally active and well positioned within the local and Austrian environment. A culturally and religiously diverse Jewish life has taken root and has attracted considerable public attention. This transformation is exemplified in this paper by the Viennese Jewish Community (Israelitische Kultusgemeinde Wien (IKG)), which accounts for 95 percent of today's Austrian Jewish population. The IKG developed from a Liquidationsgemeinde – a community that the Jews in Vienna as well as abroad planned to liquidate after the last Holocaust survivors had left the country – into an established community with a population consisting of Ashkenazi and Sephardic Jews of various origins whose religious denominations range from Reform to ultra-Orthodox, and an educational, social and religious infrastructure which could cater to a much larger population.

It also developed from a frightened and voluntarily invisible community to a self-confident and active player in the Austrian cultural and political landscape. The Jews became growingly aware of their ability to stand up for their rights, and eventually to become an integral – not assimilated – part of the Viennese society in which they not only do not feel threatened but believe that they have a future. This vision of a future in Vienna is reflected in the large project of the new community compound on a street

1 Special Report, in: Jewish Telegraphic Agency, New York 15.5.1948.

named after Simon Wiesenthal including a school, a sports area and the new home for the elderly community members.

This paper is looking for the key the key to this rather unique communal reconstruction, changed self-perception and final "unpacking of the suitcases"[2], in changes in the Jewish group identity in Vienna. It examines the communal, national and international social and political developments, which, in turn, influenced internal and external communal politics, and thus affected communal reconstruction and development.

Jewish Group-identity

In sociology and political science, the notion of identity refers to the individual's self-perception as a member of a certain group. The people in this group feel that "they have important things in common and that they differ so much from other large groups that they constitute a distinctive and self-contained society"[3]. Thus, while members of this group feel part of the surrounding society with the same rights and duties as others in it, they feel at the same time 'different from the others'. Basic to their individual group identity is the need for group recognition – the full social and political acceptance by the surrounding society of the group and its members, and of group difference.

Jewish group identity, the group's definition of itself, is characterized by the pluralism of Jewish-identity perceptions of its individual members. Jewish identity can, at the same time, be based on religion, ethnicity, culture, the identification with other Jews or just 'feeling Jewish', and common roots and history. Jewish identity is "differentiated rather than monolithic"[4] – enabling the individual to choose from its various elements – and 'voluntary' in the sense that Jews are free to choose how to define and express their Jewish identity[5]. These differing perceptions of Jewish identity stem from the fact that an individual's sense of self-identity is constantly affected by the various social influences – communal and national – to which he is exposed during his life. "Out of these influences [people]

2 The notion "sitting on packed suitcases" was common among Austrian Jews. It reflected their perception of Austria as a temporary place of residence.

3 Jos De Beus, Quasi-National European Identity and European Democracy, in: Law and Philosophy 20/3, Netherlands 2001, 283-311, here: 292.

4 Herbert C. Kelman, The Place of Ethnic Identity in the Development of Personal Identity: A Challenge for the Jewish Family, in: Studies in Contemporary Jewry 14, Oxford 1998, 3-26, here: 19.

5 Diana Pinto, Eternal Volunteers: Towards European Jewish Identity, http://hagalil.com/bet-debora/golem/identity.htm, 12.4.2005

draw beliefs, attitudes, values and expectations that, when added to their personal core, make up their emerging identity"[6]. Since it is "variable rather than fixed in meaning"[7], Jewish identity is in an ongoing formation process. Similarly, according to Kelman, Jewish group identity may have both permanent, or fixed, elements and elements that develop and change over time – or new ones that arise in particular circumstances (e.g. Holocaust memory and the state of Israel which did not exist before 1945 and 1948 respectively). What individuals choose to emphasize among the elements of group identity, what they incorporate of it – how they as individuals see the place of the Jewish group in the universe whether in past, present or future – becomes part of the core of their personal identity; in other words it is the group-identity component of their personal identity.

The research will focus on Jewish group identity, rather than on individual Jewish identity, because of its impact on communal life and reconstruction. For example, the strengthening of the Jewish identity in a particular locality is likely to lead to organizational blossoming and community building. So, too, this is likely to affect the community's internal and external politics.

Reconstructing the Jewish community in Vienna

Demographic structure

The official census of March 22, 1934, registered 191,481 Jews in Austria (3 percent of the Austrian population), with 176,034 Jews in Vienna alone (10 percent of the Viennese population)[8]. On March 13, 1938, the Jewish communities in Austria counted 181,882 members (Vienna: 167,249) from about 206,000 Jews living in the country[9].

After the Anschluss, about 130,000 Austrian Jews had succeeded in emigrating and about 65,000 were deported and murdered, some committed suicide.

In December 1945, 3,955 Jews were left in Vienna; 1,977 survived because they had special protection (e.g. members of the Ältestenrat der Juden [Council of Elders of the Jews], or because they had non-Jewish spouses), 200 as U-Boot (in hiding), 1,727 returned from concentration camps and

6 Kelman, The Place of Ethnic Identity, 5
7 Kelman, The Place of Ethnic Identity, 19
8 Martin Gilbert, Atlas of the Holocaust, New York 1993, 22.
9 Data taken from the Documentation Centre of Austrian Resistance, http://www.doew.at/projekte/holocaust/shoahengl/demo2.html, 3.3.2006

251 from abroad[10]. Additionally, a few hundred Hungarian Jews who had survived the forced marches to the West were still in Austria.

Only few former Austrian Jews returned to Vienna from their countries of exile. By April 1947, 700 Austrian Jews had returned from England (where most of them were sent in children's transports), 800 from Shanghai, 200 from Palestine and 350 from Karaganda in Russia[11].

The small number of Viennese Jews were joined by Displaced Persons (DPs) from Central and Eastern Europe who fled post-Nazi anti-Semitism and pogroms in their countries. From 1945 to 1953 about 170,000 DPs had their first stop in Vienna – most of them in the DP camps of the Western allies. The majority never registered with the community. They never intended to stay and generally continued to other countries such as the United States, Canada, Australia and Israel. By 1950, when the mass migration of DPs had come to an end about 3,000 DPs registered with the IKG[12].

In 1956, the aborted Hungarian uprising brought a significant influx of refugees into the Viennese Jewish community[13]. They were generally younger than the local average. In 1968, the incursion of the armies of the Warsaw Pact into Czechoslovakia brought another, but smaller wave[14] of new members to the community. In the 1970s and 1980s, with the easing of the emigration regulations in the Soviet Union, around three hundred thousand Jews – mainly from Bukhara and Georgia, but also from Russia and Caucasia – migrated through Austria. "95 percent of them went to Israel, the others mostly to the USA. 3,000 former Soviet Jews remained in Austria or came back from Israel"[15]. After 1990 this immigration stopped because of Austria's new restrictive immigration policy.

Negative attitudes of Austrian politicians towards Jews re-settling in Austria[16] and Jewish policies and attitudes abroad condemning such settling, as well as high death and low birth rates and the emigration of young Jews due to the dearth of eligible potential marriage partners, led to the

10 Christine Oertel, Juden auf der Flucht durch Austria, Wien 1999, 118f.

11 Evelyn Adunka, Die Vierte Gemeinde – Die Wiener Juden in der Zeit von 1945 bis Heute, Berlin 2000, 56.

12 Abraham Hyman, Central Europe: Displaced Persons, in: American Jewish Year Book 52, New York 1951, 305-312, here: 308ff.

13 Estimated numbers for Hungarian Jewish refugees are not available.

14 Estimated numbers for Jewish refugees from Czechoslovakia are not available.

15 Alexander Friedmann, Psycho-Socio-Cultural Rehabilitation in an Ethnic Subgroup: A 30-Years Follow-Up, in: World Cultural Psychiatry Research Review, 2/2-3, April/July 2007, 87-95, here: 88.

16 Susanne Cohen-Weisz, From Bare Survival to European Jewish Vision: Jewish Life and Identity in Vienna, Jerusalem 2008, 6.

small size and low population increase of Viennese Jewry from 1945 to 2007 (see table 1). Despite the various immigration waves of Jews from Eastern Europe and the former Soviet Union, the membership of the IKG did not grow beyond 10,000–12,000[17], and since the 1970s it remained between 6000 and 7000.

Table 1: IKG Membership after 1945

1945	1951	1961	1971	1981	1988	1991	1995	2001	2007
3,955a	11,224b,c	8,354b	7,747b	6,527b	6,069	7,103	6,841	6,614	7,014

Source: Official IKG numbers received from the IKG member service[18].
a. Oertel, 1999, p. 118.
b. Not yet verified numbers received from the IKG member service.
c. The number is assumed to have been significantly lower.

Despite the constantly small number of its members, the Jewish demography began to take a positive turn. The immigration from the former Soviet Union altered the age pyramid in the IKG since these mainly Sephardic[19] immigrants "came as whole families, showing mostly three generations and had at least three, in some cases even more than five children"[20]. Also the crumbling of the segregation walls due to origin lead to a growing number of Ashkenazi[21]-Sephardic 'mixed marriages' which reduced the emigration of young Jews.

Recently there has been some natural increase: in 1990, the IKG counted for the first time since 1945 more births than deaths, and the majority of the members were under the age of 50; statistics from January 25, 2008, show that of the 7,018 IKG members about 59 percent are under the age of 50 (see table 2).

17 The exact numbers of IKG members are still largely unknown. According to the member service of the IKG, various historians presented different numbers, and also IKG statistics often counted only cases of births and deaths. Only at the beginning of 2000 did the IKG engage in retroactively constructing new statistics also taking into account departures, which were numerous because of emigration. The project is anticipated to be finished by 2012; official IKG statistics are available only for the time period after 1988.

18 Statistics of IKG membership were sent to the author by email from the director of the member service of the IKG.

19 Sephardic Jews are a subgroup of Jews originating in the Iberian Peninsula.

20 Friedmann, Psycho-Socio-Cultural Rehabilitation, 89.

21 Ashkenazi Jews are descendants of the medieval Jewish communities of the Rhineland.

Table 2: Age Statistics of IKG Members from 25.1.2008

Age-group	0-10	11-20	21-30	31-40	41-50	51-60	61-70	71-80	81-90	91-100	101-110
Members	727	757	996	951	758	1,078	672	478	517	82	2

Source: Official IKG statistics.

Furthermore, an estimated 8,000-13,000 non-affiliated Jews live in Vienna[22]; the reasons of Jews not to register with the community are diverse[23].

Even so, the Viennese Jewish community must still cope with the problems associated with its size, and seemingly has little prospect of growth in the near future because of the restrictive Austrian immigration policy. The current IKG president Ariel Muzicant is working to convince the Austrian government to enact a Jewish immigration policy enabling the immigration of young educated Jews; but for the time being without success.

Jewish life and identities in Vienna

As before WWII, the IKG was re-established in 1945 along the regulations of the Israelitengesetz (legislation regulating the relations between the state and the 'Israelite Community') of 1890. Among other things, this law acknowledged the Jews as "Austrians of Jewish faith" " – not as a nationality – and foresaw for each locality a single community (Einheitsgemeinde) that represented all the Jews, which offered the state a single point of contact[24]. In the law the term "Jewish faith" is used without any further definition, especially not the Halacha (the Jewish religious law) ruling of "who is a Jew". Nevertheless only Jews recognized as such according to the Halacha are eligible to membership.

The establishment of the IKG as a Religionsgemeinschaft, a religious association, reflected the broadest common denominator within an immediate post-war Viennese community composed of Jews with varying Jewish identities, nationalities and religious denominations[25].

22 Interview with Rabbi Paul Chaim Eisenberg, Chief Rabbi of Austria, August 2005. (All the interviews in this paper were done, recorded and translated by the author)

23 Cohen-Weisz, From Bare Survival, 8.

24 Cohen-Weisz, From Bare Survival, 3ff.

25 Interview with Avshalom Hodik, former IKG Secretary General, July 2007.

Among the pre-1938 Viennese Jews who survived the war in Vienna or returned immediately thereafter were religious and secular Jews who identified themselves as Jews before the war, as well as Jews who had been living on the periphery of Judaism before the Holocaust and moved to its center only because of the historical events. Among the Jews returning from exile many were Marxists, and did not feel Jewish out of religious sentiment but out of the feeling of heredity or even the definition by others. Jews, who were religious, but not necessarily nationally minded before the Holocaust, generally emerged from it with an ethnic Jewish identity. In contrast, Jews with weak or no Jewish identity, who generally were 'made to' be Jews by the Nazis, perceived Judaism thereafter as a religion only and their identity as secular-Jewish; the stigma of being Jewish had become an intrinsic part of their own personal identity. The Jewish identity of many of the latter was mainly a feeling of belonging to a community of fate imposed upon them by the Holocaust, and a substitute for social acceptance denied to them because of their being Jewish.

The mainly traditional and religious DPs had a strong religious and ethnic Jewish identity in terms of identification with the Jewish people, culture, traditional family life and religion – similar to that of the Ostjuden, the Jews from Eastern Europe living in Austria before the Holocaust. They created religious institutions even in the DP camps.

The Orthodox groups, and especially Agudas Israel also had a strong religious and ethnic identity, and in contrast to before the Holocaust, a Zionist one as well. Their previous anti-Zionist ideology had changed into a pragmatic Zionist position towards the state of Israel. In 1948, Rabbi Ehrmann of Agudas Israel stated that "political sovereignty, the sovereign nationalism and its state were the first steps on the way to the actual goal, the state ruled according to the Torah"[26]. In the immediate post-war years the creation of religious institutions in Vienna was largely due to them, sometimes even in opposition to the IKG leadership.

Religious life in Vienna was boosted by the immigration from Hungary in 1956 which brought Jews identified with various streams within Orthodoxy, ranging from the modern-Orthodox and Zionist Mizrachi to a group of fervently anti-Zionist ultra-Orthodox Satmar Hassidim.

For some three decades after 1945, the Viennese Jewish community remained almost entirely Ashkenazi. This changed with the immigration from the former Soviet Union in the 1970s and 1980s which added a new element: Sephardic Jewish identity and culture. Most of the im-

26 Adunka, Die Vierte Gemeinde, 222

migrants are traditional Jews with a strong religious and ethnic Jewish identity who grew up in an environment with strong ties to the tradition. Even if they are non-observant, kosher food and Shabbat candle lightning are widely maintained.

Now, in contrast to the situation in 1945, sixty years after the Holocaust, Viennese Jewry is characterized by cultural, ethnic and religious diversity. The IKG is "probably the most heterogeneous [community] in the world: under a common roof there are Ashkenazim and Sephardim, atheists and agnostics, Hassidim and Mitnagdim, ultra-Orthodox and less ultra-Orthodox, people with various rites and people without rites, reformists, liberals, conservatives, Orthodox".[27]

A considerable infrastructure supports the development of the many facets of the Viennese community and of Jewish life in general. This infrastructure includes, among other things, eighteen synagogues and prayer rooms, two ritual baths, three kashrut (Jewish dietetic laws) authorities, four Jewish schools, Talmud-Torah schools, the Wiener Jeshiwah, a Jewish business school, a Jewish teachers' academy and further educational institutions, the psycho-social center Esra and a home for the elderly.

Towards a growingly self-confident community

The representatives of the Jewish community who met an Anglo-American Commission for Palestine in 1947 were described as "shrill and pathetic, self-assertive and broken", fostering the impression that the "Jewish community of Vienna would not flourish again" and that "in Europe the Jewish communities have been so thoroughly destroyed that it is impossible anyway to rebuild them"[28]. The development of the Viennese community from the small and broken group of survivors to a flourishing Jewish community with an extensive Jewish infrastructure that caters effectively to the varied needs of an increasingly heterogeneous population is a consequence of the distinctive pattern of development of Jewish identity in Viennese Jewry after 1945.

27 Jüdische Einheit 28, Wien Mai 1994.

28 Richard Crossman, Palestine Mission: A Personal Record, London 1947, 103f.

The Holocaust in the Jewish identity

The Jews in immediate post-war Vienna were mostly preoccupied with the memory of their lost relatives and friends, by the memory of the extinguished glory of the pre-1938 Viennese Jewish community or their other lost communities, by the need to share Holocaust memories and by the imperative of ensuring their own physical and material survival. The first issues of the IKG magazine, Die Gemeinde, which appeared monthly from September 1948 to December 1949, and then again after February 1953, reveals a broken Jewish community that focused on trying to find a way to survive after the Holocaust.

The Holocaust that so radically separated the Jews from the gentiles reinforced their sense of group belonging. Many Jews who began to feel Jewish only because of it, now shared a common recent past with Jews who always felt Jewish. These war-generation Jews felt that they were united by a common experience, their memories and the struggle for survival, and that these bonds differentiated them significantly from the rest of the population. Indeed, the Holocaust drew an uncrossable line between the Jews and the gentile population. The Jews in Austria saw themselves as the victims in the land of the hangman who not only disavows any responsibility for the Holocaust, but also founded its Second Republic on the myths of being the 'first victim of Nazi Germany'[29]. Moreover, it reintegrated former Nazis (including killers) into Austria's public service, politics and universities, and ignored de-Nazification.

In this situation the Jews found themselves in a vulnerable position. A significant proportion of Austrians continued to espouse anti-Semitic views and held firmly to the notion that Jews were not part of Austrian society. They also perceived the presence of the Jews as a threat to their positive self-image of suffering victims. This hostile socio-political situation strengthened bonds among the Jews who were afraid of an again rising anti-Semitism. The Holocaust became a major binding link among the survivors and the central element in their Jewish group identity; and for some the memories of the Holocaust and its apotheosis as a singular event in world history were even elevated to the rank of a substitute religion.

This centrality of the Holocaust in Viennese Jewish identity began fading in the post-war generation. The Jews, who were born after 1945

29 The declaration of independence of April 27, 1945, which is the founding document of the Second Republic, describes Austria as "the first free country, which fell victim to Hitler's aggression" (Republik Österreich, 1945) and depicts the *Anschluss* as occupation.

and grew up with the assurance that a Jewish state exists, perceived the past differently. The very existence of the State of Israel and its dramatic victories in 1948 and 1967, and the image of heroic Israeli soldiers as a strong antithesis to the Jews who went silently to their deaths, alienated many in the post-war generation from the seemingly 'weak Jews' of the Holocaust period who happened to be their parents. While critical of them, if only privately in order not to hurt the survivors, they began to say in public what their parents at most dared to think, namely, that Jews had to stand up and fight publicly, both against those who sought to harm them and in order to secure what was necessary to ensure the Jewish future. For this generation, too, the Holocaust served as a key element in their group identity and as a binding link, but unlike for their parents, their leitmotif was 'Never Again'[30]. Their outrage at the ongoing injustices Austrian Jews had faced since 1945 exacerbated their ire over what had taken place during the Holocaust, and the desire to prove themselves fueled, since the 1970s and especially the 1980s, the resolve and the self-confidence to fight publicly to secure a better Jewish future. In doing so, they reversed the pattern of non-confrontational behavior vis-à-vis the Austrian state and society that since 1945 had characterized the Austrian Jewish community and its leadership[31].

Members of the second post-war generation (the children of those born after WWII), however, have been openly critical of the central role of the Holocaust in Jewish identity. For them, Jewish identity should be based not on a past catastrophe, but rather on positive and attractive components connected to life (the central value of the Jewish religion) and not death, to Jewish continuity and the Jewish people rather than fear. In short, they sought to move Jewish culture, Jewish heritage and modern Jewish life into the foreground[32]. Put differently, Jewish identity "combines a tendency of laughing and crying, and the young second generation sees the importance in developing from the laughing while remembering the crying"[33]. A citation from the campaign platform of IKG political party Gesher, founded by second post-war generation activists, corroborates these findings: "[The community] has to present itself as an active and vital community and draw a positive picture from

30 'Never Again' is an international phenomenon that appeared at the same time throughout the world.

31 Interview with Willy Weisz, Jewish Vice-President of the Coordinating Committee for Christian-Jewish Cooperation and representative of B'nai Brith international and B'nai Brith Europe at the UN site in Vienna, August 2004.

32 Interview with Janki Grünberger, who works in an honorary position for Bnei-Akiba Vienna, January 2006.

33 Interview with Yvonne Feiger, Chairperson of the Jewish student organization in Vienna, July 2007.

the flourishing Jewish life in Austria, without defining itself solely through the horrors of the past"[34].

Israel in the Jewish identity

Significant Zionist activities were undertaken in the DP camps established in Vienna right after the end of WWII. Underground organizations trained and organized DPs for mostly illegal immigration to Palestine. The proclamation of the State of Israel in 1948 intensified these activities. As noted above, hundreds of thousands of Jews passed through Austria on the way to Israel, before the DP camps were closed down in the Kreisky era. Austria was regarded as a transit country and its Jewish community perceived itself as a Liquidationsgemeinde. Thus, in the early years, many communal properties were sold for a pittance to finance immediate needs, and communal records and libraries were transferred to Israel. The expected self-liquidation of the Viennese Jewry never occurred, however, and today more than sixty years after the Holocaust a flourishing Jewish community exists in Vienna. The bonds with the State of Israel contributed to this communal strengthening.

Now the Jew is no longer the 'vaterlandslose Geselle' (the fellow without a homeland), but, like members of other Diaspora national groups, he can turn to a real national homeland. Awareness of the existence of a state that would always accept Jews and its creation of conditions for an autonomous and viable Jewish existence played an important role in the post-war Jewish-identity formation. Israel became a synonym for Jewish future, and the Jews came to feel that they were now living in a Diaspora rather than in exile, with the possibility of moving to their spiritual homeland at a time of their own choosing.

The year 1967 was particularly significant for the post-war generation, which, as described above, did not want to identify with the 'passively suffering' Jews. Israel's victory and its emergence as David overcoming Goliath, led Viennese Jews to feel that they were 'little Davids' in their fight against anti-Semitism and in their conflicts with the Austrian government. It also gave rise to a new self-confidence of being able to provide physical security to Viennese Jews in the global fight against terrorism. This self-confidence and an the feeling of being responsible for their fellow Jews has led many young people of the post-war generations to volunteer to train and serve as security guards in front of synagogues during services. This solidarity and the conviction that "we

34 Vereinte Interessensvertretung, http://www.gesher.at/index.html, 14.3.2008

protect the Jewish people"[35] (Rabbi Eisenberg, 2005) has generated a significant degree of group pride that has become a major element in their Jewish identity and contributed greatly to its overall strengthening.

Israel's victory also gave rise to new and strong feelings of solidarity with Israel: many young Jews heeded calls to volunteer in kibbutzim and cities, and went to Israel – often against the wishes of their parents[36]. The significance of Israel in Viennese Jewish life is also manifest in various issues of Die Gemeinde. "Through the mid-1960s, about a third of the articles...addressed Israeli matters. By the late 1960s, the average was well above 50 percent and, in the course of the 1970s and 1980s,...rarely...less than 60 percent"[37]. These articles dealt with the security situation as well as with daily life and scientific, technological, social and cultural developments, enabling the Jews to identify with a new and modern Jewish state, to be proud of it and to follow its achievements. Thus, the post-war generation grew up as Israel was built up, and for them its existence was a kind of miracle, its military successes gave them inner support, and they were ready to fight for its right to exist[38].

The situation changed again, however, in the aftermath of the First Lebanon War in 1982 and especially after the outbreak of the Second Intifada in 2000. Israel no longer seemed to be in existential danger and was thus taken somewhat for granted. In addition, it appeared in the non-Jewish media as the aggressor state, which influenced the opinions and attitudes of both gentiles and Jews, especially members of the second post-war generation. In the past, Jews stood unconditionally behind Israel, irrespective of how critical they were of the politics of the Israeli government. In recent decades, however, Israel is more likely to be criticized openly. The fading of the ideal image of Israel and the lessened impact of ideology in general led to a change in the perception of Zionism. The dream of moving to Israel was replaced by support for Israel from abroad, while strengthening Jewishness outside of Israel. Die Gemeinde reflects this new emphasis on strengthening local Jewish life. Even though Israel is still the subject of much of its issues, the "Insider", the part dealing with the Viennese community grew from a single page in the mid-1980s to four pages in 1995 and eighteen pages in 2007, before appearing for the first time in July 2007 as a separate publication of twenty pages, reflecting the increased number of institutions and level of activity in Jewish Vienna. To be sure, Israel was still important, but

35 Interview with Rabbi Paul Chaim Eisenberg, 2005

36 Interview with Sonja Feiger, editor of Die Gemeinde, July 2007.

37 Matti Bunzl, Austrian Zionism and the Jews of the New Europe, in: Jewish Social Studies 9/2, Bloomington 2003, 154-173, 157.

38 Interview with Sonja Feiger, 2007

far greater weight was now attached to the need to strengthen Jewish life in Vienna, independent of Israel, and this is now viewed as a critical element in shaping the identity and ensuring the future of Viennese Jewry. While Israel is perceived as the spiritual homeland, Vienna is the physical one.

The platform of Gesher shows this wish for independence from Israeli politics, and their strong local Jewish identity: "We view a separation between Israeli politics and the IKG agenda as suitable for counteracting the equating of all the Jews with Israel. The renaming of the IKG (Israelite religious community) to 'Jewish community' is therefore not only reasonable, but also up-to-date, since it takes into account the Jewish self-confidence".[39]

Austrian politics towards its Jews

In the 1950s and 1960s, Austria sought to keep quiet issues such as the involvement of Austrians in Nazi crimes, its subsequent unwillingness to face up to its past and its behavior towards the Jewish population. The requests of the IKG for restitution and Simon Wiesenthal's campaigns against Nazis holding significant political positions were portrayed by the Austrian politicians and population as disturbing the social order and undermining the population's positive self-image. The situation worsened after the 1975 United Nations 'Zionism is Racism' resolution, which influenced the "anti-Israel actions of Bruno Kreisky"[40]. He played a crucial role in making Yasser Arafat and the PLO respectable in the West. Kreisky insisted "on presenting terrorist leaders like Gaddafi and Arafat as admirable 'patriots' and 'freedom-fighters'"[41] and at the same time called Israel a semi-fascist state[42]. The Jewish community was irritated by his attitude towards Israel and his decision to hold talks with the PLO, as well as his acceptance of the promotion of known – but mostly not convicted – former Nazis to prominent public positions, and his fight against Wiesenthal. Nevertheless, the Jewish community remained quiet out of fear that criticizing the popular chancellor would heighten anti-Semitism. Further contributing to this quiescence was the

39 Vereinte Interessensvertretung, http://www.gesher.at/index.html, 14.3.2008.

40 Manfred Gerstenfeld, Jews against Israel, in: Nativ Online 8, October 2005/Tishrei 5766; http://www.acpr.org.il/ENGLISH-NATIV/08-issue/gerstenfeld-8.htm, 12.8.2007

41 Robert Wistrich, Anti-Zionism and Antisemitism: The Case of Bruno Kreisky, Jerusalem 2007, 14

42 Chancellor Kreisky on Saddat/Israel, in: Journal of Palestinian Studies 13/ 3, Washington 1984, 143-151, here: 148.

fact that Kreisky himself was born (and still considered by many) as a Jew, and that the IKG leadership was Social Democratic and strongly linked to Kreisky's party, the SPÖ.

The situation changed in the 1980s, when the Austrian population began to discuss publicly the period of the National Socialist (NS) regime. The series The Holocaust directed by Marvin J. Chomsky, which was broadcast by Austrian TV in 1979 and seen by millions of Austrians was the catalyst of this new public discourse, which peaked in the mid-1980s in the Waldheim affair. During the campaign for the 1986 Austrian presidential elections, the ÖVP (the Christian-oriented, conservative Austrian People's Party) candidate Kurt Waldheim was accused by the World Jewish Congress (WJC) – most probably instigated by the SPÖ – of having concealed or, at least, incompletely disclosed his membership in the Sturmabteilung (paramilitary wing of the Nazi Party) and NS student federation, as well as his role as liaison officer in the German Wehrmacht. Waldheim justified himself by stating that "I just performed my duty", and that after more than forty years it had slipped his mind. The WJC accused – but without ever providing any proof – Waldheim of having committed war crimes in the Balkans while he was a German-army lieutenant in Greece and Yugoslavia at a time of brutal campaigns against Yugoslav partisans and the large-scale deportation of Jews to death camps. These accusations moved the IKG unwillingly to the center of Austrian politics and forced Israel to downgrade its diplomatic representation to avoid the spectacle of an Israeli ambassador presenting his credentials to a person suspected of Nazi crimes.

The accusations triggered the Austrian government's establishment of a commission of historians (see below) to research Waldheim's role as a Wehrmacht officer in the occupied Balkans and Greece. Even before the official publication of the commission's results, its work and findings gave rise to extensive public discussions in Austria concerning Waldheim's past, the validity of his self-exoneration and the acceptability of Nazi perpetrators in influential political positions, and split the Austrian population into two camps: those who wished to continue to remain silent about the past and those who wanted the past, including Austria's post-war denial of guilt, to be examined critically. The Waldheim affair also brought young Jewish and non-Jewish Austrian intellectuals to form protest groups such as Neues Österreich to try and change deeply ingrained Austrian attitudes. For the first time since WWII, the Austrian public and politicians discussed and criticized the 'first victim' theory as a problematic element of the national ideology. This polarization of the Austrian population strengthened the Jewish community, since, in contrast to the previous post-war years, it was not alone in its fight against the country's failure to face up to its past and its attempt to whitewash the guilt of a non-negligible part of its population.

During the election campaign, for the first time since 1945, anti-Semitism, mainly cautiously formulated, was used as a political weapon. Anti-Semitism did not increase but became more manifest. Anti-Semitic political speeches were followed by an immediate increase in anti-Semitic statements in the media – "Formerly Joseph Goebbels agitated against Austria. Today it is Edgar Bronfman"[43] – and incidents on the streets. Rabbi Biderman reported that "previously I had been verbally attacked once or twice a month, now two to three times a week"[44]. These anti-Semitic outbursts spread a certain panic among the Jews and an increased consideration of emigration, but also enabled the community to fight back more effectively[45].

To the dismay of the Jewish community, Waldheim was elected Austrian president in May 1986. Nevertheless, "since 1987, the federal government and municipal authorities have sought to improve relations with Austrian Jews, world Jewry, and Israel"[46]. The government and the authorities increasingly supported the construction and renovation of synagogues, research projects on the Holocaust, Jewish cultural activities, scholarly conferences on Jewish topics and Holocaust memory projects. They launched further educational programs – which had already begun in the Kreisky era – and asked for the rewriting of school textbooks, to counteract anti-Semitism and improve the understanding and knowledge about the Holocaust. Moreover, they seriously entered talks about restitution. In 1986, the mayor of Vienna, Helmut Zilk, announced the establishment of a Jewish museum, and the fiftieth anniversary of the Anschluss in 1988 was marked by several high-profile public commemoration ceremonies. The same year, the commission published its findings: though no concrete evidence could be found that Waldheim was guilty of explicit war crimes, it was proven that, contrary to his assertions, he was placed high enough to know about the crimes committed by the Nazi occupier in the Balkans and Greece, that given his education in legal matters he must have been aware that some of the actions of the German army and other German paramilitary groups were defined as crimes even by the German military law of the time, and that no document contained any indication that he opposed such crimes or

43 Staberl, in: Neue Kronen Zeitung, Wien 2.2.1988.

44 Österreichs Juden haben wieder Angst, in: Der Spiegel 28, Hamburg 1987, 94-96, here: 95.

45 Interview with Willy Weisz, 2004

46 Robert Wistrich, The Roots of Haiderism, http://www.aijac.org.au/review/2000/253/essay253.html, 9.7.2007.

even tried to hinder their execution. As a result of the findings, which were partly made public already before the official publication, and the public discussion they aroused, Waldheim became internationally isolated: he was banned from entering the United States, Canada and Israel, and many other countries declared a state visit unwanted; only in the Vatican and the Arab states was he a welcome visitor.

However, more important, Austria admitted for the first time its Mitschuld, co-guilt, for what had happened during the Holocaust. In his speech at the parliament in June 1991, Federal Chancellor Franz Vranitzky qualified the official 'first victim' thesis, acknowledged the co-responsibility of the Austrian population for the suffering they inflicted on other individuals and peoples, and apologized to the survivors and the descendants of the victims. In June 1993, Vranitzky, who more than compensated for Waldheim's inability to represent Austria abroad, became the first Austrian chancellor to visit Israel. In a speech at the Hebrew University in Jerusalem, he repeatedly acknowledged the role of Austrians in the Nazi machinery and spoke about the responsibility of each and every Austrian to remember and to seek justice.

In 1995, Austria created the National Fund of the Republic of Austria for Victims of National Socialism, which makes direct payments to Austrian victims of Nazism and supports research and remembrance projects concerning the Holocaust. And in 1998, sixty years after the Anschluss, the Austrian government created an official commission of historians to research the issue of Jewish property confiscated during WWII. "New legislation passed by the Austrian parliament on stolen art objects still in Austrian museums and collections places Austria ahead of most other countries on this issue"[47].

As a result of this radical turnabout in the attitudes and public stance of the Austrian government and populace, the Jews began to anticipate social integration despite or because of their being Jews, and to foresee a better future for themselves in the country. Even many of the former émigrés and communists, who hid their Judaism and facts about their life during the Holocaust, or even left the IKG soon after the war, declared themselves publicly as belonging to the Jewish community and many of them and their descendants joined the IKG[48]. Furthermore, the Jews were now eager

47 The Roots of Haiderism, http://www.aijac.org.au/review/2000/253/essay253.html, 9.7.2007.

48 Interview with Eleonore Lappin, historian, associated with the Institut für Geschichte der Juden in Österreich (Institute for the History of Jews in Austria) and Vice-President of Or Chadasch, July 2007.

to present their culture and Judaism itself to the non-Jewish population, and were ready to give public expression to their Jewish identity and to live their Jewish life more openly. In addition, the IKG gained a good standing within Austrian public opinion, as was manifest at the festivities for the 150-year jubilee of the IKG in 1999, in which the entire 'official Austria' – the governing elite – and people from all spheres of Austrian social life were present.

Had those festivities taken place "a year later, only the 'other Austria' would have been there, but not the governing one, since in 2000, Haider's Freedom Party and the People's Party joined to form a coalition government"[49]. IKG president Muzicant, European and American Jewish representatives now positioned themselves against the new government. The speeches of Muzicant and other Jewish and non-Jewish Austrian and European public figures at the demonstration against the coalition government under the title "Nein zur Koalition mit dem Rassismus" (No to the coalition with Racism) at the Heldenplatz in Vienna in January 2000 had their effects on the Viennese Jews, and dampened the good mood of the 1990s. Furthermore, Muzicant was now portrayed by the rulers as an enemy of the state since he opposed the Austrian government's position on restitution negotiations, which, as in the past, was to seek to drag the issue out and reach agreements on class-action suits in the United States at the expense of Austrian Jewry. This the IKG could not accept.

Jews again began to suffer from anti-Semitic activities, such as 'Jews out' graffiti, desecration of Jewish tombstones, and verbal and physical attacks (see the section "Rechte Ecke" [right corner] in each publication of Die Gemeinde). This anti-Semitic eruption was triggered by the racist and SS (Schutzstaffel, a major Nazi military organization) nostalgic statements of Haider and the FPÖ, which gave sections of the Austrian population the legitimacy to reveal their deep anti-Semitic roots. Jews again began to feel they might have to pack their suitcases; some even bought apartments in Israel. As a consequence the Jews felt separated, if not excluded from Austrian society and an urge to meet in Jewish circles, leading to increased activities at the community center[50].

This tense situation relaxed after the elections in 2006 which ended the ÖVP-FPÖ (since 2005 its offspring BZÖ) coalition government. This led to some improvement in the relationship between the IKG and the government, but it did not bring about a return to the situation of the 1990s. Public expression of anti-Semitism declined with Haider's removal from

49 Interview with Doron Rabinovici, politically engaged Jewish writer, July 2007.

50 Interview with Rabbi Josef Pardes, Rabbi of Mizrachi in Vienna, August 2005.

federal power. Restitution negotiations continued in a quarrelsome manner, but concluded successfully.

Talk of emigration died down. Moreover, the IKG leadership, with the financial support of the Austrian government, engaged in constructing a large compound which includes the communal school, the new elderly home of the IKG and the Hakoah sports and leisure center. The latter was inaugurated by Austrian governmental and IKG leaders in March 2008 as part of the high-profile public ceremonies commemorating the seventieth recurrence of the Anschluss. On the eve of the parliament's commemoration session the IKG, the federal and Viennese governments reached an agreement on the location and financing of the Vienna Wiesenthal Institute for Holocaust Studies hosting Simon Wiesenthal's archives.

The IKG leadership

The significant transformations that Viennese Jewry underwent since 1945 are clearly reflected in the changes in the membership, objectives and patterns of operation of the IKG's leadership group over the years.

The politics of the IKG towards Austrian authorities in the immediate post-war years reflected low Jewish identity and self-confidence. Until the late 1970s the IKG, led first by communists and then by Social Democrats, kept a low profile in order not to arouse anti-Semitism, and complied fully with the wishes of the federal and regional governments. They sold or leased communal real estate for almost nothing, and even gave away properties of religious importance, such as the remains of destroyed synagogues and cemeteries[51]. They adopted a non-confrontational stance in an effort to ensure tolerance for the Jews in Austria and gain state support. For the first four decades representatives of the Jewish community absented themselves from Vienna's public spheres. The IKG focused solely on internal religious administration and made itself 'invisible' publicly.

This changed after the mid-1980s when the IKG leadership began to assert their Jewish identity in public, as evidenced by their determined battle in the 1990s for restitutions, and currently for the Eruv[52] project. Initially the restitution negotiations were conducted quietly by the old IKG leadership in order not to arouse anti-Semitism. The new leadership, however, believes that it is its duty to fight publicly for the rights of the robbed victims, and is of the opinion that openness and a self-confident public stance

51 Interview with Willy Weisz, 2004
52 An Eruv is a symbolic fencing of parts of a city which allows observant Jews to carry (e.g. babies in a pram) on Shabbat within its limits.

will enhance the gentile public's respect for and acceptance of Jews. It is not surprising therefore that in order to receive the needed approval for establishing an Eruv, the IKG embarked on a campaign to explain the need for it to various Austrian authorities and the public[53], an action unthinkable two decades earlier.

The leadership and the Jewish population have also sought to make Jewish culture an integral part of Vienna's cultural landscape. The many public Jewish events, such as the yearly Jewish street festival and the Chazzanut (Jewish liturgical chanting) concerts have become cultural highlights for Jews and gentiles alike, and the Chanukah candle lighting next to St. Stephan Cathedral in the very heart of Vienna, as well as the opening of the Jüdisches Institut für Erwachsenenbildung (Jewish Institute for Adult Education) in 1989 that caters mainly to non-Jewish students, are all evidence of this strengthened self-confidence and new public self-understanding.

The IKG politics around the Waldheim affair in 1986 reveal the differences between the different post-war generations. Before the Austrian presidential elections, IKG president Ivan Hacker preferred to "follow a strategy of non-partisanship in the hope that a low profile would aid the country's progressive forces"[54]. The IKG did their best to avoid anything that could be understood as an electoral endorsement, and issued a general and mild declaration that appealed to the candidates' campaigns not to let themselves be tempted to stir up destructive emotions[55]. Hacker believed that the fight against anti-Semitism and neo-Nazism had to be coordinated with and assisted by the Austrian government – "not the IKG and not the Austrian Jews have to take a stand against anti-Semitism, but the non-Jews"[56] – and that the IKG was not a political forum. As a reaction to this non-confrontational policy, the IKG faction Junge Generation (JG) established by members of the post-war generation introduced a no-confidence motion against Hacker in 1987. The generation of Jews born after the Holocaust was unwilling to continue with the strategy of appeasement and sought to articulate a clear Jewish position independent of the expectations of the country's political leaders. The young generation refused to accept the victim role, opposed suffering in silence and head-in-the-sand

53 All of Austria's broadcast channels and printed media dealt with the Eruv project e.g. 'Eruv' soll Innenstadt symbolisch umzäunen, in: orf.at (website of the Austrian broadcasting corporation ORF), Wien 14.12.2007; Thomas Egerer, Wien erhält symbolische Stadtmauer, in: Die Presse, Wien 24.11.2007; Orthodoxe Juden wollen City 'umzäunen', in: Kurier, Wien 14.12.2007.

54 Matti Bunzl, Political Inscription, Artist Reflection: A Recontextualization of Contemporary Viennese-Jewish Literature, in: The German Quaterly 73/2, Durham 2000, 163-170, here: 166

55 Die Gemeinde, Wien 9.5.1986.

56 Hacker in an interview in the Jüdische Rundschau, Zürich 10.7.1986.

policies and was determined to stand up for the rights of the Jews, even if this meant criticizing Austrian politicians and politics. They advocated a publicly outspoken Jewish community with "more Jewishness and more Jewish self-confidence"[57]. After the elections of 1998 Ariel Muzicant became the first IKG president born after WWII.

The controversies between Muzicant and Haider provide a good illustration of the changes in IKG leadership style. Ariel Muzicant personifies the self-confidence of the post-war generation. He openly criticizes Austrian politicians and politics and makes frequent and outspoken media appearances. Thus he did not remain silent in the face of Jörg Haider's declarations that the Third Reich had a "reasonable employment policy" (1991), that the members of the Waffen-SS were "respectable persons with character" (1995), and his reference to the concentration camps as "detention camps" (1995). At a press conference in March 1999 before the election for the prime minister of the state of Carinthia, in which Haider was a candidate, Muzicant declared, "I do not agree to this, I am not going to keep my mouth shut". He recalled the situation in 1938 and asserted that democracy also includes the right to self-protection[58]. In contrast to Hacker during the Waldheim affair, Muzicant thus sought openly to influence national elections. He also campaigned openly against Haider in the 2001 Viennese municipal council elections. In an IKG publication, Muzicant writes that Haider's politics of racism and anti-Semitism discredits Austria and that "only the voters can put an end to this spook"[59]. Muzicant confronted Haider in the media and the courts, and sued him for various statements he made during the run-up to the Vienna elections, such as that he could not understand how anyone called Ariel – also the brand name of a well-known washing powder – could have so much "dirt on his stick" – equivalent to the English 'to have a skeleton in the closet'.

Also the communal objectives of the IKG changed with the self-perception of its leadership. Until the 1970s the IKG leadership's main concern was the physical survival of the Jews and their relation to the ruling politicians – who did not have any interest in a strong Jewish community. Therefore, the IKG established only the basic infrastructure needed for a religious association, such as synagogues, religious education, youth organizations and an elderly home, to maintain the Jewish community physically and spiritually. Before the IKG elections in 1972, the Zionist bloc published a list of what was lacking, which included a Jewish school, a kindergarten,

57 Ariel Muzicant, Editorial, in: Atid, Wien Januar 2007/Schwat 5767, 1-2, here: 1

58 Demokratie heißt auch, dass man sich wehrt, in: Die Gemeinde, Wien 1999, http://www.hagalil.com/austria/gemeinde/artikel/99/muzicant.

59 Christian Eder, Muzicant: Haider läuft Amok, in: Der Standard, Wien 22.03.2001.

cultural programs, a real understanding of the needs of the youth, and the upkeep of Jewish memorials[60].

With their entry into IKG politics in the late 1970s, the post-war generation was committed to altering the Viennese community's self-perception as a Liquidationsgemeinde. They focused particularly on building in Vienna a sound Jewish infrastructure beginning with the establishment of Jewish educational institutions. Their proposal that the IKG set up such a school – private ultra-Orthodox schools existed already since 1946 – became a major point of disagreement between the old and the young leadership generation[61]. This generation, which had grown up in Vienna and chose freely to live there, and whose parents had already succeeded in ensuring their physical and economic survival, saw the establishment of a Jewish school as "an axiom for Jewish thinking"[62], critical for Jewish-identity formation and for securing future Jewish life in Vienna. In many cases, the young adult Jews whose Jewish identity was formed and whose leadership skills were honed in Jewish youth and student organizations in the 1960s and 1970s were those who now pushed for and established a kindergarten (1973), a Jewish school (1980) and a Jewish professional development center, the JBBZ (1998) under the auspices of the IKG.

The 1981 elections marked the entry into IKG leadership for the first time of members of the post-war generation. They stood for a more Jewishly self-confident policy, in which more critical involvement in Austrian politics, as well as physical self-defense and the defense of Jewish values and interests, and an improvement of Jewish education received high priority. The IKG and Jewish organizations have been very involved in stimulating the formation of a strong Jewish identity through the study of Judaism, associating with other Jews, creating an ongoing and well-rooted local religious and cultural leadership, and promoting communal co-operation and institutional consolidation.

'We, the Jews, are here and will stay here' – the Establishment of an Austrian-Jewish identity

In the immediate post-war years, the Jews saw no future for Jewish life in Austria and certainly did not feel part of an Austrian society that itself was in search of its national identity[63]. The Jewish survivor generation in

60 Adunka, Die Vierte Gemeinde, 348

61 Interview with Avshalom Hodik, 2007

62 Interview with Avshalom Hodik, 2007

63 During the time of the first Austrian Republic (1918-1938), many Austrians identified more with a "German Nation" then with Austria, thus leading even Socialist Demo-

Vienna did not regard Austria as its homeland; on the contrary, many survivors hated Austria but stayed in the country for various personal reasons. Often they felt guilty for having stayed and passed on these feelings to the next generation. Their sense of guilt was heightened by the universal Jewish condemnation of Jews who chose to live in the land of the murderers. A good indication of the fact that they did not see their future in Vienna, and were not ready to consciously settle there was their unwillingness to donate funds for the reconstruction of Jewish infrastructure in Vienna, while contributing to the Jewish homeland in the State of Israel.

The alienation from the Austrian society began to gradually phase out in the late 1970s. The construction and inauguration of the Gemeindezentrum (communal center next to the main synagogue) in 1980 reflected a growing feeling that 'we, the Jews, are here and will stay here'. An intra-Jewish discourse on the Austrian identity of the Jews began and gathered momentum following the Waldheim affair, promoted on the one hand by the active dealing of the Austrian population with its own history and the place of the Jews in it, and on the other hand by the conscious desire of many members of the post-war Jewish generation to live in Vienna and build their future in the city as Viennese.

These discussions on the question of Austrian identity were conducted primarily as an intra-Jewish affair in order to avoid being stamped 'non-Austrian' by the Austrian population. In general, Jews have difficulties defining the Austrian component of their identity: most Jews feel loyal Austrian citizens, yet in intra-Jewish discourse still refer to the gentile population as 'Austrian'. Depending on the context of the discussion, they define themselves as Jews in Austria, as Jews with Austrian citizenship, as Austrian Jews, meaning that they are part of Austrian Jewry, or feel Austrian but not patriotic. It should be noted that since the Austrian identity is itself a development of the Second Republic, many gentiles also do not feel patriotic; a 1993 survey found that only 61 percent of Austrian citizens indicated that they were proud Austrians[64]. Moreover, the Viennese Jews' identity is Viennese rather than Austrian, echoing the rather weak commonality between persons living in the different provinces, reflected in the federal nature of Austria's constitution. Furthermore, for many local and international Jews, Vienna which stands for culture and beauty has a more positive connotation than Austria which is commonly associated

cratic politicians, like Karl Renner, to welcome the *Anschluss.* This changed gradually as a consequence of the memories of the Nazi terror regime with the creation of the Second Republic in 1945.

64 Ernst Bruckmüller, Österreich-bewußtsein im Wandel: Identität und Selbstverständnis in den 90er Jahren, Wien 1994, 26.

with the Holocaust, Waldheim or Haider. A 'Viennese Jew' therefore has higher status than an 'Austrian Jew'. Thus, in Austria they are Viennese, and abroad they emphasize the Viennese and Viennese-Jewish elements of their identity.

Many Jews see Israel as their spiritual homeland in parallel to their connection to Vienna as their physical place of abode. Some gentile circles have used this argument to cast doubt upon the Jews' loyalty to Austria. The emotional attachment to more than one country is unknown to most of the Austrian gentiles but is becoming a general phenomenon in Europe due to the increased proportion of migrants and the growing importance of a new European identity, and of new transnational group identities.

Most of the Jewish immigrants from the former Soviet Union lived in Israel before moving to Vienna. They did not experience the trauma of the Holocaust and the post-war years in Vienna, and thus have a more open attitude towards Austrian identity than the Jews of Viennese and Central European origin. They feel thankful to the state for having accepted them and given them the opportunity to build new lives[65]. They see Austria alongside Israel as their homeland – the Soviet Union is only part of their memories[66]. The Austrian identity is thus more easily adopted by the Jews from the former Soviet Union than it was for the Holocaust survivors and partly their descendants, and is added to their Bukhara or Georgian, and Israeli identities. In contrast to the Jews arriving after WWII and in migration waves thereafter, these immigrants came to Vienna intending to settle and build their future in the country. By the end of the 1990s, they had enriched Vienna's Jewish infrastructure by establishing the Sephardic center with a Bukhara and a Georgian synagogue, several cultural and religious institutions, and an array of Sephardi-owned kosher shops, butchers and restaurants (see the yearly service booklets of the IKG). These activities indicate that these immigrants feel settled and envision their future in the country.

The immediate post-war generation's main contribution to the process of Jewish-identity formation was institutional – building up a Jewish infrastructure – and psychological – a newly found personal and group self-confidence. The second post-war generation's distinctive contribution to the process comes via the renewal of interest in Judaism as a religion and a new look at Jewish identity, and via the further strengthening of Jewish self-confidence in Vienna. Having grown up in a secure economic environment and in a Jewish community with the necessary infrastructure,

65 Interview with Benni Gilkarov, responsible for youth matters in the IKG, July 2007.

66 Interview with Roman Ascherov, Secretary General of the Association of Bukhara Jews, July 2007.

the members of the second post-war generation continue to examine their Jewish identity in depth and to promote study and discussion of Judaism among the youth, as evidenced by the increase in the number of sites of teaching and a manifest tendency towards greater personal religiosity. In addition to the Talmud-Torah school and other ultra-Orthodox educational institutions, lessons are offered daily for ultra-Orthodox as well as for Modern Orthodox to secular youth and adults by rabbis and teachers from various Orthodox groups which in general are well attended[67].

This generation also displays its Jewishness more openly than their parents. They are not afraid to wear kippot (skullcaps) in the street, in contrast with their parents who generally wear caps or hats in public. Similarly, the previous generation's habit of using the expression 'mishelanu' (one of us) to refer to Jews in public, so as not to attract the attention of non-Jews, has largely given way to the self-conscious public use of the word 'Jew'. This shows that the Viennese Jews feel increasingly secure in the country, comfortable with Viennese society and more accepted as Jews.

This feeling of well-being in their place of residence and the strengthening of the Jewish identity that is openly displayed paved the way for an active participation as Jews in the Austrian economy, politics, science and culture. This interest in securing the well-being of the greater Austrian society of which they feel an integral, but not assimilated, part is the result of the development of what can be termed Austrian-Jewish[68] identity. The latter is based on both the feeling of being part of the World Jewry and of sharing the interests of the other groups of the Austrian society.

This Austrian-Jewish identity, however, does not include Austrian patriotism. The Jews insist that they are loyal Austrian citizens and that they increasingly feel connected to Austria as a democratic state, but they do not feel connected to the Austrian land or the Austrian nation. "It is unlikely that an IKG politician would declare himself as patriot. The Jews perceive themselves Austrian citizens but do not as patriots" (Lappin, 2007). "A patriotic statement as was recently expressed by the President of the Zentralrat of Jews in Germany Charlotte Knobloch is unimaginable in Austria" (Hodik, 2007). Before 1938 the well-assimilated or at least well-acculturated Austrian-born Jews (not the Ostjuden) were deeply devoted Austrian patriots. This patriotism, which is also expressed in their definition as 'Austrians of Jewish faith' was extinguished with the Holocaust, and was not

67 Interview with Sonja Feiger, 2007

68 'Austrian-Jewish' refers to a distinctive identity pattern in which both Austrian and Jewish components are present, as opposed to 'Austrian Jewish' identity which applies to the Jewish identity of Austrian Jews that may or may not have a Austrian component.

revived thereafter. The Austrian-born survivors could not revive their love for Austria since they had been disappointed by their country and felt betrayed by it. They had learned that patriotism and assimilation did not make them 'Austrians' and that they had remained 'Jews' in the eyes of their fellow citizens, who had not stood up to protect them. The DPs and immigrants from the East and their descendants as well as the Austrian-born descendants did not establish an Austrian identity because they felt that "Austria was the country of the perpetrators and had for a long time not dealt with its historic responsibility" (Fastenbauer, 2007). "Austria improved significantly in the last fifteen years, but there is still a long way to go. Austria still perceives itself as victim and does not want to acknowledge its moral and historic guilt. This will still take decades" (Muzicant, 2005). Furthermore, the Austrian populace continued perceiving the Jews as a collective entity, 'the Jews', and thus distinct from themselves, 'the Austrians'. These Austrian attitudes complicated the formation of an Austrian identity that goes beyond the loyalty to the democratic state as well as the development of trust in the political leadership and society. The Viennese Jews are permanently looking out for anti-Semitic tendencies and activities in Austria. These tendencies are constantly monitored by the IKG and other organizations and are published monthly in the Gemeinde under the title Aus der Rechten Ecke (from the right corner).

The Jews in Vienna have surely unpacked their suitcases, but the empty suitcases are still stored at hand for the case of emergency. They are positive that if Austria should once again cease to be a democratic country, they will immediately pack their suitcases to leave the country on time. But for the time being they feel at home in the Viennese Jewish community and in the democratic Austria, and are actively participating in developing the Jewish and the general life in Austria

Conclusion

The development of the Jewish community in Austria as exemplified by the Viennese community shows how the development of a group's self-confidence produces a group identity that is strongly influenced by its already existing group particularities, rooted in its history and traditions, as well as the attitudes of the surrounding society towards the group.

Despite the predictions in 1945 that the Viennese Jewish community would soon disappear, it has developed a new self-confidence and strong group identity that are at the base of the birth of a new – not the rebirth of the pre-1938 – Jewry. In the 1970s and 1980s, the generation born after the Shoah, unlike its predecessor, began to view positively the possibility of a Jewish future in Vienna. The legacy of the Shoah, the existence and strength – as exemplified by the victory in the Six-Day War of 1967 – of the State of Israel, as well as changing national politics and friendlier attitudes towards the Jews strengthened their search for identity and their decision to stay and live an active life in Vienna, as Jews and as Austrian citizens. They also have begun to look beyond the national borders to enhance trans-European-Jewish contacts and cooperation.

Like the Jews, groups can, at the same time, belong to transnational greater entities with strong ties, as well as feel attached to the well-being of the society, region and nation in which they integrate themselves – without attempting assimilation. This is the situation countries of the European Union face more and more often, when groups reach out to their kin in other countries to set agendas on the transnational level. The better the reception of a group – which is ready to integrate itself into the basic European values like human rights, freedom of belief and expression, and democracy – is in its country of residence, the more it will not only see its group interests, but also take care of the national interests when lobbying at the European level.

Eva R Hudecova
(University of Minnesota)

The Witness Who May Not Have Been There: Eastern European Authors Looking Westward

"There is no content, no formal category of the literary work that does not, however transformed and however unawarely, derive from the empirical reality from which it has escaped"

-Theodor Adorno

"Poetry is one of the places where a rewriting of subjectivity can happen"

-Harriet Davidson

"My corner of Europe, owing to the extraordinary and lethal events that have been occurring there, comparable only to violent earthquakes, affords a peculiar perspective. As a result, all of us who come from those parts appraise poetry slightly differently from the majority of my audience, for we tend to view it as witness and participant in one of mankind's major transformations"

-Czeslaw Milosz

Interactions between the former Eastern Block and the West as reflected in the literature of this region highlight its status as a point of contact between the still largely non-Western world, and a world which is quickly being westernized. Through an analysis of the writings of the Slovak poet Milan Richter whom I have translated into English, the work of the Polish author Dorota Maslowska, the Croatian writer Slavenka Drakulic, as well as the German writer Thomas Brussig, my dissertation reframes testimonial literature such as poems, memoirs, or autobiographies, thus opening a channel of communication between the eastern writer and western reader. I call this reframing of testimonial literature removed witnessing, since it is a witnessing very different from the narrow legal definition of testimony. In removed witnessing, the bodily presence of the witness is possible but not absolutely required. My dissertation is a study of the Central and Eastern European witness as a key figure facilitating cultural testimony to the events leading up to and immediately following the revolutionary year 1989.

In the acts of removed witnessing that I examine and theorize in my dissertation, eastern writers typically also anticipate the expectations of western readers. Writers such as Drakulic consider the perception of Eastern Europe in the west and attempt to transform it. If the dialogue between the authors and their implied Western readers is successful, the readers of narratives written by removed witnesses will form a culturally literate and passionate collective of their own. In addition to looking westward, the author as witness is also looking towards a future in which the West will lose the fear of its eastern other and gain an interest in understanding this other, thus also itself.

My dissertation develops the thesis that the Eastern European witness is formed through faithfulness to the event which may have been witnessed from afar. This is particularly the case in poems such as Milan Richter's "The Dream of the Man Who Dived," where the narrator – and in this case also the author – is a witness to Alexander Dubcek's involvement in the events of the Prague Spring by witnessing Dubcek's presence at an unrelated event only days before August 21st, 1968.

The following analysis of the aforementioned poem by Milan Richter is an excerpt from Chapter Two of my dissertation, entitled "The Eastern European Poet as Witness:"

In the poem "The Dream of the Man Who Dived," the Slovak poet Milan Richter discusses his encounter with the leader of Prague Spring, Alexander Dubcek. The location of this encounter is quite informal: a spa, more specifically, a pool with a diving board. The historical moment of this encounter is more telling, however: it is the summer of 1968, an ominous prelude of sorts to the Warsaw Pact invasion. Dubcek is the only one brave enough to dive off the high diving-board and is admired by his onlookers until a crisis occurs, in which the circumstances would require the random onlookers to act. (Although the most important part for my purposes here is the third stanza, I am including the poem here in its entirety. The caption under an enclosed photo reads: The man who dived in summer 1968: / Alexander Dubcek / The place: Spa Santovka, Western Slovakia):

The Dream of the Man Who Dived

One of the daughters had suddenly aged, she was twenty
like me (I'd suddenly grown younger by those years),
she's sitting with me on the edge of the pool,
we dangle our legs...

Who is that gentleman with the long nose,
why are they photographing him?
And why is he the only one to dive?

The man dived all the way to us,
the water splashed us, just as if it were
live water, all around us came to life,
at all the little tables, on the towels
there is discussion, and I see some friends
but they are very young,
my enemies, too, have become younger
and in their applause the diver
could have bathed...

For God's sake, Dad, do help him!
I can hear my daughter. And I see the diver
under the water, trying to swim up,
but the rippling surface has now turned
into smooth glass, he beats his fists against it,
he screams but no one hears him, no one helps him,
the people round us have all disappeared
or else have suddenly aged
and now pretend they've not seen anything,
the ones who kicked their feet in the pool
are fettered to the glass
I too, my daughter with me, have grown
into the surface,
the diver, that long-nosed gentleman,
is beating at the glass, ever more weakly,
ever more weakly,
and all the time he's looking straight at us,
he's motionless, but all the time
he's looking at us...
as we are growing old now in the falling dusk,
my daughter's getting younger, smaller, vanishing...

And for a long, long time there's nothing,
except grey twilight and grey glass,
and trapped in it hundreds of heads
and pairs of legs...

And the springboard is still trembling.

November 1988

The crisis here is not only the fact that Dubcek is drowning. It is as significant that the onlookers find themselves unable to act, unable to transform their looking into doing. Having failed at this just as all the other onlookers did, the narrator makes a point of gaining back some agency from the terrifying event he and his daughter have just witnessed by retelling it.

It is clear that it is not the water which entraps Dubcek. Rather, it is the onlookers' unwillingness to see, which hurts Dubcek. It is just as important that this unwillingness does not just capture Dubcek: quite poignantly, it entraps the onlookers themselves, draining them of agency. Dubcek's inability to move, to act, is directly related to the onlooker's unwillingness to help. Richter's bold line "And all the time he's looking straight at us" is an unabashed, urgent call to witness, a call emphasizing the moral responsibility of witnessing: Dubcek, this fearless leader, is frozen and "we" will remain thus as well unless we see and acknowledge the responsibilities that are implicated in active seeing. Dubcek was, as Richter points out, in a state of anticipatory commitment to a variety of possible events. He was living dangerously, so to speak, and was calling on the onlookers to participate in freeing him almost as a practice run (exploration of potential) of the same onlookers were a revolutionary event to occur.

This poem also incorporates one of the most significant contradictions a witness has to deal with: there is always an irreconcilable juxtaposition of the everyday life (no matter how "exotic" by outsider standards) to the urgency and monumentality of the moment of change, transition or trauma encountered by the witness. There is a diametrical opposition between the nondescript flow of the witness' (literally) uneventful life and the events which radically interrupt this mundane state. Witnessing, however, becomes impossible without an indivisible merging of these opposites, as can be seen in the poem at hand.

In this poem, as well as in other countless pieces of Eastern European literature of the late twentieth and early twenty-first century, it becomes clear that the actual bodily presence at a particular event is not necessary in order for witnessing to occur. In fact, the poem, written in 1988, is a sort of post-script to the traumatic events of the Warsaw Pact invasion, while the moment of the poem's narrative (Summer 1968) is an anticipation of the same event. What is narrated thus is a memory, but not a detached or closed one: this is a memory with a purpose, and in that sense, it is still unfinished.

To complicate matters further, the moment of the author's willing confrontation with these sets of events and witnessings (November 1988) can also be viewed as an anticipatory moment to the events of 1989. The author is taking it upon himself to work through a set of promising potentialities as well as failings, in a year that was certainly a prelude to the most important changes in Eastern European societies since 1968. Following this line of reasoning, a call to responsibility and action in fidelity to the events of 1968 can also be seen as a rehearsal for the same kinds of challenges the society would have to face only a few months after the poem at hand was published. Since the moment of writing is 1988, and thus after Dubcek's removal from office and after the harsh period of normalization in the 1970s, Richter's intervention is more of a call to witness than a call to action on behalf of 1968. It could, however, be read as a call to action and witness on behalf of some of the gradually developing changes happening a year before the Velvet Revolution. As Harriet Davidson argues in her essay "Poetry, Witness, Feminism," "the witness, while perhaps speaking of the past, is most concerned with the future" (164).

With the complicated four-fold temporality of this poem (narrator's present, Dubcek's impending future, author's present, the impending future of Eastern Europe), the event proper remains a "silent" subtext. The author manages to speak about it by speaking around it, more poignantly than he would if he provided a detailed narrative of tanks rolling and soldiers marching down the historical center of Bratislava while he stood on the sidewalk, observing. What occurs in the poem then is both a more direct (and better documented) witnessing of Dubcek's day at the pool in the summer of 1968, as well as a more removed, anticipatory witnessing of the failure of witnessing (the onlookers not budging when Dubcek remains trapped in the pool, drowning). Via the pool, more specifically, via the frozen water in the pool which reflects the passive attitude of the onlookers, all – including the narrator – have been transformed into one, powerless, stagnant entity. Significantly, the fact that the frozen water is referred to several times as "glass" is evocative of a window, or a screen, where the possibility to watch is granted, but the momentum to act is taken away. The onlookers' refusal to act when they had the chance is now being punished – they have squandered their potential at becoming a true removed witness, which is a role that the narrator consciously took upon himself.

Any narrators' immediate presence at an actual event becomes unimportant and irrelevant, while the narrators' moral responsibility to recount, express and witness from within her/his specific cultural, historical, and political moment about and around these actual events becomes all the more important. It is here that a narrator of an event, an often uninvolved, ambiguous witness becomes a passionate removed witness: removed only in bodily presence – not in the ability to recount an event from a culturally literate position[1]. Shoshana Felman in her book Testimony: Crises of Witnessing in Literature, Psychoanalysis and History introduces so called "second-degree witnesses," a concept which has some aspects in common with my figure of the removed witness:

> Like professional interpreters, although in very different ways, the filmmaker in the film and the historian on the screen are in turn catalysts – or agents – of the process of reception, agents whose reflective witnessing and whose testimonial stances aid our own reception and assist us both in the effort toward comprehension and in the unending struggle with the foreignness of signs, in the processing not merely (as does the professional interpreter) the literal meaning of the testimonies, but also, (some perspectives on) their philosophical and historical significance (213).

Felman's constellation of the "second-degree witness" alongside the translator and the interpreter is telling: this witness (like my removed witness) becomes a more sophisticated interpreter, one who facilitates the understanding of the "foreignness of signs" and "philosophical and historical significance." However, the removed witness is not only limited to be a "witness of a witness" or a "witness of ... testimonies."

A chain leading back to the original event is not necessary. While some may argue that this makes the removed witness less trustworthy or relevant because of the lack of connection to the original event, I argue that it is this very lack of connection which can potentially liberate the removed witness' point of view (provide a kind of birds'-eye view) as well as open up her/his potential to contextualize and interpret the original event. (According to a Slovak proverb, it is darkest right underneath the lamp). Based on this interpretation, the removed witness can have a lot in common with a medium: s/he is someone who channels messages and experiences, albeit in a less supernatural and more pragmatic manner. (After all, this removed witness is not furthering a "message" revealed or imposed in the manner of a deus ex machina; s/he is relaying his/her actively gathered and lived knowledges and experiences). As James E. Young argues in his essay "Between History and Memory: The Voice of the Eyewitness" when analyzing the Holocaust narrative of Saul Friedlander,

1 Rather than the more traditionally implied connections with class or a certain level of education, I am using the phrase "cultural literacy" throughout this piece to mean 'knowledge acquired' by decades of *lived experience* involving a fluency in the particular country's language, investment – whether willingly or by force – in that particular country's legal system, and the continuous exposure to the media. The issue here is not as much erudition as it is a cross between knowledge, experience and passion.

As a hidden child survivor whose parents were murdered at Auschwitz, Friedlander could have distinguished between those historians whose lives were directly affected by events and those shaped only indirectly by events. But he does not. Indeed, he seems also to be speaking for a generation of historians born after the Holocaust, as well, whose lives have been shaped not by the history of this time, but by the memory if others, as passed down to them (276).

What Young touches on here is an insertion of a kind of oral quality into written narratives (whether they are historical, autobiographical, or otherwise). This oral quality represents precisely a greater concern with a "passing down" (and in my specific argument also a "passing across") of cultural literacy than cut-and-dry written narratives normally have.

Here my project clearly branches off from Holocaust studies and towards the problem of the consciousness-forming events in Eastern Europe spanning from the late twentieth century until today (in my case mostly the events leading up to, happening in, and resulting from the crucial year 1989). This region was (and is) faced with a multitude of perhaps at times less disastrous, but vastly more varied, and nonetheless (occasionally) traumatizing series of events.

In order to situate and locate the removed witness of Eastern Europe vis-à-vis the vast amounts of literature produced under the rubric of Holocaust or trauma studies, one should ask the question: What makes the Eastern European removed witness specific? Whence the need to define her/him and speak about her/him? The answer which I outline both theoretically and with the examination and close reading of essential literary texts throughout my dissertation involves the way in which this witness has experienced crucial events and/or traumas in a fundamentally different manner from the way in which a typical Holocaust victim would have. This is the difference between the Holocausts' witness/victim narrating an account of an immensely traumatic event and its extensive consequences that nonetheless had a shorter duration, versus the Eastern European witness narrating a multitude of extremely varied accounts with varied degrees of trauma inflicted over decades and generations. In the Eastern European narratives, there is also a critical concern not only with the past, but also with the way in which these narratives can become crucial interventions on the way to a future, which is always imagined or alluded to as more than the past or the present. Thus, often times dystopic narratives also include crucial utopias.

The specification of the Eastern European witness' trauma is not an attempt to essentialize the types of trauma or narratives that this witness goes through (in fact, removed witnessing is possible and absolutely necessary in other geographical and historical spaces). Rather, it is an attempt to locate the specificity of this experience in the limit-space/outskirts of Holocaust and trauma studies. Since, as mentioned, the original traumatic event is much vaguer, multiple, and dispersed over time in Eastern Europe, its digestion warrants a different approach as well. Jacob D. Lindy and Robert Jay Lifton explain the near impossibility and simultaneous need to formulate the Soviet and post-Soviet era trauma as separate from other traumas of the century in their volume Beyond Invisible Walls: The Psychological Legacy of Soviet Trauma, a work which gives voice to local professionals (mostly psychologists or psychiatrists), and through them, also to their patients. When explaining the overwhelming central goal of their work, Lindy and Lifton introduce the idea that the twentieth century in Eastern Europe produced three "successive waves of violence and death" (15). They continue:

> For those caught in these waves, there were traumatic losses and radical discontinuities in their experience of themselves, their families, and their world. Soviet political repression is the...primary source of trauma and loss for the patients and their therapists. But political repression became so folded in with war, genocide, famine, natural and man-made disasters, and disease that precise distinctions are difficult. Survivors find that they cannot isolate an atmosphere of political repression from these additional catastrophic traumas which complicate them (15).

While the literal sorting out of Soviet-era traumas may not be possible or even desirable, it can be deduced from the above that in order to give voice to such traumas, one needs to have at least an inclination towards this task. It is less important here to place blame than it is to allow for alternate retellings of history and experience, ultimately and ideally resulting in at least partial cures of trauma.

Apart from the scientific dialogue-style accounts such as that of Lindy and Lifton's, a multitude of fictional autobiographies, slightly altered historical narratives (courting the event instead of nailing it down) are prevalent. These fluid styles are different from the more straightforward diary-style narratives much more common with Holocaust survivors. Yet another source of complication is the fact that while the crimes of the Nazi regime (excepting the events which occurred on German soil itself), were done by "others" (i.e. by entities stemming from outside a particular nation), more often than not, the crimes of the various socialist regimes were done by "us" to "ourselves."[2]

2 This may be a partial answer to the question regarding the reasons for the disinterest of the current Eastern European vis-à-vis his/her *most recent* history. It is more

Within Trauma Studies, the emergence of a serious approach to the events in Eastern Europe after and not related to the Holocaust has become an all but impossible challenge for several reasons. First, Trauma Studies have gradually become equated exclusively with Holocaust Studies. Secondly, although Trauma Studies do deal with Eastern Europe, this region gets treated almost exclusively as a crime scene. The actual Eastern Europe is effaced with an implied suggestion that all Eastern Europeans are guilty by association for stemming from a barbaric place. My goal is to complicate and add dimension to this reading, thus bringing Trauma Studies, Eastern European Area Studies and Literature into a closer and less tortured relationship.

Works Cited/Works Referenced

- Theodor Adorno, Commitment, in:.New Left Review I, London 1974, 87-88.
- Harriet Davidson, Poetry, Witness, Feminism, in: Ana Douglass and Thomas A. Vogler (Ed.), Witness and Memory. The Discourse of Trauma, New York 2003, 153-172.
- Shoshana Felman, Testimony: Crises of Witnessing in Literature, Psychoanalysis, and History, New York 1992.
- Jacob D. Lindy, Beyond Invisible Walls: The Psychological Legacy of Soviet Trauma, New York 2001.
- Tyrus Miller, The Burning Babe: Children, Film Narrative, and the Figures of Historical Witness, in: Anna Douglass and Thomas A. Vogler (Ed.), Witness and Memory: The Discourse of Trauma, New York 2003, 207-232.
- Czeslaw Milosz, The Witness of Poetry, Cambridge 1983.
- Milan Richter, Five Seasons of Life, Bratislava 1998.
- Thomas A. Vogler, Poetic Witness: Writing the Real, in: Anna Douglass and Thomas A. Vogler (Ed.), Witness and Memory: The Discourse of Trauma, New York 2003, 173-206.

---

comfortable to leave the direct or implied guilt of the self (or those close to oneself) unexamined.

• James E. Young, Between History and Memory: The Voice of the Eyewitness, in: Anna Douglass and Thomas A. Vogler (Ed.), Witness and Memory: The Discourse of Trauma, New York 2003, 275-284.

Nina Paulovičová
(University of Alberta)

"Her way among the higher things..." Scrutinizing female agency in the 19th century Slovak National Revivalism.

"Discovering women in history" is how we can describe the contemporary approach to gender studies among scholars in Slovakia. This approach is marked by efforts to extrapolate women as a new category from what they saw to be depersonalized frameworks of historical narrative. Although such efforts reinforced women's status as historical agents, they also posed some dangers: the women-centered treatment tended to sever women's subtle links to other historical agents and to their own milieu. Feminist theorists frequently resorted to a dichotomous "us" and "them" treatment that essentialized women as either "do-gooders" or victims of masculine oppression. The "us" and "them" dichotomy oftentimes failed to shed light on the ways gender operates.[1] It paralyzed the inner workings of the category of women, its viability within and connection to the larger social milieu. In the course of the "discovering" phase, the approach to the issues of gender has yielded a divide between the "powerless female" and "powerful male" or a "victim" and a "victimizer." The gendered victimization rhetoric permeates the post-communist milieu in multiple forms. For example, the female disobeying characters in the novels of Božena Slánčiková-Timravá led to the recognition of Timravá as an ideal symbolic "mother' of female victims of the nineteenth century patriarchal society. Božena Slánčikova Timravá's oversized motherly portrayal on the second page of the first issue of Aspekt in 1993 was to initiate a pantheon of Slovak "unwomanly women" who in one way or another revolted against the "sweet obeying female" construct disseminated by their contemporaries. The effort to highlight the victimization discourse is not a unique phenomenon of Slovak milieu. In April 2006 scholars from Poland, Hungary and Czech Republic met in Pardubice, Czech Republic to discuss representa-

1 The failures of the "us" and "them" dichotomy are pointed out in several works that deal with gender issues within the context of imperial history. Antoinette Burton, Burdens of History: British Feminists, Indian Women, and Imperial Culture, 1865-1915, Chapel Hill 1994; Catherine Hall, Civilizing Subjects: Colony and Metropol in the English Imagination, 1830-1867, Chicago 2002; Kathleen Wilson, (Ed.), A New Imperial History: Culture, Identity, and modernity in Britain and the Empire, 1660-1840, Cambridge/New York 2004; Antoinette Burton, Gender, Sexuality and Colonial Modernities, London 1999; Philippa Levine, (Ed.), Gender and Empire, Oxford 2004; John M. MacKenzie, Orientalism: History, Theory and the Arts, Manchester 1995.

tion of women in historiography. The title of the two day conference "So called history of women or European female from Middle Age to 20th century in the captivity of historiography" explicitly postulates the theme of victimization as a viable methodological tool in gender approach.[2] Such debates have spurred the questions about terminology. Some scholars insist on the wider usage of the term "gender history" as opposed to "history of women," which, in the view of some connotes either the idea of "history of women's oppression," or the history of feminist movement. [3]

The victimization rhetoric naturally poses the question of its origins. The fall of communism followed by the revival of ethnic nationalism in 1990s introduced "the slump in female representation in public sphere, the decanting of women out of the formal economy and their consequent loss of job security, together with a widespread adoption of pro-natalist policies."[4] With the restoration of the Catholic Church's influence after the fall of communism, patriarchal values in Slovak milieu proved to be even more resilient.[5] Secondly, victim-victimizer dichotomy is partly a result of the post-1989 confusion over the applied methodology in historiography: Marxist paradigm's heavy focus on economic and class organization of society, "exploiter and exploited" divide together with the staunch belief in historical "objective forces," have only slowly abated. Hesitance and reluctance, rather than excitement over the transition to new theoretical paradigms, describe the current state within Slovak gender studies as well. Ľubica Kobová's remark that the primary sources cannot simply speak for "themselves" without being tried through the prism of various methodological paradigms is poignant in this regard.[6] The juxtaposition of the "exploiter" with a nineteenth century middle class male – national awakener, and the "exploited" with a female – both, middle and working class, indicates the reluctance to step out from the convenience that the accepted/excluded discourse readily offers. Thirdly, the persistence of the victim-victimizer gendered dichotomy can be seen as a result of a general reluctance to draw a comparative framework with gender theme in "Western" historiography, which, in most part, has managed to abandon dichotomous categorization especially due to the application of the postmodern paradigm in analysis of gender. Gender scholarship in Slovakia has

2 Ľubica Kobová, Dejiny žien – takzvané, alebo jednoducho dejiny žien? in: ASPEKTin - feministický webzin, May 9, 2006, http://www.aspekt.sk/aspekt_in.php? 30.8.2008.

3 Irena Jenčová, Spoločenské postavenie žien v procese sociálnych zmien. Societal status of women in the process of social change, in: Slovak Ethnology (Slovensky Narodopis), 03/2005, www.ceol.com, 4.9. 2008.

4 Rick Wilford, Women, Ethnicity and Nationalism: The Politics of Transition. Surveying the ground, in: Rick Wilford, Robert L. Miller, (Eds.), Women, Ethnicity and Nationalism: The Politics of Transition, London/New York 1998, 7.

5 Ibid.

6 Kobová, Dejiny, http://www.aspekt.sk/aspekt_in.php? 30.8. 2008

been recently attentive to the calls such as Gabriela Dudeková's who challenged the self-centered approach and highlighted the benefits of situating Slovak feminist movement in a dialogue with other feminist movements within the Habsburg Empire.[7] The self-centered approach and distancing of Slovak gender scholars from productive comparative frameworks can be in part ascribed to a general "Eastern" repugnance to "Western" feminism. Gender historians in post-communist era draw a visible line between the "derogatory Western feminism" on the one hand, and the "positive," "humanitarian," and widely appraised concept of the emancipation concept on the other. Nadežda Lindovská puts it bluntly: "To be a feminist is bad. To be emancipated is good."[8] The post-communist identity of female is clearly mobilized against multiple constructed countertypes, of which Western feminism is but one representative. The last, but not least obstacle in our analysis of the workings of gender and nationalism in the nineteenth century Slovakia has its roots in the realm of collective memory. Collective memory represents the focal point in both, "nation's memory" reconstruction and the parallel process of Europeanization. According to the French sociologist Maurice Halbwachs, present concerns determine what of the past we remember and how we remember it. Due to its ability to simplify the past, collective memory is in many ways ahistorical, or even anti-historical.[9] In Halbwachs line of thought, by refusing to acknowledge the existence of the pastness, collective memory insists on continuing presence of past events and themes. As a result, the juxtaposition of the present with past helps to shape "eternal truth" and "eternal identity" for the members of the group.[10] I approach the gendered victimization discourse in Halbwachsian fashion, i.e. I look at the gendered victimization rhetoric as being a simple political tool that chisels the present concerns onto the surface of the past. I approach masculinity and femininity as being constructs specific to historical time and place. They are categories continuously being forged, contested reworked and reaffirmed in social institutions, social practices and a range of ideologies.[11] To avoid dichotomous narrative one might rely on the Foucauldian theorem of the multiplicity of power discourses.

7 Jenčová, Spoločenské postavenie žien, 334.

8 Nadežda Lindovská, 'Feminism' is an insult in Slovakia, in: Theatre Journal, 47/3, Oct. 1995, 381. More nuanced analysis of "Czech style feminism" see Marrianne A. Ferber, Phillis Hutton Raabe, Women in the Czech Republic: Feminism, Czech Style, in: International Journal of Politics, Culture & Society, Spring 2003, 16/3, 407; Vilma Iggers, Women of Prague. Ethnic Diveristy and Social Change from the Eighteenth Century to the Present, Providence/Oxford 1995, 8.

9 Peter Novick, The Holocaust in American Life, Boston 1999, 3.

10 See for example Eduard Krekovič, Elena Mannová, Eva Krekovičová (Eds.), Mýty naše Slovenské, Bratislava 2005; Zuzana Kiczková et al., Pamäť žien. O skúsenosti sebautvárania v biografických rozhovoroch, Bratislava 2006.

11 Leonore Davidoff and Catherine Hall, Family Fortunes. Men and Women of the English Middle Class, 1780 – 1850, Chicago 1987, 29.

Power does not function within the dual model, which is so widespread in political discourse precisely because of convenience that the dichotomy of accepted/excluded discourse or dominant/dominated discourse offers.[12] Foucault advises that it is important to conceive discourses as a multiplicity of various elements that can enter the game with various strategies. My aim is to look at female agency in the period of the nineteenth century national revivalism as being defined by multiple discourses: respectability, Christian principles, emancipation and education of women, pragmatism and economy.

In particular, my aim is to grapple with the female stereotype as constructed by the nineteenth century audience against the political needs of Slovak National Revivalism. The deliberate restructuring of the idealized apotheosized female into a new type of femme national yields some interesting insights into our understanding of the contemporary discourse surrounding the issues of female agency, the theme which stood out as the most compelling area of study.[13] The careful analysis of the general understanding of the male and female agency within the targeted milieu would eventually challenge the simplified dominant/dominated or accepted/excluded dichotomy as the core of the gendered victimization discourse. This essay articulates the idea that "passive female" as envisaged by nineteenth century nationalists does not necessarily connote negative meaning and henceforth does not necessarily situate female in the role of victims. How is female agency imagined within the context of what Benedict Anderson defined as "imagined community"?[14] What are the signifiers of "active" and "passive" female as understood by Slovak men involved in the nationalist project? How crucial is female agency to Slovak national revival in the course of the nineteenth century? These are the general questions that frame this research.

12 Michel Foucault, The History of Sexuality. An Introduction. New York/Toronto 1990, 100.

13 Some recent interesting works on female agency vis-à-vis nationalism: Ida Blom, Karen Hageman, Catherine Hall, Gendered Nations. Nationalisms and Gender Order in the Long Nineteenth Century, Oxford/New York 2000; Nira Yuval-Davis, Gender and Nation, London 1997; Andrew Parker et al. (Eds.), Nationalisms and Sexualities, New York 1992; Rick Wilford and Robert L. Miller, Women, Ethnicity and Nationalism: The Politics of Transition, London/New York1998; Gisela Brinker-Gabler, Sidonie Smith, Writing New Identities: Gender, Nation and Immigration in Contemporary Europe, Minneapolis 1997; on women's participation in nationalism in Yugoslavia in "a less violent form" see Rada Iveković, Women, Nationalism and War: Make Love not War, in: Hypatia, 8/ 4, Autumn 1993, 113 – 126.

14 Benedict Anderson, Imagined Communities: Reflection on the Origin and Spread of Nationalism, New York/London 1991.

Slovak gender scholar Jana Cviková implicitly suggests that what is masculine is in the center of politics, whereas what is rendered feminine is relegated to the periphery. Cviková believes that Slovak "women were excluded from national culture no matter what they did."[15] "Men," Cviková continues, "articulated the norm of women's acts and behavior in national life."[16] Quite the contrary, American scholar Norma Rudinsky highlights the phenomenon of "men asking for women's help."[17] "Men," Rudinsky continues, "offered women an important role to play, and women accepted that role enthusiastically."[18] She emphasized the element of shared momentum when "men's recognition of their political needs coincided with women's increased confidence in their own ability to contribute to national cause." [19] In a similar fashion Andrea Šalingová argues for the "deliberate emergence" of female emancipation that occurred concurrently with the intensified national upheaval. She argues that the eventual coalescence of the emancipation and nationalism materialized in August 1869, when the first female organization Živena was established.[20] In her effort to define male and female domains and the nature of gender tension within the middle class society Šalingová clearly refutes the notion of a passive female. Whereas Cviková, Rudinski and Šalingová negotiate the loyalties to Slovak nation through the lens of gender, Nora Weber refutes to recognize the category of gender as the primary factor determining the loyalties of women to Slovak cause. Her argument runs along Anthony Smith's insistence that gender, as such, is "relatively impotent as a basis for collective mobilization."[21] Weber argues that women developed their own unique concept of gender equality based on the discourses of motherhood, domestic duties and religion. Nora Weber's argument refutes the interpretation that runs along the gender scheme of duality of power which implicitly suggests the binary between "rulers and ruled." Instead her argument reminds us of Linda Gordon's own refusal to interpret the history of female experience as powerless. Gordon concludes that "being less powerful after all, 'is not to be powerless, or even to lose all the time.'[22] How shall we

15 Jana Cviková, Po boku muža a národa, in: Aspekt, 1/2003-2004 "(Her) stories of Women" (Príbehy žien), 15.

16 Ibid.

17 Norma L. Rudinsky, Incipient Feminists: Women Writers in the Slovak Nation Revival, Ohio 1991, 10.

18 Ibid.

19 Ibid.

20 Andrea Šalingová, Združovanie a spolkový život žien na Slovensku (od polovice 19. do polovice 20. storočia), in: Aspekt, 1/2003 – 2004, " (Her) stories of women" (Príbehy žien), 5.

21 Wilford, Women, 10.

22 Janaki Nair, Agency in Indian Feminist Historiography, in: Gender & History, 6/1, April 1994, 83.

come around such a different views about the role of female within the context of the nineteenth century Slovak nationalism?

"Hungarus sum." This is how one can describe the identity of the seventeenth and eighteenth century members of Slovak ethnic within the context of Habsburg monarchy. In the course of the second half of the nineteenth century Slovaks were loyal to both, a Hungarian[23] political nation and the Slovak cultural and linguistic nationalism imagined in various ways as Pan-Slavic, Czechoslovak and Slovak.[24] In the course of the nineteenth century Slovak national movement did not seek to establish its own Slovak or Czechoslovak state but promoted the idea of a multi-ethnic and multilinguistic Hungary.[25] By 1918, the political loyalty of Slovaks to Hungary, ("Uhorsko") had withered away under the pressure of Hungarian cultural and linguistic assimilation policies.[26] Slovak national movement could not rely on the state institutions and the process of the "inventing of the nation" was carried out by private voluntary associations and individuals, rather than public networks and government.[27] In Andersonian sense, the newspapers and literature was a means of the marking a "familiar" landscape by communicants of "imagined community."[28] Jozef Miloslav Hurban, one of the forerunners of Štúrist's generation, claimed that "literature paves the path to the establishment of community and a state."[29] Ľudmila Riznerová-Podjavorinská, the famous Slovak female writer of the nineteenth century, opined that literature represents the nation per se, especially at times when the political conditions were not feasible for the idea of statehood.[30] Poetry, in particular, is generally recognized as "a purely

23 Slovaks use the term "Uhorsko" for Hungary prior to 1918, and "Maďarsko" (Hungary) for Hungary after 1918. Hungary as a monolithic national state is thus distinguished from multi-national "Uhorsko." See for example István Kollai, Shattered Past. Socio-Psychological Aspects of Slovak – Hungarian Relations, in: International Issues & Slovak Foreign Policy Affairs, 03-04/2006, 28 – 29.

24 Alexander Maxwell, Multiple Nationalism: National Concepts in the Nineteenth Century Hungary and Benedict Anderson's "Imagined Communities," in: Nationalism and Ethnic Politics, 11/2005, 385.

25 Ibid., 385 - 387.

26 Peter Macho, O Slovenskej identite trochu inak," in: Slovenská otázka dnes, Bratislava,2007, 72 – 77.

27 Geoff Eley, Culture, Nation and Gender, in: Ida Blom, Karen Hageman, Catherine Hall, Gendered Nations. Nationalisms and Gender Order in the Long Nineteenth Century, Oxford/New York 2000, 30.

28 Anderson, Imagined Communities, 35- 36.

29 Stanislav Šmatlák, Literárnohistorické predpoklady typológie slovenského romantizmu, in: Oskár Čepan et al., Literárny Romantizmus, Bratislava 1974, 45.

30 Peter Petro, A History of Slovak Literature, Montreal/Kingston/London/Buffalo1996, 113.

symbolic act in a culturally saturated environment," and a "perfect model to describe the human mental condition...."[31] The poems and novels serve as a crucial tool of policing nineteenth century community's everyday acts vis-à-vis the expected behavioral norms that the carefully constructed stereotypes readily display. Slovaks' perception of themselves as "manlier creatures" was highlighted in Ľudovít Štúr's rhetoric. Not rarely were "manlier creatures" further glossed in veneer of "civilizers." In this regard Slovak nationalists nurtured the myth of Slovaks as teachers of "uncivilized intruders" of Magyar tribes who settled in the Carpathian basin after 895. According to this myth, which survived well into the twentieth century, Slovaks taught Magyars how to plough the land and build the dwellings. Slovaks were also imagined as the first agents who mediated converting of Magyars into Christian faith.[32]

With respect to our goals, the dissemination of imagined female stereotype as a messenger of desirable normative behavior bears far reaching political consequences. Stereotypes, in general, have a power to turn the invisible into visible and public, which is precisely the way how stereotypes gain their social and political importance.[33] Not only did nationally gendered stereotypes merge political and sexual contexts into a broad cultural phenomenon. At the same time, gendered stereotypes served as a means of defining relationships between nationalities within the Habsburg Empire.[34]

The female as inspiration was the social construct that emerged as an outcome of national ideologies in the nineteenth century European milieu. George Mosse views the emergence of a new female representation as a consequence of mutual dialogue between nationalism and respectability. Nationalism as an effective ideology of modern times, the author argues, absorbed all that men thought meaningful. Nationalists advocated a variety of flexible means to reach their goal. Whether the means were liberalism or conservativism, tolerance or repression, or even a combination of them, the nature of possible means to reach specific national dream was of secondary concern. Yet, according to Mosse, there was a value that nationalism hardly wavered about – its advocacy to respectability.[35] Navigation between the existing dichotomies of respectability - normality and abnor-

31 Indrek Tart, Poetry and Gender: Mindscapes and Publishing Opportunities, in: Interlitteraria, 05/2000, 306. www.ceeol.com, 26.8. 2008.

32 Robert B. Pynsent, Questions of Identity. Czech and Slovak Ideas of Nationality and Personality, Budapest/London/New York, 153 - 154.

33 George Mosse, The Image of Man. The Creation of Modern Masculinity, New York/Oxford, 6.

34 Alexander Maxwell, Nationalizing Sexuality: Sexual Stereotypes in the Habsburg Empire, in: Journal of the History of Sexuality, 14/ 3, July 2005, 269.

35 George Mosse, Nationalism and Sexuality: Middle-Class Morality and Sexual Norms in Modern Europe, New York, 1985, 9.

mality, morality versus immorality, manliness and unmanliness - were to ensure the control and security of a national community. Overt expressions of sexuality would be deemed unmanly, abnormal and immoral. In this light, Mosse continues, sexual urges and men's passions were redirected to a higher purpose by projecting a new stereotype of human beauty that was to transcend sensuousness.[36] Therefore, the concept of a woman as inspiration emerged not only as a response to the romantic ideal of the Herderian nation but also as a response to concerns about respectability.[37] The wide attention that the issues of female agency received in the course of longue durée lies at the core of the debate about the role of traditional society. This is not to say that tradition represents the ground on which the status of women was being contested. Rather the reverse seemed to be the case: female agency represents the platform against which the traditional society becomes tested.

Some scholars adhere to the view that the female as a depersonalized ethereal type could hardly embrace the needs of women. According to Norma Rudinsky, female embodiment in the stereotype of "inspiration" was an abstract concept unattainable for women to reach, or as Cviková claims "a pompous role often taking on absurd images."[38] Mosse implies that the construction of this type of the ethereal ideal female was the result of male desires. The unreal female being was to nurture their dedication to the national cause. However, it would be misleading to conclude that women were excluded from the process of constructing the apotheosized female, even if it was a model too distant from their own needs. The famous Slovak female writer Ľudmila Riznerová-Podjavorinská, who used mythology as a didactic tool, saw Slovak culture embodied in a feminine image of the goddess Živena. Motherhood and passive suffering were codes of behavior enunciated through the image of this goddess, who was so profoundly embraced in Slovak cultural symbolism.[39] The concept of female as inspiration attained various forms of ancient mythological beings, goddesses, or Muses. The Muse of the Slovak Mountains, a traditional form of ethereal female in Slovak poetry, as presented by Palkovič and Šafárik, might have embraced the "pure hearts" of the mountain population of pastoral regions,[40] while the old agricultural society of Slovak lowlands was probably more responsive to the image of the Mother Earth goddess. According to Norma Rudinski, in the context of traditional patriarchal society, Mother Earth does

36 Ibid., 11.
37 Rudinski, Incipient Feminists, 11.
38 Cviková, Po boku muža, 11.
39 Nora Weber, Feminism, Patriarchy, Nationalism, And Women in Fin-De-Siecle Slovakia, in: Nationalities Papers, 25/1, 1997, 39.
40 Rudinski, Incipient Feminists, 18.

not promote only the beauties of motherhood; her functions of nurturer and lover are equally essential.[41]

The scale and intensity of body symbolism through which women were idealized is truly remarkable and deserves our attention. According to Katherine Verdery, body symbolism, or "symbol system by which bodies enter into sociality" not only "makes bodies social," but also represents a means through which "gender enters into an organization of power."[42] Similarly Irena Malec offers a thorough research of female body symbols in Slovak poetry, which uniquely repressed the dominant eroticized signifieds in favor of newly attained meanings representing nonphysical spiritual qualities.[43] One might have expected that moral concerns in the face of respectability, as depicted by George Mosse, would naturally result in the purge of sexually toned cultural symbols. But the research of Malec demonstrates that the elements of strong eroticization are present, although their delicate presence is instantly de-eroticized by attaching new signifieds of higher moral national values. Therefore, the reader's sensuousness is cautiously guarded while he encounters the perfect breasts of Andrej Sládkovič' famous "Marína". Her breasts that lack physicality are transformed into ideal breasts symbolizing the inner spiritual values of an adored Goddess. De-personalized female faces in Slovak poems can represent virgin innocence, noble pain, or justified anger. In this context, married women presented in poetry do not have physical bodies; their motherhood is in fact impersonal, veiled by a national-religious gown. Nursing also bears cultural-political signs. Mother's milk is the source of patriotism and nationalism. Quite remarkably, while female body stands out as nonphysical and for that matter unreachable, a womb does acquire a physical form in poetry. It bears highly abstract and contradictory meanings connoting either protection or death followed by redemption.[44] Overall, female physical beauty, as represented in Slovak poems signifies high moral values and national symbols, while the aspects of female agency and individualism are carefully undermined. Slovak poetry portrays the female through her disciplined non-physical body as idealized and passive whereas the male, through the presence of his physical body, is presented as an active contributor to the process of national awakening. Not surprisingly in this regard, women's own will is frequently associated with a Satan.[45] Will and desire of men to act in the name of the nation, quite contrary, are constantly being encouraged through the gaze at unreachable, ethereal

41 Ibid., 17.

42 Kathrine Verdery, What Was Socialism and What Comes Next?, Princeton 1996, 65.

43 Irena Malec, Telo ako znak, Ženské postavy v poézii slovenského romantizmu, in: Aspekt, 1/2003 – 2004 "Her Stories of Women" (Príbehy žien), 1.

44 Malec, Telo, 8.

45 Ibid., 15.

and de-erotized goddesses. Worshiping and adoring ethereal female as the perfect embodiment of nation's virtues seem to consume energies of some Slovak awakeners, including Ľudovít Štúr himself, to a degree when they consciously reject relationships with beautiful women in order to commit their lives to the national cause.

According to George Mosse feminine images remained usually untouched by changes within the nation and that the passive image of female had been constant and generally unchallenged, despite the raising wave of women's movements, well into the twentieth century interwar period.[46] In his view female public symbols "did not reflect the needs and hopes of society directly" as male symbols did.[47] The following lines, quite the contrary, will shed some light on the political changes in Slovak milieu which had a tremendous impact on the emergence of a new female stereotype in Slovak milieu. Although the new female stereotype has significantly moved from the image of an apotheosized female, the meaning of its newly constructed agency remains rather ambiguous.

As in the second half of the nineteenth century Slovak society plunged into a state of political turmoil and the trappings of reactionary backlash which threatened the fragile existence of Slovak culture and the nation per se, a new type of female stereotype emerged. The construct of apotheosized female underwent the process of radical modification as the old image failed to cope with new pressures within society. Domestic political battles oscillated around the question of the codification of Slovak language. A bitter confrontation ensued between those who viewed Slovak language as a vernacular of Czech and those who claimed the uniqueness and authenticity of Slovak language and culture. The vitality of internal policy was both weakened and revitalized by the shift from "Slavic"- oriented to "Slovak"- centered policy. Despite his respect and love of Slavs, Ľudovít Štúr found Ján Kollár's idea of Slavdom[48] a "dry, dead theory."[49] More importantly however, it was their own unique understanding of nationalism that set both, Kollár and Štúr's followers on their own distinguished paths. In Kollár's understanding, nation was but one of the forms in which universal intellect was to be expressed, whereas Štúrists believed in nation as a being. Stanislav Šmatlák saw these ontological differences as roots behind the further disagreement over the historical and sociological function of nation between Kollár and Štúr's followers.[50] While Kollár's nation as a form of universal

46 George Mosse, The Image, 13.
47 Ibid., 8.
48 About the myth of Slaveness see Pynsent, Questions, 44 – 96.
49 Petro, A History, 67.
50 Stanislav Šmatlák, Literárnohistorické predpoklady typológie slovenského romantizmu,, in: Oskár Čepan et al., Literárny Romantizmus, Bratislava 1974, 44.

intellect was an apolitical messenger of a higher culture and science, Štúr's circle emphasized a pragmatic role of the nation and its social and political activities. Whereas Ján Kollár does not enter nationalist discourse with the polarized "other", Štúr's understanding of otherness displays more sharper edges.[51] That the national movement refrained from political projects pertaining to the larger Slavic milieu and maintained cooperation on cultural level might have weakened the livelihood of the national process. But when one reconsiders the psychological impact of a self-centered combat for survival of its cultural heritage, it is easy to imagine the engine of revitalization that ran Slovak national movement into a higher gear. Patriots of the Štúrist tradition (1835 - 1875) naturally turned to a larger social spectrum for support. Female hubris of national agitators of Štúrist generation is almost non-existent in the late 1840s and 1850s. Only in 1870s the number of women participants in national revival, mostly from the families of Protestant priests and teachers, increased.[52] The daughters, wives and sisters of famous Slovak patriots played an active part in the national revival as their lives were naturally affected by the activism of their fathers, husbands and brothers. In Liptovský Svätý Mikuláš, much in the fashion of 'platform women' in the nineteenth century London, Marína Hodžová "in a fervent indignation" publicly castigated a "terrible crime of "magyarons" who hurt and beat her father Michal Miloslav Hodža.[53] When "Magyar ploughboys" built gallows in front of J.M. Hurban`s house threatening to hang him, his wife was ready to sacrifice anything to support her husband in his national efforts.[54] Hodža's daughters Marína and Ľudmila organized a theatrical society and contributed to the establishment of "Beseda dievčenská," a society of girls "longing for spiritual health."[55] The aim of the Beseda was to educate women and girls to love the nation by means of reading of wide variety of literary genres, encouraging debates and systematic education.[56] In the political realm, women helped to promote the idea of Slovak Memorandum in 1861. They were visible agents in Matica's public gatherings and they took part in small scale activities in the country.[57] But such a mobilization of women from the families of nationalists as we could see in the course of 1860 and 1870s was unheard of in the first half of the nineteenth century. The roots of the transition to more agile roles of women in public

51 Bohuslava Ferenčuhová, Zmieri sa Slovensko so svojím nacionalizmom? in: László Szigeti, (Ed.), Slovenská otázka dnes, Bratislava 2007,185.

52 Kačírek Ľuboš, Vnímanie emancipácie žien v slovenskej spoločnosti v 60. a 70. rokoch 19. storočia, in: Jolana Darulová, Katarína Koštialová, (Eds.), Sféry Ženy: Sociológia, História, Etnológia, Banská Bystrica 2004, 400.

53 Štefana Votrubová, Živena: Jej Osudy a Práca, Turčiansky Sv. Martin 1931, 11.

54 Ibid. 11.

55 Šalingová, Združovanie, 3.

56 Miloš Ferko, Prvá slovenská dáma: Osudy Maríny Hodžovej na pozadí slovenského ženského hnutia v 19. storočí, in: Historická Revue, 6 - 7/ 13, 2002, 22 – 23.

57 Andrej Mráz, Literárne dielo Terézie Vansovej. Štúdia, Turčiansky Sv. Martin 1937,15.

sphere could be partly traced in the introduction of a new female stereotype of a "cultured mother."

The introduction of a new female stereotype in Štúrist's period represented a means to mobilize a wide female audience in the process of national revival. A similar process had been under way in other parts of the monarchy as well -- Hungarian, Czech and Croatian patriots respectively appealed for women's help. The imperative of national survival consequently made women respond and contribute to the makeover of an apotheosized ideal female into its humanized earthier counterpart. Within the context of "imagined community" anonymous ethereal female is juxtaposed with what Anderson defined as a more familiar "socioscape."[58] While the model of the female as inspiration was impersonal and passive, the new female stereotype was physical and appeared to be active. It is precisely the notion of female agency, however, that led to controversial opinions and a series of published debates. While examining the degree of female agency, one constantly comes across disputes concerning women's expected involvement in the national cause. On the one hand Slovak women were to expected help the national movement, while on the other, they were expected to play essential role. How shall we come to terms with these deliberately different modes of agency?

Norma Rudinski has already pointed to the phenomenon which can be dubbed as a "false visualization of female agency in public sphere." Poems or pamphlets as a means of addressing women in these tumultuous times were not unusual medium. What is striking though is an effort of these poets to conceal their male identity and claim female authorship in order to appeal to wide female audiences. The idea of men appealing to female audience by opening phrase "we Slovak women" may seem somewhat amusing to a modern reader.[59] Such poems carried educational, ethical, moral as well as political messages. These poems and pamphlets not only promoted images of women being a part of the national dream but also eschewed and even harshly chastised those who preferred Magyar rather than Slovak spouses and lovers. The aim was to prevent de-nationalization of the female, to thwart the fragile ethnic balance in favor of the relatively small Slovak population and to establish national identity within more definite ethnic boundaries. The tactics of the abovementioned purposeful gender juxtaposition is also evident from the list of the constituent membership of "Živena," the first Slovak female organization established upon the incentive of Ambro Pietor. Readers cannot help but smile over the name Vilma Paulíny-Tóthová, a female version of Viliam-Paulíny Tóth, a famous Slovak patriot and a participant in the preliminary meeting of

58 Anderson, Imagined Communities, 35.

59 Rudinsky, Incipient Feminists, 49.

Živena. These men's attitude to Slovak women was undoubtedly positive, as Elena Maróthy-Šoltésová notes in her autobiography Sedemdesiat rokov života, (Seventy Years of Life). She highlights Viliam Paulíny Tóth, Ambro Pietor and Jozef Nedobrý's "almost leading role" in the establishment of the Živena.[60] Women and men, respectively, subscribed as members of the first women's national-educational organization. Yet, the examination of published opinions of male patriots clearly confirms the focus on visual rather than physical aspect of female agency. The concept of women as seen rather than heard stands out from Štúr's editorial note published in Slovenskje narodnje noviny (Slovak National Newspaper) in March 1846:

> "A wife should be a good housekeeper, and a stimulating, pleasant companion and careful, serious cultured mother. In general, a wife should make her way among the higher things, not actively (which we are not in favor of) but rather passively...."[61]

"Passive" female connotes the idea of cultured mother whose motherly care, love and passion are to bring up the new nationally aware generation. Cultured mother is a symbol of national virtue, a silent moral agent that inspires by its mere symbolic presence in a public sphere. It is believed that with these fragile and vulnerable bearers of Slovak cultural heritage Slovak nationhood becomes mobilized. Yet, their help is seen as both, symbolic in the public realm and essential at the core of the private realm and family. The tension between "symbolic help" and "essential role" and "passive" and "active" notion of female agency is inherent in the core of the debates about visualization of female agency. Why do the media such as literature or newspaper, as well as some Slovak awakeners including Štúr himself prefer the visualization of female agency over actual activities of women in the spotlight of public sphere? The answer lies in the gravity of the public concern with the actual presence of female in public sphere. Rather than constraining the independence of women, men shielded them from harsh vicissitudes of public life. This phenomenon was certainly not bound to Central European milieu. In her analysis of the representations of women in Victorian Britain, Lynda Nead claims that "...female purity can only be guaranteed within the confines of the home. Outside the home is knowledge and knowledge undermines innocence. Better then, for the bourgeois woman to stay within her domestic sphere and donate money to charity,

---

60 Želmíra Handzová, Elena Maróthy Šoltésová. Život a dielo v dokumentoch, Bratislava 1989, 38.

61 Rudinsky, Incipient Feminists, 34.

than to leave a sanctuary and come into contact with sin..."[62] The access of women to knowledge within the context of Slovak milieu represents a focal point of contemporary debates, a key medium in reaching out towards national goals. Ľudovít Štúr was aware of the problem:

"....Already, even among our women, the female sex had begun to talk of the nation, fatherland, and so on, pretending to understand these terms. But with few exceptions, these words in our women's mouths are only empty sounds, without meaning. Our women lack enough education to understand and appreciate them, and they only mouth them from others, usually a few months before and a few months after their wedding."[63]

"Love Thy Nation" lied at the core of national behavioral norms of the imagined Slovak community. Yet, love of one's nation was predetermined by knowledge about one's nation. In his public speeches Štúr insisted on knowing oneself and knowing one's nation to be premises of unconditional love of nation. One could truly love nation only by understanding both, human and national destiny.[64] Love represents a means through which the imagined nation enters into the imagined being. And as Benedict Anderson reminds us, love and nation are mutually interwoven since it is also "nations [that –NP] inspire love, and often profoundly self-sacrificing love."[65] But given the poor state of female education, women's love of nation stood on shaky grounds and posited dangers to national survival.

The new challenges of Slovak-centered policy of Štúrist awakeners brought a new paradigm of "cultured mother" to the spotlight of the day. A "cultured mother" whose role was to bring up a nationally self-confident generation replaced the unreachable, non-physical female image imbued with rich national symbolism. The "cultured mother" has been given a crucial task to "resurrect" – or in Andersonian sense "invent," the Slovak nation.[66] Public discourse displays rather ambiguous views about female agency. On the one hand, the preference of a passive mode of female agency is expressive of an effort to safeguard and protect pure hearts of Slovak women which was a moral, religious as well as cultural-political imperative. Fears that cultured and educated women would be "desensitized" and deprived of virtues such as self-sacrifice, humbleness and modesty was all-pervasive in traditional Slovak society. General public was concerned that woman's

62 Lynda Need, Myths of Sexuality. Representations of Women in Victorian Britain, New York 1988, 202.

63 Rudinsky, Incipient Feminists, 34.

64 Ľudovít Bakoš, Ľudovít Štúr ako vychovávateľ a bojovník za slovenskú školu: školské pomery na Slovensku v tridsiatich až päťdesiatich rokoch 19. storočia, Bratislava 1957, 62.

65 Anderson, Imagined Communities, 141.

66 Mráz, Literárne dielo, 11.

"brightness of the mind" rises to the detriment of her feelings, motherhood and marriage.[67] In this regard, female agency was to be disciplined in order to preserve female virtues. At the same time however, a "cultured mother" was assigned a vital role of producing and eo ipso mobilizing Slovak nation. Such contradictory views on female agency understandably shifted women into the center of public debates about women's education and emancipation. A "cultured mother's" vital role to raise a new generation of "kriesiteľov a kriesiteľky národa"[68] was put on the pedestal. The motherhood was venerated as "the most beautiful role of Slovak woman, the most ample field of her salutary activities."[69] All aspects of women's lives were to be subordinated to women's leading role as custodians of Slovak nationalist heritage.[70] As one of the contemporaries noted, the failure to transform females into "cultured mothers" would posit a threat of the "demoralization of our age"[71] and eventually put the nation's future in jeopardy. Education clearly represents a discursive platform where women's essential contribution to Slovak nation were negotiated:

> " A woman lacking the understanding of human activities – and without education such understanding can be hardly attained – cannot be beneficial to a family whatsoever, or, better to say, to community as such."[72]

The discourse about beneficiary aspect of educated women to Slovak community runs along an effort to protect females. By a means of proper education, Slovak women were to be protected from what Andrej Mráz described as a "passive absorbance of foreign culture."[73] Women's education turned out to be a new kind of experiment within the multiethnic milieu. The problem was not the access of women to education as such, but rather an access to Slovak education.[74] Given the almost non-existent schooling in Slovak language, female literati received their education in foreign languages. At the age of twelve, Terézia Vansová was sent to Girls's Institute in Banská Bystrica to learn German. A year later she spent a year in Rimavská Sobota to learn Hungarian.[75]. When she was ten years old, Maróthy Šoltésová studied at local Hungarian Calvin school in Lučenec to gain fluency in Hungarian language.[76] Six moths later Maróthy Šoltésová

67 Marcela Mikulová, Ženy a národ na prelome 19. a 20. storočia, in: Aspekt 1, 1994, 73.

68 Mráz, Literárne dielo, 11.

69 Kačírek, Vnímanie, 393.

70 Weber, Feminism, 40.

71 Kačírek, Vnímanie, 393.

72 Ibid., 392 – 393.

73 Mráz, Literárne dielo, 15.

74 Owen Johnson, Slovakia 1918 - 1938: education and the making of a nation, New York 1985, 37.

75 Mráz, Literárne dielo, 22.

76 Handzová, Elena, 23.

joined German Institute of Žaneta Friedlová to master German language.[77] In the words of Šoltésová "with rare and happier exception of few, perhaps all village priests and teachers' daughters received similar education."[78] Female literati were fully aware of the importance of "spisba" – literature for national goals. Maróthy-Šoltésová claimed: "...we also long for the higher [spiritual spheres and knowledge - NP] ,.. our next duty, in this regard, is diligent reading of Slovak books and journals...."[79] However, the task to keep up spirits of national awareness within the context of multicultural milieu was rather problematic. On a political platform, the 1867 Ausgleich and the upsurge of Hungarian nationalism resulted in the forced closing of three Slovak gymnasiums and the cultural institution of Matica Slovenská. On a cultural platform, let us just underscore the widespread popularity of German literature in 1860 and 1870s among Slovak women. Even Šoltésová and Vansová loved to reach to "non-Slovak" literary production. As many other female readers, they admitted being strongly influenced by German novels, and its "moral tendency and emotionality."[80] Vansová herself, was "guilty" of frequently reaching out to "exotic elements" in her own work. She did not try to purge her texts of so called "czechisms."[81] Such literary "sins" readily revealed Vansová's diversion from the established norm in Slovak national literary production.[82] The dissemination of a national message was secondary to her own fascination with moral aspects of human relations. Only at the beginning of the twentieth century, the voice of Božena Slánčiková Timravá, stood out on purely national grounds. In her novel Experience (1902) Timravá was not afraid to reveal a phony side of Slovak nationalists. She also voiced her critical views of the conservative Slovak national leadership prior to 1918 in her later autobiographical novel Everything for Nation.[83].

Nationalists were generally dissatisfied with a poor level of girls' enrollment in Slovak schools.[84] Although many leading Štúrists received their education at the universities in Göttingen, Halle or Jena, there were multiple voices in society that discouraged young Slovak girls to learn French, Hungarian, German or English, since acquiring the ability to speak foreign languages would "poison her heart."[85] Even mediocre language skills would

77 Ibid., 24.

78 Mráz, Literárne dielo, 22.

79 Zlatý Fond Sme, http://zlatyfond.sme.sk/dielo/310/Marothy-Soltesova_Clanky/2, 17.9. 2008.

80 Mráz, Literárne dielo, 54.

81 Ibid., 63 - 64.

82 Petro, A History, 110.

83 Ibid., 115 – 117.

84 On the poor state of Slovak education see Bakoš, Ľudovít Štúr, 24 – 30.

85 Kačírek, Vnímanie, 398.

turn young women into "maznavé fifleny nemeckých románov"[86] - "spoilt coquettes of German novels," who were "reckless, proud and susceptible to renegade behavior."[87] "Renegade behavior" - "odrodilectvo" - was denounced as a sin against language and "blood."[88] The association of "odrodilectvo" with nihilism and degeneration undoubtedly reveals racial dimension of nationalism of this period – the theme hardly tackled by Slovak historiography. The public denunciation of "odrodilectvo" was to thwart the process of mass assimilation of Slovaks with Hungarians. According to László Szarka, after Germans and Jews Slovaks represented the third largest group of willing assimilates with Hungarian speaking milieu.[89] Slovak nationalists failed to thwart the ongoing process of cultural and political "hungarism" of lower nobility and middle classes due to their meager economic prospects in Slovak milieu.[90]

The education of girls in Slovak language was central to the discourses about the role of family. Slovak sons and daughters who were brought up by "philological maids" and uttered their first words in foreign language were marked as a threat to Slovak nation. The future generation of non-Slovak speakers was put on a par with drunkards who wasted their parents' fortune, "proletariats without acquaintances," or backward losers. And it was a "careless, from the world just returned, girl" who was fully responsible for bringing up "intellectually neglected," non-Slovak speaking generation of sons and daughters.[91] Yet, even within the camp of staunch Slovak nationalists, the importance of the efficiency in foreign languages vis-à-vis modernity[92] and its economic challenges was reluctantly acknowledged. For example girls attending Girls' school in Revúca established in 1870/1871 received a "special education" in the form of French lessons. Moreover, during the embroidery classes they communicated in German and Hungarian on a regular basis. The communication in foreign languages,

86 Ibid., 397.

87 Ibid., 399.

88 Miloslav Szabó, Predohra Kulturkampfu. Uhorsko cirkevno-politické debaty v rokoch 1883 – 1884 na stránkach Národných novín, in: László Szigeti, (Ed.), Slovenská Otázka Dnes. Výber textov z časopisov OS 1997 – 2006, Bratislava 2007, 452.

89 Ibid. 451.

90 On the workings of pragmatism, modernity and national identity see Tibor Pichler, Národovci alebo občania. Inštitunalizácia ako problém, in: László Szigeti, (Ed.). Slovenská otázka dnes: Výber textov z časopisov OS 1997 – 2006, Bratislava 2007, 104; Jan Rychlík, Moravské Slovensko a Záhorie v letech 1939 – 1945, in: Veľká politika a malé regióny (1918 – 1939), Prešov/Graz 2002, 229 – 241; Chad Bryant, Either German or Czech: Fixing Nationality in Bohemia and Moravia, 1939 -1946, in: Slavic Review 61/4, 2002, 683 - 706.

91 Szabó, Predohra, 453.

92 About the workings of modernity and modernization in Slovak milieu see for example Ľubomír Lipták, Changes of changes: Society and Politics in Slovakia in the 20th Century, Bratislava 2002, 51 – 59.

according to the instructor Helena Botová, was to help young girls to become familiar with foreign technical terminology.[93] But nationalists mostly feared the "foreign" and "non-traditional" influences that modernity and liberalism might have exercised on those whose national consciousness was rather questionable. Increased mobility and transition of ideas, discoveries and experiences, posited both, the benefits and risks to Slovak national movement. Let us just mention a public discussion about the proposed marriage law between Christians and Jews which was denounced in Národnie noviny (Slovak national newspaper) in November 1883 as a "thoughtless liberalization." What is interesting in this regard is the confidence that nationalists invested in virtues of Slovak "cultured mothers." While the author of the article expressed his concerns about marriages of male Christians with Jewesses, it was believed that the number of marriages between female Christians with male Jews would be much smaller as a result of virtues of Slovak cultured mothers. The confidence in Slovak "cultured mother" thus reflects the power of its symbolic investment acquired in the course of several decades. Slovak cultured mother's virtues were further embraced against the otherness of a luscious "beautiful Jewess" with erotic charisma."[94]

The discourse about the female education naturally overlapped with the emancipation discourse. The notion of the emancipation in the latter half of the nineteenth century acquired a range of negative connotations. In the eyes of Svetozár Hurban Vajanský, the emancipation was a threat to the morality, marriage and motherhood. When twenty nine years old Mária Kopová defrauded three hundred "zlatý", her case was published in newspaper under the title "Emancipation" and Kopová herself was described as a "very emancipated lady."[95] Banšel also expressed some doubts when he compared emancipation to "self-deceit," "crossroad" and a "tree without roots, without soil".[96] How did Slovak women reconcile Slovak national cause and the emancipation? How did Slovak female writers cope with ambiguous efforts to discipline female agency?

Slovak female literati in the course of the second half of the nineteenth century cautiously kept a distance from the emancipation concept that was imbued with a range of negative meanings. Ľudmila Riznerová-Podjavorinská promoted the idea of so called "solídna emancipácia" - "reasonable emancipation" that did not undermine the pillars of traditional society. The concept of so called "reasonable emancipation" was built upon the no-

93 Kačírek, Vnímanie, 398.
94 Szabó, Predohra, 454.
95 Mráz, Literárne dielo, 35.
96 Mikulová, Ženy, 73.

tion of benign patriarchy and collective nationalism.[97] Under the auspices of Christian values both, men and women respectively, were to contribute to the building of Slovak nation. Podjavorinská's concept underlined the idea of women's domesticity, modesty, and undying loyalty flavored with a nationalist penchant for voluntary self-sacrifice on behalf of the nation. She believed that all members of Christian community respectively should be involved in the nation building project. At the same time, however, Podjavorinská insisted on a complete separation of male and female domains in Slovak "imagined community." The idea of divided gendered domains was reflective of her awareness of "male superior capacities" and effort to preserve the traditional patriarchal model:

"If both sexes refuse to stick to their own domains then the nation cannot survive. Consequently women's emancipation cannot infringe upon these boundaries; quite the opposite, it must go along with these traditional lines and be reasonable."[98]

In Podjavorinská's view, the uncurbed emancipation would disrupt the traditional family and undermine the nation. In her novel Žena (A Woman) Podjavorinská situates female agency in the role of a moral "policeman" of Slovak imagined community's vices, embodied in the character of a widower Štefan, an insecure procrastinator with five children. It is through his wife Iva, a good-hearted hard worker, that Štefan becomes a better man.[99] In Podjavorinská's line of thought the radius of female agency was firmly grounded vis-à-vis the expectations of traditional patriarchal society. At the same time however, female agency stands out as a moral agent in nation-building process.

Maróthy-Šoltésová, like Podjavorinská, remained loyal to the core of traditional patriarchal values. She blended the idea of domesticity and Christian morality and laid the basis for a concept of so called Christian feminism.[100] But unlike Podjavorinská, she did not believe that higher education would "de-womanize" or "unsex" women.[101] Maróthy-Šoltésová called for a kind of education that would not distract women's role as mothers or undermine their feminine nature, but rather foster their Christian morality.[102] It was Christian ideology that made Maróthy-Šoltésová believe that women's role in society should not be auxiliary: "Man and woman are two

97 Weber, Feminism, 38.
98 Ibid., See also Michal Kocak, (Ed.), Listy Ludmily Riznerovej-Podjavorinskej, Martin 1988, 232.
99 Petro, A History, 113.
100 Weber, Feminism, 35.
101 Ibid., 43.
102 Ibid., 44.

different halves that together form one whole person". In her view, the sexes were equally valuable, complementing and mutually supporting each other: "The husband is often strong and active – the wife, weaker, softer, and passive. ..."[103] Quite remarkably, weakness and passivity do not undermine female value in society, nor do they make it a less valuable "half." Woman, in her line of thought, remains an equal partner of her male counterpart. The differences between male and female should stimulate personal and spiritual self-education and self-improvement of women.[104] Here, the reader is already aware of the crux when the process of self-improvement evokes the notion of a more active rather than passive woman:

> That difference (see between woman and man – NP), however, absolutely does not confer a right of domination or exclusive activity in the spiritual realm. Women, too, are called to this activity, and it has not been given to men's will, nor their power, to decide how far women may go. (As long as God's law is not repealed that each woman is also her father's daughter, not only her mother's, and that each man is also his mother's son, not only his father's, then human beings cannot presume to divide and separate the psychological characteristics and roles of men and women in such a way that women never receive men's qualities and roles and men never receive women's. [105]

As Nora Weber correctly noted Šoltésová's immediate concern stems from the threat of general immorality rather than from gender inequality. Similarly, in Terézia Medviecká-Vansová's value system, the nationalist ideology stood above gender concerns.[106] She also adhered to the concept of Christian feminism emphasizing a more traditional image of the female. The mother as a guarantor of the strength and health of the family and nation is at the core of Vansová's attention. A philosophy of essentiality of motherhood is promoted by Vansová in "Denica", the journal that aimed to disseminate the nationalist ideology among less educated women. [107] Here, any views that lured woman away from the responsibility of the motherhood were condemned. And yet, the magazine was considered a hotbed of "dangerous emancipation" which, according to Rudinsky, reached out to its female audience by means of emotional rather than relevant factual argumentation. The ideal female portrayed in Vansová's novels was attractive, spirited and, as Rudinsky comments, "unusually (and probably unrealistically)" independent.[108]

103 Ibid., 47. See also Lea Mrázová, (Ed.), Začatá cesta, Martin,1934, 107.

104 Weber, Feminism, 47.

105 Ibid., 48. See also Rudinsky, Incipient Feminists, 127.

106 Weber, Feminism, 52.

107 Weber, Feminism, 51.

108 Rudinsky, Incipient Feminists, 117.

So far we have paid attention to the female agency as disseminated by the female stereotype of ethereal non-physical female and physical cultured mother. We have also looked at the way how leading Slovak male and female literati approached female agency within the discursive fields of education and emancipation vis-à-vis nation-building process. Given the failure of nationalists to reach out towards wider middle classes (meštianstvo) in urban areas and lower nobility (zemianstvo) in the country, their energies were naturally channeled to lower social strata, i.e. mostly the population living in villages. In this regard, the idealization of peasant, folklore culture and Slovak rural milieu was a natural outcome of imagining Slovak nation from bottom up. [109] The following line of inquiry demonstrates how pragmatism, through the practice of needlework, affected gender relations, enforced inter-regional relations, and brought the national cause to a new supranational level.

Although the participation of working class women in the process of Slovak National Revival might not have been immediately recognized due to the paucity of studies, over time the contribution of these women was crucial. Let us just mention Slovak cultural heritage inherent in the knowledge of hundreds of songs, stories, ballads, lullabies, riddles, and proverbs that women provided to such famous collectors of folk oral heritage as Pavol Jozef Šafárik or Ján Kolár.[110] Whereas vernacular "involves people negotiating with one another by drawing on the practices of the past as a means of addressing the present," folk culture "stands in contrast at every level with the construction of official culture."[111] The unique colors and patterns of regional needlework became a truly mobilizing venture with unprecedented consequences resulting in national unification on all societal levels and spheres. Mary B. Kelly who examined embroideries in Eastern Europe noted the huge profusion of design and embroidered fabric in all Eastern Europe in the nineteenth and twentieth centuries as a result of increased economic opportunities.[112]

Marína Ormisová-Maliaková, a prominent Slovak female intellectual, picked up dress-making as a vocation related to nationalist work.[113] Her sewing courses could be readily called national agitation courses as she encouraged political and cultural discussions, singing of national songs, and the recitation of Slovak poems while keeping female hands busy with

109 Pichler, Národovci, 104.

110 On how folkloristic thinking has encouraged nationalism see Roger D. Abrahams, Phantoms of Romantic Nationalism in Folkloristics, in: The Journal of American Folklore, 106/ 419, Winter 1993, 3-37.

111 Abrahams, Phantoms, 6.

112 Marry B. Kelly, Embroidering The Goddesses of Slovakia. A Handbook of Patterns and commentary on their history and usage, Denver 1995, 5.

113 Weber, Feminism, 53.

work. Clearly, pragmatism was not only the most efficient means of extensive female mobilization but it had a profound impact on national, cultural, and even economic mobilization of the nation as such. Štefana Votrubová's Živena jej Osudy a Práca (Živena, her Fate and Work) published in 1931 is a precious account of needlework's importance. Turkische Vorhange, Altdeutsche Betdecken, Arabische Kopfhauben, Bulgarische Schurzen, Chinese Arbeit were names flavored with hints of orientalism frequently attached to Slovak needlework in order to attract buyers in major European town markets.[114] No wonder that such an obvious "stealing" of national artwork attracted Živena's attention. In order to reclaim its own name, Živena worked out a plan to organize an exhibition of Slovak needlework. The exhibition, however, was postponed until 1885 due to the outbreak of the cholera and disastrous reactionary backlash of monarchic policy. Despite the delay, the event was carefully prepared with help of Prague colleagues who shared their experiences of organizing a similar venue. The scale of advertising, preparations and public interest in the event from all corners of "Felvidek"(northern part of Habsburg monarchy, today's Slovakia) greatly surpassed the expectations of its organizers. The exhibition was opened from August to September 3, 1885 in Turčiansky Svätý Martin and surprised its visitors by the richness of techniques, wide range of color schemes, and high artistic value. One thousand and six hundred needle work artifacts, besides the number of photographs, drawings and pattern diagrams for needle work, were collected and displayed.[115] Catholic and Evangelic Masses were served on the opening day. Jozef Miloslav Hurban preached from the pulpit: "The nation whose women can create such a beautiful art work cannot die!"[116] The exhibition sent two important messages. Firstly, it increased the demand for Slovak needlework which was on a par with its popular application on garments and household decorative objects. This was certainly essential not only to the process of self-identification of the community but also to the process of understanding of key role of female agency by contemporaries. Secondly, the positive reviews of the exhibition in the foreign press transformed its success into an ideological message of Slavic solidarity among Czechs, Serbs, and Croats.[117] The widespread popular application of needlework motifs on garments or in households increased the demand for quality work and therefore helped to accumulate financial capital. Money earned through the exhibition was reinvested in such social and cultural venues as the publication of books, support of women in need, and preparations to establish a one-year domestic-economic school for women. Some exhibitors were awarded with honor diplomas and Živena's Exhibition Committee, consisting of eight

114 Votrubová, Živena, 20.
115 Ibid., 30.
116 Ibid., 32.
117 Ibid.

male members and sixty (!) additional members from all around Slovak milieu, decided to provide financial donations to poor needle workers. The basis for a precious collection of needlework and an international exchange of needlework art was established.

There is no doubt that by this time all social classes of women were mobilized. The element of pragmatism linked to the national cause put women in a new light. Needlework's close link to the traditional ideal of domesticity helped to sooth the friction over passive female that was to be seen but not heard and "active" female's actual presence in public sphere. Needlework bridged both perceptions into a notion of active female contributing to national cause safely contained within the realm of their households.

Conclusion

The anxieties and tensions that accompanied female agency often pertain to contemporary polemics about "the old" and "the new," feudal and capitalist, traditional and modern, and also Christian and anti-Christian. My effort was to highlight the complexity and various dimensions that accompany the issue of female agency vis-à-vis nationalism. We have seen earnest efforts to mobilize women for the national cause as well as various interpretations and views of female agency. The connotations linked to the notion of active female contributing to national cause in the nineteenth century Slovak milieu differ from the expectation of the twentieth century audience. What we nowadays understand as active female contributing to the nationalist cause was in nineteenth century an unacceptable notion. General expectations dictated containment of female agency within their households. Although crossing the threshold of the household into public sphere was no taboo, yet in the public sphere the notion of women "seen rather than heard" was accepted norm of traditional patriarchal society. Similarly as an unreachable apotheosized female construct has made demands upon men, the new female stereotype of cultured mother challenged traditional society due to a very proximity of female in public sphere. Yet, as we could see, the presence of women in public sphere is indicative of something more than merely a "passive agency." The leading political echelons of Slovak nationalists consciously acknowledged the need to incorporate women in the process of nation-formation and realized that it was the lack of education that hindered the attainment of this goal. Prominent female intellectuals approved traditional patriarchal norms which, in their view, embraced the strength of Slovak nation. At the same time they agitated for availability of higher education to women in order to widen their spiritual horizons. By doing so, they not only implicitly blurred the boundaries between what was seen to be passive and active female but unwillingly helped to create the cracks in the traditional patriarchal hierarchy.

Although Slovak awakeners' reaction to the female contribution to the national cause was often ambivalent, overall Štúr's generation of male patriots did respect women's efforts. As Jana Juráňová rightly claims Slovak patriots' acceptance of female writers such as Vansová, Šoltésova, Podjavorinská did not always run smoothly. These women oftentimes transgressed against disciplining of female agency by entering the public debates under the names of their husbands, (Terézia Vansová), fathers (Maróthy-Šoltésová) or pseudonyms (Božena Slánčiková Timravá).[118] Yet, as Juráňová concludes, the Slovak nationalists' acceptance of female "was desirable and relatively positive."[119]

Overall, the presented research questioned the recent production of simplified gendered victimization rhetoric for political purposes. It revealed a complex gendered terrain of the nineteenth century national turmoil and pointed to the problems that certainly deserve more attention of scholars in Central European milieu.

118 Cviková, Po boku muža, 10.

119 Jana Juráňová, Hľadanie stratenej autorky. Témy, motívy a osudy próz Hany Gregorovej, in: ASPEKTin-feministický webzin, Februray 14, 2005. http://www.aspekt.sk/aspekt_in.php?content=clanok&rubrika=18&IDclanok=194, 27.8. 2008.

Richard Lein
(University of Vienna)

The "betrayal" of the k.u.k. Infantry regiment 28.

Truth or legend?

In his well-known play "The last days of Mankind", which is dealing with Austria-Hungary in World War One, the famous Austrian writer Karl Kraus let one of his Characters say: "When a soldier at the front fails to do his duty, you can be sure he is of Czech nationality".[1] This statement, however, doesn't express the authors own point of view, but merely shows us the public opinion in the newly erected Austrian Republic after the end of World War One. Back in these days many people in Austria and Germany thought that the majority of the Slavs belonging to the imperial and royal monarchy had not only openly questioned the aims of the war from the first day on, but had also weakened the Austro-Hungarian army severely by not showing proper resistance in combat and had therefore contributed to the military collapse of the Central Powers in October 1918. These accusations were not entirely new, since even before the war many people, including members of the Austro-Hungarian High Command, had harboured the fear the deployment of Czech troops against Russia or Serbia, which were the potential enemies of the Habsburg monarchy in the upcoming conflict, could endanger the entire k.u.k. Army. These fears had resulted from several incidents with units dominated by Czechs, Ruthens and Serbs, which had occurred since the beginning of the 20th century. In most cases the soldiers of these regiments had joined radical political movements, revolted against their commanders, participated in protest marches or openly expressed the wish not to fight against their "Slavic brothers" (meaning the Russians or the Serbs) in a future war.[2] These worries were,

---

1 In the original German Version: „Wenn ein Soldat seinen Pflichten als Vaterlandsverteidiger nicht nachkommt, so ist es immer ein Tscheche!", Karl Kraus, Die letzten Tage der Menschheit. Tragödie in fünf Akten mit Vorspiel und Epilog. Suhrkamp- Taschenbuch 1320, Frankfurt am Main 1986, 622.

2 Richard Plaschka, Zur Vorgeschichte des Überganges von Einheiten des Infanterieregiments Nr. 28 an der russischen Front 1915, in: Hugo Hantsch (Hg.), Österreich und Europa – Festgabe für Hugo Hantsch zum 70. Geburtstag, Graz/Wien/Köln 1962, 455-464, here: 458; Richard Lein, Das militärische Verhalten der Tschechen im Ersten Weltkrieg, Wien 2009, 55-60; Johann C. Allmayer-Beck, Die bewaffnete Macht in Staat

however, quickly dispelled, when in August 1914 the k.u.k. army was being mobilized without any severe problems and the Czech troops were willingly marching into battle for emperor and fatherland.[3]

It was only in mid-April 1915 during the battle in the Carpathians, when the k.u.k. High Command received the message that the whole k.u.k. Infantry Regiment [IR] 28, which had originally been garrisoned in Prague and consisted to 98% of Czechs[4], had not only failed to do its duty during a Russian attack near the Hungarian town Bartfá (today Bardejov), but had been nearly wiped out by the enemy. Some time later it was even alleged that the whole regiment, including nearly all soldiers and most its non-coms and officers, had not only surrendered, but literally deserted to the enemy without having fired at least a single shot.[5] The High Command reacted quite quickly and disbanded the IR 28 without any further delay, an act of state, which was later even confirmed by Emperor Franz Josef I.[6] This incident, which was from a military point of view insignificant, nevertheless fostered in the k.u.k. Army as well as in the German part of the Austro-Hungarian population sore feelings against the Czechs, although the majority of them continued to do their duty in the armed forces and in the factories at home.[7] The atmosphere became even worse when until summer 1915 three other Czech-dominated units either collapsed or fled the battlefield during enemy attacks.[8] Although even the High Command could not find any proof for disloyal behaviour of these regiments, the majority of the people in the Austro-Hungarian Empire now looked upon the Czechs as traitors and blamed them for the severe military setbacks of the Central Powers on the Russian front.

Even before the end of the war the "betrayal" of the IR 28 was openly discussed by the public and was also used by Pan-German circles within the Habsburg Monarchy as well as by Czech nationalist leaders, who had

---

und Gesellschaft, in: Adam Wandruszka – Peter Urbanitsch (Hgg.), Die Habsburgermonarchie, 1848–1918, vol. 5, Die bewaffnete Macht, Wien 1987, 1-141, here 115-116.

3 Manfried Rauchensteiner, Der Tod des Doppeladlers. Österreich-Ungarn und der Erste Weltkrieg, Graz/Wien/Köln [2]1994, 104-106.

4 Maximilian Ehnl, Ergänzungsheft 9 zum Werke Österreich-Ungarns letzter Krieg. Die Österreichisch- Ungarische Landmacht nach Aufbau, Gliederung, Friedensgarnison, Einteilung und nationaler Zusammensetzung im Sommer 1914, Wien 1934, 22.

5 Bericht III. Korps [Kps] an k.u.k. 3. Armee, III. Korps Op. 359/32, 1915 April 8, Österreichisches Staatsarchiv Wien [ÖStA Wien]/Kriegsarchiv [KA]/Neue Feldakten [NFA]/III. Kps.

6 Allerhöchster Befehl zur Auflösung des IR 28, Militärkanzlei Seiner Majestät [MKSM] 69/6/14/1 ex 1915, 17. April 1915, ÖStA Wien/KA/MKSM.

7 Jan Křen, Tschechen und Deutsche 1780 – 1980, München [2]2000, 337-345;

8 Christian Reiter, Der Untergang des IR 36. Der „Verrat" der tschechischen Soldaten im Gefecht bei Sieniewa 1915, Wien 2008.

fled Austria at the beginning of the war, for their political aims. The German nationalists claimed to have found the ultimate proof for the disloyal behaviour of the Czechs living within the Austro-Hungarian Monarchy, who, in their opinion, could therefore no longer be trusted.[9] The exiled Czech leaders, on the other hand, praised the soldiers of the IR 28 as heroes, who had deserted the Austro-Hungarian army in order to fight with the Russians for the liberation of the Czech nation and for the foundation of an independent Czechoslovak state after the war.[10] Both versions of the events around the battle of April 3, 1915 found their way into national historiography on both the Czech and the Austrian/German side and still dominate popular works and manuals. It was, however, the post-war Austrian Republic, where the case of the IR 28 was remembered with great bitterness for a long time as an example for the treacherous behaviour of the Czech nation during the war, which was supposed to have ultimately led to the defeat and the destruction of the Habsburg monarchy.[11] In Czechoslovakia, on the other hand, the "betrayal" of the IR 28 was also well remembered by the people[12], but the event never became as important to the nation and the official historiography as the famous battle of Zborów.[13] Nevertheless the event was soon glorified by artists and writers, many streets throughout the country were renamed "Dvacátého osmého pluku"[14] (28th Regiment) and an infantry regiment of the Czechoslovak army, which was garrisoned in Prague, bore again the number 28.[15] Hardly anybody on the Austrian or the Czech side was interested in the fact that the collapse of the regiment had not been caused by a betrayal of its soldiers, but by fatal strategy errors of the officers in command, who had later let the unit take the blame for their own mistakes. Fortunately, there is an extensive and complete dossier of files on the case of the IR 28 in the War Archives in Vienna and Prague, enabling us to shed more light on the battle in question than it was done until today in Czech, German and Austrian historiography.

9 Deutschnationale Geschäftsstelle (Hg.), Das Verhalten der Tschechen im Weltkrieg. Die Anfrage der Abg. Dr. Schürff, Goll, Hartl, Knirsch, Dr. v. Langhan und K.H. Wolf im österreichischen Abgeordnetenhause, Wien 1918.

10 Edvard Beneš, Bohemia's Case for Independence, London 1917.

11 Zur versuchten Ehrenrettung des ehem. IR 28, Österreichische Wehrzeitung, 1926 June 11, 4.

12 Vladimir Klecanda, Slovenský Zborov, Praha 1934.

13 Jan Galandauer, 2.7.1917 Bitva u Zborova. Česká Legenda, Praha 2002; Vladimír Klecanda, Bitva u Zborova, Praha 1927; Lein, Verhalten, 221-374.

14 A street by name „Dvacátého osmého pluku" can still be found in Prague.

15 Martin Zückert, Zwischen Nationsidee und staatlicher Realität. Die tschechoslowakische Armee und ihre Nationalitätenpolitik 1918-1938, München 2006, 88.

The cause of events until spring 1915

In summer 1914 many officers and soldiers of the great Austro-Hungarian army believed that it would take them only a few weeks to crush the Russian forces and that a peace treaty would be signed even before Christmas. This assumption was, however, wrong, since the k.u.k. High Command had not only underestimated the enemy's strength, but had also failed to prepare its own army for modern warfare properly. Instead of realizing that the introduction of machine guns and rapid firing field artillery had changed the situation on the battlefield completely, many commanding officers of the k.u.k. armed forces still believed in the battle tactics of the 19th century, which were hopelessly outdated.[16] The Russian army, on the other hand, had gained vast experience from its defeat in the Russo-Japanese war of 1904-1905 and had therefore been able to properly prepare its troops for the war to come.[17] Needless to say, the first battles in Eastern Galicia in summer 1914 ended in a disaster for the Austro-Hungarian army. While the Russians knew exactly how to make use of rapid-firing artillery and machine guns, the k.u.k. soldiers were attacking the enemy lines in a way which reminded observers of the battles of the first crusade in the middle ages. As a consequence of this, the Austro-Hungarian forces suffered severe losses and, although a great victory was achieved in the battle of Komarów, were forced to withdraw to the west, letting big territories fall into the enemy's hands.[18] The retreat was only halted on the Galician-Hungarian border, where the badly beaten k.u.k. army set up a new line of defence in the Carpathian Mountains. Here the High Command planed to halt the Russian assault until a counteroffensive could be launched by the united armies of Germany and Austria. Unfortunately, the German forces didn't arrive on time, so the Austro-Hungarian troops were forced to hold their position in the mountains during the entire winter. Since the soldiers had neither been trained for alpine combat nor been equipped for the harsh weather conditions, the units suffered further critical casualties. Until January 1st 1915 the k.u.k. army on the eastern front, which had originally consisted of 1.2 million officers, non-coms and men, had lost 994.883 soldiers due to death, injury, capture and sickness and was practically no longer operational.[19] At the same time the Russian army, which had also sustained severe losses, but still had enough reserves to keep its troops operational,

16 Walter Wagner, Die k.(u.)k. Armee – Gliederung und Aufgabenstellung, in: Wandruszka/Urbanitsch (Eds.), Habsburgermonarchie, vol. 5, 142-633, here 606-628.

17 Johann C. Allmayer-Beck, Bewaffnete Macht, in: Wandruszka/Urbanitsch (Eds.), Habsburgermonarchie, vol. 5, 1-141, here 134.

18 Österreichisches Bundesministerium für Heerwesen – Kriegsarchiv Wien [BMHW/KA] (Eds.), Österreich-Ungarns letzter Krieg 1914 – 1918 [ÖUlK], 7 vols., Wien 1930-1938, vol. 1, 155-598.

19 BMHW/KA (Hgg.), ÖUlK, vol. 2, supplement 1, table 3.

prepared for a new offensive to finally break through the Austro-Hungarian frontline and to open the way towards the Hungarian capital Budapest.

The IR 28 itself, which had consisted of 2.952 officers and men at the beginning of the war[20], was as well mobilized in August 1914 and subsequently participated in most of the battles in eastern Galicia, including the victorious battle of Komarów.[21] In this time the unit, which belonged to the k.u.k. 4th army, was never suspected of nationally motivated disorderly conduct, but was, on the contrary, repeatedly commended by the k.u.k. High Command. During these battles, however, most of the regiment's well trained officers and man were slain, wounded or captured, which caused the IR 28 to lose most of its combat strength over the course of only four months. The greatest casualties were sustained in the three-day battle of Limanowa-Łapanów, during which the unit lost more than two thirds of its men and consisted only of 15 officers and 193 soldiers after the fighting had ended.[22] These losses had to be made up with replacement battalions[23], which consisted of about 700 recruits, trained by the regiment's home garrison stationed in Prague, and were sent to the front every month. These replacements, however, had in most cases received only eight weeks of training, were therefore inexperienced and sometimes didn't even know how to handle a rifle properly.[24] Due to this fact, although the IR 28 received replacement battalions on a regular basis, the unit's combat strength remained quite low. Despite this fact the IR 28 could not be pulled out of the front, since in March 1915 the k.u.k. High Command prepared to launch a major offensive in the sector of the k.u.k. 3rd and 4th army. The objective of this operation was to liberate the garrison of the Austro-Hungarian fortress Przemysl, which was situated near the river San, 80 kilometres behind the frontline, and which had been under siege by the Russian army since autumn 1914. To rescue the more than 100.000 soldiers, who had been left behind in the fortress, the k.u.k. armies were now ordered to break through the Russian defences near the town Gorlice and advance on Przemysl at any cost.[25] The IR 28, which was at that time part of the k.u.k. 3rd infantry division of the k.u.k. 4th army, also had to participate in the offensive, where the regiment, again, fought with great courage, but at

20 Frührapport der 3. Infanterie-Truppendivision [ITD], 16. August 1914, ÖStA/KA/NFA/3. ITD.

21 IR 28. Tagebuch ab 25. Juli 1914 [Tagebuch], 14-15., Vojenský ústřední archiv Praha [VUA Praha], Fond Vojsková tělesa – Pěší pluk 28,

22 Frührapport der 3. ITD, 1914 December 13, ÖStA Wien/KA/NFA/3. ITD.

23 In the original German version: „Marschbataillone".

24 Ludwig Vogelsang, Das steirische Infanterieregiment Nr. 47 im Weltkrieg, 2 vols., Graz 1932, vol. 1, 218; Viktor Dankl, Mehr Klarheit und Wahrheit, Der Österreicher, 1937 February 12, 5.

25 Rauchensteiner, Tod des Doppeladlers, 204-205.

the same time suffered further losses. The severest casualties were sustained by the unit on March 18, when the 3rd battalion of the IR 28 participated in the final assault against the Russian lines of defence near the town Sękowa. Major Julius Meergans, the adjutant of the regiment, later reported to headquarters about the outcome of the attack:

> "At 5am we received the order to advance on the enemy's position. Unfortunately we were soon discovered by the Russians, who stated shooting on us from all sides. After having suffered extreme losses, the 3rd battalion reached the graveyard of the town, but was not able to gain any additional ground. During the day the men had to take cover in the snow while they were being fired upon by the enemy artillery. Due to the hopeless situation, the command finally decided to order the retreat of the unit after sunset. On the 18th of March the regiment sustained severe casualties, approximately 100 soldiers were killed, 270 wounded."[26]

Despite all efforts, the offensive, which had, cost the Austro-Hungarian army thousands of officers and men, had to be stopped some days later[27], which forced the starving garrison of Przemysl to surrender on the 22nd of March 1915.[28] After these battles, the command of the k.u.k. 4th army ordered the IR 28 to be pulled out of the frontline and sent to the hinterland for recreation. This step had become necessary, since the regiment had lost 680 officers and men in the past two weeks[29] and was virtually no longer operational. Therefore the unit was being transferred to the town Grodek some kilometres behind the front, where it was supposed to get some rest and to be joined by its 8th replacement battalion, which was expected to arrive in the hinterland anytime soon. On the 23rd of March 1915 the IR 28 was, however, suddenly transferred from Grodek to the town Bartfá, 50 kilometres to the south of the unit's original position.[30] There, in the sector of the k.u.k. 28th infantry division, which was part of the k.u.k. 3rd army, the enemy had managed to break through the lines of the Austro-Hungarian forces some days before. During their retreat the troops of the 28th infantry division had been forced to abandon some key positions on top of a mountain range, which had subsequently fallen into enemy hands.[31] Since the defence of these mountains was vital to the stability of the entire

26 Tagebuch, 108-109, VUA Praha, Fond Vojsková tělesa – Pěší pluk 28.

27 Rauchensteiner, Tod des Doppeladlers, 204-205; BMHW/KA (Hgg.), ÖUlK, II, 141-201.

28 BMHW/KA (Hgg.), ÖUlK, II, 216.

29 IR 28, Namentliche Verlustliste Nr. 1-62 für den Zeitraum 1.März – 31. April 1915, k.u.k. Kriegsministerium [KM], ohne Zahl, ÖStA Wien/KA/KM/Verlustlisten.

30 Tagebuch, 112-113, VUA Praha, Fond Vojsková tělesa – Pěší pluk 28.

31 Meldung 28. ITD an III. Korps, 28. ITD Op. 259/9, 1915 March 25, ÖStA/KA/NFA/28. ITD.

frontline in this sector, the Austro-Hungarian High Command ordered the k.u.k. IIIrd corps to carry out a counterattack and take back these positions as soon as possible. For this purpose the 28th infantry division was reinforced with four additional infantry units (including the IR 28), which were supposed to advance on the Russian’s position in the morning of the 27th of March and to take back the mountain range within two days.[32]

The situation before the battle

The Austro-Hungarian counteroffensive in this sector, although the k.u.k. High Command failed to realize it, had all along only limited chances of success. The reason for that was basically the fact that the enemy forces stationed on the mountain range northeast of Bartfá were much stronger than the k.u.k. forces in that sector. Most of these troops had some weeks ago still besieged Przemysl and had afterwards been transferred to various sectors the front. These reinforcements had subsequently increased the pressure on the Austro-Hungarian frontline severely, in the sector of the k.u.k. 28th infantry division, as was pointed out before, with catastrophic effects.[33] The k.u.k. High Command was, unfortunately, not aware of these facts, which is why it ordered the troops of the 28th infantry division to launch an attack against a well-defended enemy of superior strength.[34] Over and above that the weather conditions, which had already been unpleasant during the entire month, worsened shortly after the preparations for the offensive had begun. The temperature suddenly dropped below minus 20 degrees Celsius and heavy snowstorms set in, which soon covered the entire landscape, including all streets and paths, under three meters of snow. The commanding officers of the k.u.k. IIIrd corps knew very well how critical the situation had become since the troops of the 28th infantry division informed them on a regular basis about the harsh weather conditions and their soldier’s deteriorating strength. Some days before the operation started, the commanding officer of the IR 97 described the situation of his unit as follows:

> “The men, who are on guard duty every day and night, are no longer capable of reinforcing our trenches or doing any other kind of work, since they have become so weak that they are barely able to stand upright. The heavy snowstorms of the last days have com-

32 Befehl des Kommandos III. Kps an 28. ITD betr. die Durchführung des Gegenangriffs, 28. ITD Op. 260/19, 1915 March 26, ÖStA Wien/KA/NFA/28. ITD.

33 Vogelsang, IR 47, 218-224.

34 Meldung 8. ITD an 28. ITD betreffend die aktuelle Feindlage, 28. ITD Op. 261/9, 1915 March 27, ÖStA Wien/KA/NFA/28. ITD.

> pletely covered all trenches and bunkers, which is why the soldiers had to use their remaining strength to clear them out. During every snowstorm some men are freezing to death since our small stoves are useless under these extreme weather conditions. It is so cold that the fabric of the uniforms becomes solid like wood and breaks when it is being touched. It is therefore my duty to inform you that if nothing is done to improve the situation, the fighting strength of my unit is going to deteriorate severely!"[35]

Against the backdrop of these facts was evident that it would be very difficult for the k.u.k. troops to move on the battlefield and to climb the ice-covered slopes of the mountain range. Despite all this the k.u.k. High Commando decided to launch the offensive at any cost, since it seemed to be the only way to prevent a Russian breakthrough in that sector. The commanding officers furthermore hoped that if they were able to surprise the enemy, the Russian forces would not have the chance to react quickly enough and play the trump cart of their superior strength.[36] Therefore the commanding officers of the 28th infantry division, including the Commander of the IR 28, received the order to prepare their men for battle and to launch the attack according to plan in the morning of the 27th of March 1915.[37] One day before the offensive started, the 8th replacement battalion of the IR 28 finally arrived in Bartfá and joined the regiment at the frontline.[38] Unfortunately, as the officers, who had guided the transport, pointed out, the replacements had only received five instead of eight weeks of training. What is more, most of the recruits were lacking winter equipment and had, due to ammunition shortages, never fired a rifle before.[39] Although these soldiers were not really fit for combat, the commander of the Regiment, Lieutenant Colonel Florian Schaumaier, nevertheless decided to take them into battle in order to strengthen his unit and to raise the operation's chances of success.

The Austro-Hungarian counteroffensive

When the attack began in the morning of the 27th of March, the IR 28 advanced as planed on the Russian positions east of the small town Eszteb-

35 Lagebericht des IR 97 an das Kommando der 55. Infanteriebrigade [IBrig], 28. ITD Op. Nr. 248/6 Beilage 2, 1915 March 13, ÖStA Wien/KA/NFA/28. ITD.

36 Meldung 8. ITD an 28. ITD betreffend die aktuelle Feindlage, 28. ITD Op. 261/9, 1915 March 27, ÖStA Wien/KA/NFA/28. ITD.

37 Befehl des Kommandos III. Kps an 28. ITD betr. die Durchführung des Gegenangriffs, 28. ITD Op. 260/19, 1915 March 26, ÖStA Wien/KA/NFA/28. ITD.

38 Tagebuch, 115, VUA, Fond Vojsková tělesa – Pěší pluk 28.

39 Rauchensteiner, Tod des Doppeladlers, 206.

nekhuta (today Stebnícka Huta). The town itself lay in a valley surrounded by mountains[40], which had only one exit southwest of the mountain range. The other units of the 28th infantry division, which had also begun their advance early in the morning, closed in on the mountain range as well and stared to climb up towards the crest. During the first three hours, the operation seemed to go according to plan, but soon the Austro-Hungarian units met heavy resistance by strong Russian forces, which had dug in on top of the mountains.[41] Although the attack was carried out several times that day, the k.u.k. troops were not able to break through the Russian lines of defence at any point of the sector. Finally, in the late afternoon, the units were ordered to stop their attacks and to dig in close to the enemy lines. Owing to this order the IR 28 came in a quite unfavourable situation, since two thirds of its troops were now standing on the slopes of the mountain range near Esztebnekhuta, while its left flank and the valley's exit were only being protected by four companies of infantry.[42] In the face of this situation the commanding officers of the regiment feared that the enemy, if he succeeded in crushing the unit's left flank in the course of a surprise attack, could easily surround large parts of the IR 28 in the valley, which, due to their position on the slope, wouldn't be able to defend themselves properly. Lieutenant Colonel Schaumaier informed the command of the IIIrd corps division about his concerns, which, nevertheless, didn't allow him to transfer his troops to a position easier to defend, since it had already decided to resume the operation the following day.[43]

Due to the fact that the Austro-Hungarian troops hadn't been able to take back the mountain range on the first day of the offensive, it would have been the best choice to drop the entire operation. In the evening of March 27 the commanding officers of the 28th infantry division must have realized that the Russian forces were much stronger than they had expected, which greatly limited the offensive's chances of success. What is more, the enemy commanders were now on full alert and were expected to bring in additional troops in order to strengthen their positions on top of the mountain range. Despite these circumstances the command of the k.u.k. IIIrd corps decided to resume the offensive the following day, but at the

40 Skizze „ Angriffsgruppierung 28. März vormittags", 28. ITD Op. 262/11, 1915 March 28, ÖStA Wien/KA/NFA/28. ITD.

41 Gefechtsbericht der k.u.k. 56. IBrig über die Ereignisse vom 27. März – 2. April 1915, 1-2, ÖStA Wien/KA/GB/56. IBrig; Berichte des III. Kps über den Fortschritt des Angriffs am 27. März, III. Kps, 1915 March 27, ÖStA Wien/KA/NFA/III. Kps.

42 Skizze „ Angriffsgruppierung 28. März vormittags", 28. ITD Op. 262/11, 1915 March 28, ÖStA Wien/KA/NFA/28. ITD.

43 Befehl Kommando III. Kps an 28. ITD betreffend die Fortsetzung des Gegenangriffs am 28. März, 28. ITD Op. 261/27, 1915 March 27, ÖStA Wien/KA/NFA/28. ITD

same time slightly changed the battle plan. The troops, which had attacked along a wide front the day before, were now ordered to start coordinated attacks on two key positions of the Russian defences in the morning of the 28th of March.[44] By that way the commanding officers hoped to outnumber the enemy forces at these points and to achieve the desired breakthrough.[45] This plan, which was in fact carried out the next day, nevertheless wasn't successful, since the hilly landscape and several breakdowns of the field telephone system reduced the communication between the troops of the 28th infantry division to a minimum and so made coordinated attacks almost impossible.[46] These difficulties were also experienced by one battalion of the IR 28, which was supposed to carry out an attack against a mountain designated "elevation 794" near Esztebnekhuta together with a Tyrolean infantry regiment. An officer of the unit later reported to headquarters:

> "Detailed situation of the battalion of the IR 28, which is supposed to attack in the direction of elevation 794: One company attacking together with Tyrolean infantry regiment No. 4, one company advancing from Esztebnekhuta in the direction of elevation 794. The remaining two companies appear to have gotten lost in the woods near Esztebnekhuta; we are currently searching for them."[47]

Although the two companies were shortly afterwards found nearby in the woods, the attack on the key position of the mountain range could not be carried out as planned. Since the advances on the other crucial positions in the sector failed as well, the second day of the offensive ended without any positive results for the Austro-Hungarian forces. In the evening of March 28 it finally became clear to the commanding officers of the 28th infantry division that the offensive was hopelessly stuck, since the k.u.k. troops were obviously not strong enough to advance any further. The Russians, on the other hand, had strengthened their positions on top of the mountain range and were now able to repeal all attacks launched by the Austro-Hungarian forces. Despite these facts the command of the k.u.k. IIIrd corps still wasn't willing to drop the offensive and ordered to continue the operation on the 29th of March.[48] This order was, however, not car-

44 Tagebuch, 115-116, VUA, Fond Vojsková tělesa – Pěší pluk 28.

45 Befehl 28. ITDs an 55. und 56. IBrig betr. die Fortsetzung des Gegenangriffs am 28. März, 28. ITD Op. 262/1, 1915 March 28, ÖStA/KA/NFA/28. ITD.

46 Gefechtsbericht der k.u.k. 56. IBrig über die Ereignisse vom 27. März – 2. April 1915, 3-6, ÖStA Wien/KA/GB/56. IBrig.

47 Meldung 55. IBrigKdo an 28. ITD, 28. ITD Op. 262/17, 1915 March 28, ÖStA Wien/KA/NFA/28. ITD.

48 Meldung III. KpsKdo an 28. ITD betreffend die Fortsetzung der Offensive am 29. März, 28. ITD Op. 262/31, 1915 March 28, ÖStA Wien/KA/NFA/28. ITD.

ried out by the k.u.k. units, since their commanders not only openly criticized the command's decision, but also declared their refusal to launch any further attacks. In most cases the officers informed their superiors about the overwhelming strength of the enemy forces, the bad weather conditions and the critical situation of their troops, which is why most of them stated that it would be suicidal to resume the operation. Some officers even declared that they were no longer willing to bear the responsibility for the outcome of the operation[49], which greatly enraged their superiors. Despite the High Command's lack of understanding, the Austro-Hungarian forces were, indeed, in a critical situation. Most of the soldiers, who had been on combat duty for more than two days, were lying freezing in the snow while it was nearly impossible to supply them properly. In case of the IR 28 the situation was even worse since the unit's field kitchens hadn't yet arrived in Bartfá, so the regiment had to be supplied with food by other troops.[50] Due to the fact that it took a long time to get the supplies to the valley near Esztebnekhuta, the food often arrived there in frozen condition, so the soldiers, who weren't able to reheat the meals, were starving.

Since it was not possible to reinforce the troops of the 28th infantry division significantly, the general staff of the IIIrd k.u.k. corps finally decided to break off the offensive in the evening of the 30th of March and ordered the units to hold the position they had reached at any cost.[51] Simultaneously the k.u.k. High Command pulled the Tyrolean Infantry regiment No. 4 out of the front since it was planed to use it for an offensive in a different sector of the front.[52] The former position of this unit, which lay on top of a mountain near Esztebnekhuta, now had to be occupied by the IR 28, so the already weakened left flank of the regiment now became even thinner. The commander of the IR 28 protested against this decision since two thirds of his unit were still standing on the sloops of the mountain range in the valley near Esztebnekhuta.[53] Lieutenant Colonel Schaumaier argued that since the offensive had been dropped, it was no longer necessary to keep his troops in such an exposed position and asked the command of the

49 Regimentskommando TJR 3 an 55. IBrig, 55. IBrig Op. ohne Zahl, 1915 March 29, ÖStA/KA/NFA/55. IBrig.

50 Tagebuch, 117, VUA Praha, Fond Vojsková tělesa – Pěší pluk 28.

51 Befehl 28. ITD an 55. und 56. IBrig betreffend die Umgliederung der Truppen, 28. ITD Op. 265/7, 1915 March 31, ÖStA Wien/KA/NFA/28. ITD

52 Situationsmeldung Gruppe Fischer an 55. IBrigKdo, 55. IBrig Op. Ohne Zahl, 1915 March 30, ÖStA Wien/KA/NFA/55. IBrig

53 Gefechtsbericht der k.u.k. 56. IBrig über die Ereignisse vom 3. und 4. April 1915, Supplement 1, ÖStA Wien/KA/GB/56. IBrig

k.u.k. IIIrd corps for the second time permission to withdraw them from the valley, unfortunately without success. Due to this decision most of the regiment's soldiers, starving and freezing, remained concentrated on the slopes of the mountain range, while the regiment's left flank was left almost unprotected. The troops stationed there, three companies of infantry, consisted mainly of the insufficiently trained replacements. They were neither equipped with machine guns nor was their position protected by barbed wire. Even the commander of the 28th infantry division realized that the unit was in immediate danger and asked the k.u.k. IIIrd corps for help, which, unfortunately, didn't take the officer's doubts seriously. The members of the corps' general staff argued that the Russians had never before attacked in such an unfavourable terrain as it could be found around Esztebnekhuta, so they believed that the IR 28 was not in any kind of danger.[54] Needless to say, this assumption was totally wrong.

The battle of Esztebnekhuta

In the morning of the 3rd of April 1915 strong Russian forces suddenly attacked the three companies guarding the IR 28's left flank, overran their position and threw what was left of the units back to the west. Only 50 men of the battalion, including the officer of duty, Captain Kloucek, managed to beat retreat, since the Russians had managed to break through the unit's left flank quickly and so had surrounded most of the Austro-Hungarian soldiers in their trenches. Other soldiers, who had managed to beat retreat on time, had gotten stuck in the snow and had subsquently been slain or captured by the enemy soldiers. The commander of the battalion later reported to Lieutenant Colonel Schaumaier about the cause of events as follows:

> "At 5am in the morning, when I was just inspecting the trenches on our left flank, the men suddenly reported that a large crowd of Russians was gathering near our position. I immediately reinforced my left flank by calling in all available reserves, but it was already too late. The enemy advanced on my position quickly, broke through our lines and immediately flanked and surrounded my men which were still holding out in the trenches. I have to emphasize that the attack didn't take us by surprise, but it was not possible to repulse

54 Befehl III. KpsKdo an 28. ITD, III. Kps Op. 353/2, 1915 April 2, ÖStA Wien/KA/NFA/III. Kps.

an onslaught of at least 2.000 enemy soldiers with only 400 men of our own."[55]

When the left flank of the IR 28 collapsed, the fate of the unit's remaining troops, which were stationed on the slopes of the mountain range near Esztebnekhuta, was ultimately sealed. Immediately after the Russians had succeeded in crushing the regiment's defences further to the north, they started advancing southwards in order to gain control of the valley's exit. When the Austro-Hungarian soldiers realized that they were in immediate danger of being surrounded by the enemy, they started withdrawing chaotically to the west in order to escape. Unfortunately, only a few men managed to get out of the trap, the rest ran right into the arms of the Russian soldiers, who were advancing on their position both from the north and the east.[56] Since there was no other way to get out of this situation alive, most of the k.u.k. soldiers in the valley subsequently surrendered to the enemy.[57] Those men, who managed to get out of this fiasco on time, retreated further to the west, where they were some time later gathered by Lieutenant Colonel Schaumaier. The Russian attack, which was only halted some kilometres further to the west, forced the Austro-Hungarian troops to retreat along a wide front and let all ground that had been gained during the costly two-day offensive fall into enemy hands again.[58] Naturally, the commander of the k.u.k. IIIrd corps was furious and ordered to investigate who was to blame for the disaster, which had nearly led to the collapse of the entire Austro-Hungarian frontline.

Even before the investigations started, the first rumours were spreading that the reason for the major military setback had been the passive attitude of the Czech soldiers of the IR 28, who were supposed to have surrendered or, as some people even suspected, deserted to the enemy without showing any signs of resistance.[59] In fact, on the evening of April 3rd only 120 soldiers of the unit, which had in the morning of the day consisted of 1.800 officers and men, reported back for duty.[60] The great number of soldiers missing in action, who had most likely been captured by the enemy, obvi-

55 Bericht Hptm Kloucek an 55. IBrig, 55. IBrig Op. ohne Zahl, 1915 April 3, ÖStA Wien/KA/NFA/55. IBrig.

56 Tagebuch, 118, VUA Praha, Fond Vojsková tělesa – Pěší pluk 28.

57 Gefechtsbericht der k.u.k. 56. IBrig über die Ereignisse vom 3. und 4. April 1915, 3, ÖStA Wien /KA/GB/56. IBrig.

58 Meldung 28. ITD an III. Kps, III. Kps Op. 354/59, 1915 April 3, ÖStA Wien/KA/NFA/III. Kps.

59 Bericht 28. ITD an III. Korps, 28. ITD, Sammelakt „Affäre IR 28", Res. 314, 1915 April 4, ÖStA Wien/KA/NFA/28. ITD.

60 IR 28, Namentliche Verlustliste Nr. 1-62 für den Zeitraum 1.März bis 31. April 1915, KM, ohne Zahl, ÖStA Wien/KA/KM/Verlustlisten.

ously fuelled the rumours about the betrayal of the Czech troops. Even the commander of the IIIrd k.u.k. corps did not set any measures to clarify the cause of events during the battle, but reported falsely to his superiors that large parts of the IR 28 had deserted to the enemy.[61] It is most likely that the officer knew that this statement was wrong, but since he feared to be held responsible for his own strategy errors, he obviously decided to let the Czech Soldiers take the blame for the military setback. His report, however, greatly enraged the commander of the k.u.k. 3rd Army, General Svetozar Boroević von Bojna, who subsequently asked the High Command permission to disband the IR 28 permanently.[62] The High Command agreed with the General and ordered the disbandment of the regiment on the 14th of April 1915.[63] This order was later even confirmed by Emperor Franz Josef I, who decided to have the unit struck from the register of the Austro-Hungarian army two days later.[64] The regiment's remaining officers and men were shortly afterwards transferred to other, German- or Magyar-dominated units, where they were kept under close surveillance. The IR 28 itself was completely disbanded until the end of April 1915 and – due to its alleged betrayal – never supposed to be re-erected again.

The trials

Although the circumstances of the battle seemed to be quite clear, the k.u.k. High Command nevertheless decided to set up two fact finding committees in order to clarify what had really happened during the battle of Esztebnekhuta and to find out why an insufficiently trained replacement battalion had been sent to the front in the first place. While the investigation of the field court of the 28th infantry division, which was supposed to clarify the cause of events during the battle of April 3, 1915, right from the beginning failed to the testify the assertions made by the commander of the k.u.k. IIIrd corps, the officers in the IR 28's home garrison became more and more suspicious. Especially the commander of the regiment's home garrison, Colonel Karel Krček, who had been reactivated from retirement in August 1914[65], was accused by a former subordinate, Captain Alexander

61 Bericht III. Korps an k.u.k. 3. Armee, k.u.k. Armeeoberkommando [AOK] Op. 8886, 1915 April 5, ÖStA Wien/KA/AOK.

62 K.u.k. 3. Armee an III. Korps, III. Korps, Sammelakt „Affäre IR 28", Res. 652, 1915 April 10, ÖStA Wien/KA/NFA/28. ITD.

63 Bericht AOK an Kriegsministerium, KM-Präs 49/2/1 ex 1915, 1915 April 14, ÖStA Wien/KA/KM-Präs.

64 Allerhöchster Befehl zur Auflösung des IR 28, MKSJ 69/6/14/1 ex 1915, 1915 April 17, ÖStA Wien KA/MKSM.

65 Haupt-Grundbuchblatt Josef Krček, ÖStA Wien/KA/Grundbuchblätter/Diverse.

Bornemisza, for not having kept his officers and men under control. The Captain accused Krček not only of having spent more time with his fellow officers in the wine taverns of Prague than inside the barracks, but also of not having looked after the men's discipline and moral, which had therefore stayed constantly low.[66] Regarding the soldier's discipline Bornemisza further stated in his report to the military court in Temesvár:

> "In the first months of the war the men were obviously of good moral, a condition, which unfortunately subsided rather quickly. Already the second replacement battalion was lacking discipline, a phenomenon that became even stronger during the following months. One time the soldiers were singing "Hrom a peklo, Russ je s námi" [Thunder and hell, the Russians are with us] and could barely be brought to the railway station. In September 1914 the soldiers of two replacement companies, which were supposed to be sent to the front the next day, were repeatedly disturbing a farewell speech held by Colonel Krček. Not only did they verbally assault the Colonel, they even threw beer glasses at him, but failed to hit. The following day, while the men were marching to the railway station, they suddenly dropped their rifles and ran away into the streets of the city. It took the police hours to bring all soldiers back, against some of them force had to be used. When the train finally departed the station, some of the men were calling out "Dolu, Hejtman Bornemisza" [Down with Captain Bornemisza!] and two shots were fired. Colonel Krček declared that the noise hadn't been caused by rifles, but by fireworks and immediately after that went to the nearest beer hall."[67]

Bornemisza also alleged that not only the Colonel and his officers, but also the replacements had been constantly drunk and had on top of that had frequently left the barracks without permission. What is more, the Colonel was supposed not to have reported these incidents to the Military Command of Prague since he allegedly had feared to lose his position as commander of the regiment's home garrison. The Captain further stated that even after the home garrison of the IR 28 had been transferred from Prague to Szeged, Krček and his fellow officers had continued their pleasant lifestyle and had had wagons of food and beer brought from Prague to their new post.[68] Bornemisza also criticised the Colonel's decision to make a young Lieutenant named Matejka, who had been a well-known alcoholic,

66 Protokoll aufgenommen mit Hptm Bornemisza über Zustände im IR 28, 1, KM-Präs 49/2/4 ex 1915, 1915 April 22, ÖStA Wien/KA/KM-Präs.

67 Protokoll aufgenommen mit Hptm Bornemisza über Zustände im IR 28, 2-3, KM-Präs 49/2/4 ex 1915, 1915 April 22, ÖStA Wien/KA/KM-Präs.

68 Protokoll aufgenommen mit Hptm Bornemisza über Zustände im IR 28, 3, KM-Präs 49/2/4 ex 1915, 1915 April 22, ÖStA Wien/KA/KM-Präs.

commander of the last replacement transport. He even alleged that the officer in question had had to be carried out of taverns repeatedly during the battalion's journey to the front and had therefore been unable to further train or discipline his men. Due to these circumstances, as Bornemisza concluded, the soldiers of the IR 28's last marching battalion hand not only been poorly trained, but had also been of bad moral, which had later led to the collapse of the unit during the battle of April 3.

Based on this report, the military court pressed charges against Colonel Krček, who, as it could be expected, repudiated Bornemisza's accusations. Surprisingly the Colonel admitted the fact that he and his fellow officers had indeed ordered more than 6.000 litres of beer for the officers' mess in Szeged every month, but at the same time denied that he had organized drinking sessions on a regular basis.[69] Krček further stated that the IR 28's last replacement battalion had in fact been poorly trained, but blamed the lack of time, material and ammunition for the resulting flaws. These statements were for the most part confirmed by other high-ranking officers, who were questioned by the court some time late. Nearly all of them denied the accusations of Bornemisza and declared that the Captain was a slawophobe person, who had always wanted to damage the reputation of the Czech soldiers.[70] Colonel Krček was in most cases described as an officer who had done his best to fulfil his duty, but was far too old to cope with the difficulties that had occurred since the beginning of the war.[71] Some commanders even confirmed the fact that the lack of experience of the IR 28's last replacement battalion had been the result of ammunition shortages and a too short amount of time for training, two facts the Colonel could not be blamed for by the court. For that reason it would have been logical to acquit Krček of all charges. On the other hand it was obvious that the Colonel didn't have the physical and mental power to stay at his post as commander of the IR 28's home garrison any longer, which is why a more or less "creative" solution had to be found. Due to these considerations, Krček was cleared of charges in April 1916, but was shortly afterwards declared medically unfit for military duty and pensioned off some weeks later.[72]

---

69 Sammelakt, Aussage Krček, 28-29, Feldgericht [FG] 28. ITD, Res. No. 496/16, 1915 June 2, ÖStA Wien/KA/Gerichtsakten/28. ITD.

70 Untersuchungsergebnis beim IR 28, Bericht Militärkommando Prag, KM-Präs 49/2/4/3 ex 1915, 1915 April 26, ÖStA Wien/KA/KM-Präs.

71 Zweiter Bericht Militärkommando Prag, KM-Präs 49/2/7 ex 1915, 1915 May 13, ÖStA Wien/KA/KM-Präs.

72 Oberst Josef Krček – Gesuch um Rückversetzung in den Ruhestand vorlegen, KM-Präs 2/20/77 ex 1916, 1916 May 22, ÖStA Wien/KA/KM-Präs.

Surprisingly the court now brought up charges against Captain Bornemisza, who was accused of having made a false testimony against the Colonel and his fellow officers.[73] This lawsuit, which lasted almost another year, interestingly enough didn't end with a conviction of the captain, who was, on the contrary, acquitted of charges as well. The judges later stated in their verdict that despite the fact, that the accusations of Bornemisza had turned out to be wrong, the Captain could not be blamed of having made up the whole story. In their opinion Bornemisza hadn't made a wrong testimony, but had simply exaggerated in his report about the events that had occurred in Prague and Szeged, which is why he couldn't be accused of having lied to the court. Interestingly the testimonies of the captain's former comrades, who had accused him of being slawophobe, were not taken into consideration by the military court, since the judges argued that some of these officers could have made wrong statements about Bornemisza in order to harm his career or to defend the honour of the IR 28.[74] The court further stated that at least in some cases the captain's reproaches against Krček had been justified, which is why it had been his duty to report his detections to the military court. Bornemisza was finally cleared of charges on February 3, 1917 due to the lack of evidence and retired some time later from military service.[75] Since the two lawsuits ended without any concrete results, the only outcome was the insight that on one hand obviously no one could be blamed for the lack of training of the IR 28's last replacement battalion while on the other hand a person, who accused the commander of the regiment's home garrison of being responsible for these flaws, was cleared of charges as well. It's still a mystery why the military court in Temesvár made these two conflicting decisions; it is, however, possible that the judges were under influence of the k.u.k. High Command, which had wanted to put an end to the whole matter as soon as possible. Unfortunately, although there is no other logical explanation for the attitude of the Austro-Hungarian authorities in this case, no proof can be found to support this theory.

At the same time the investigation against colonel Krček started, another lawsuit concerning the case of the disbandment of the IR 28 was about to begin. Only two months after the regiment's dissolution, its former commander, Lieutenant Colonel Schaumaier, received a letter from one of his former subordinates, Major Praschak. In his letter Praschak informed

73 Beschluss des Militärgerichts Temesvár, 5-6, VUA Praha, Fond Vojsková tělesa – Pěší pluk 28.

74 Beschluss des Militärgerichts Temesvár, 30-31, VUA Praha, Fond Vojsková tělesa – Pěší pluk 28.

75 Bornemisza, Alexander, Hptm a.D, Ehrenrätliche Untersuchung, KM-Präs 14/627/2, 1918 May 23, ÖStA Wien/KA/KM-Präs.

Schaumaier about the fact that the field court of the 28th infantry brigade had not found any evidence for a disloyal behaviour of the regiment's soldiers, which is why he expected the unit to be rehabilitated anytime soon. At the same time the Major heavily criticized Schaumaier of having made a false testimony to the commander of the k.u.k. IIIrd corps, due to which the IR 28 had been disbanded in the first place.[76] Schaumaier, who wanted to protect his honour, forwarded the letter to the honorary commission of the Austro-Hungarian army, which subsequently stared an investigation against the two officers. During the enquiry, which lasted almost three years, the commission finally approached the question why the commander of the k.u.k. IIIrd corps had wrongly reported to his superiors that the IR 28 had surrendered to the enemy without firing a single shot.[77] The former commander of the corps, who was questioned by the commission, stated that he couldn't remember what exactly had occured in the days after the battle, but claimed that he had received the information regarding the fate of the regiment from Lieutenant Colonel Schaumaier.[78] Although Schaumaier denied strictly that he had made such a statement, it has to be mentioned that the Lieutenant Colonel had suffered a nervous breakdown some days after the battle.[79] It is therefore possible that the regiment's commander, who had not had full control of his senses at that time, unintentionally had made a false statement about the conduct of his unit, which had let the commander of the k.u.k. IIIrd corps come to wrong conclusions. The commission, however, didn't blame the Lieutenant Colonel of having made a wrong testimony, since it obviously hadn't been his intention to do his unit any harm and he had later tried to persuade the High Command not to disband the IR 28, unfortunately without success. Schaumaier was finally cleared of all charges in August 1918, only two months before the end of the war.[80]

The re-erection of the IR 28

Even before the trials against Krček, Bornemisza and Schaumaier came to an end, the IR 28 was surprisingly re-erected at the explicit request of

76 Schaumeier, Ehrenratsakt – Abschlussbericht, 12, KM-Präs 14/226/2 ex 1918, 1918 August 16, ÖStA Wien/KA/KM-Präs.

77 Schaumeier, Ehrenratsakt – Abschlussbericht, 15, KM-Präs 14/226/2 ex 1918, 1918 August 16, ÖStA Wien/KA/KM-Präs.

78 Schaumeier, Ehrenratsakt – Abschlussbericht, 28, KM-Präs 14/226/2 ex 1918, 1918 August 16, ÖStA Wien/KA/KM-Präs.

79 Gefechtsbericht der k.u.k. 56. IBrig über die Ereignisse vom 3. und 4. April 1915, 5, ÖStA Wien/KA/GB/56. IBrig.

80 Schaumeier, Ehrenratsakt – Abschlussbericht, Supplement 2, KM-Präs 14/226/2 ex 1918, 1918 August 16, ÖStA Wien/KA/KM-Präs

the k.u.k. High Command.[81] Decisive for this act of state was the performance of the regiment's 11th replacement battalion, which had also been supposed to be disbanded, but was in May 1915 sent to the Isonzo front after Italy had declared war on Austria-Hungary. There the commander of the 93rd infantry division, to which the troops had been assigned to, decided not to disband the battalion, but to use it as fighting unit[82] in the defence of the plateau of Doberdo near the town Görz. During the battles of the following months the battalion's soldiers, all of them Czechs, performed in an exemplary manner and repeatedly managed to repulse the attacks of superior Italian troops.[83] In that time the unit suffered extensive losses due to enemy artillery fire[84], but nevertheless kept good moral and stayed at its post. Due to the exemplary conduct of the battalion, the commander of the 93rd infantry division wroth a report to the k.u.k. High Command, in which he informed his superiors about the units' outstanding performance. At the same time he requested not to disband the battalion in the near future, but to preserve the unit in order to honour the sacrifice of the IR 28's officers and men.[85] This report could, however, not be sent to the High Command directly, but first had to be confirmed by the commander of the k.u.k. 5th army, General Svetozar Boroević von Bojna. Although the General had only six months before requested to disband the regiment, he now had obviously changed his mind and forwarded the application of the commander of the 93rd infantry division to the High Command together with the following statement:

> "With the same convictions like in April, when I ordered the disbandment of the IR 28, I now want to stand up for this batallion and its brave soldiers. During the past two months the men of the units' 11th replacement battalion have performed in such an exemplary manner that, at least in my eyes, they have earned the right to be pardoned by the emperor. I therefore request not to disband this battalion in the near future, but to rename it "Field Battalion of the IR 28" and keep it as a fighting unit."[86]

81 IR 28 – Antrag auf Wiederaufstellung, 2, AOK Op. 17859, 1915 December 18, ÖStA Wien/KA/AOK.

82 Meldung k.u.k. VII. Korps an 93. ITD, 93. ITD Op.724/29, 1915 July 23, ÖStA Wien/KA/NFA/93. ITD.

83 Bericht über das Verhalten des XI/28 an der Front, KM-Präs 49/2/11 ex 1916, 1915 August 10, ÖStA Wien/KA/KM-Präs

84 XI. Marschbataillon/IR 28, Namentliche Verlustlisten für den Zeitraum 23. Juni bis 7. Juli 1915, KM Verlustgruppe [VG] Nr. 17907, ÖStA Wien/KA/KM/Verlustlisten.

85 Schreiben MKSM an AOK, MKSM 69/6/14/6 ex 1915, 1915 July 26, ÖStA Wien/KA/MKSM.

86 Die Klammer des Reiches, 483-484, ÖStA Wien/KA/Nachlässe, B/726/I, Nachlass Nowak.

Although even the emperor was impressed by the battalion's performance, the High Command argued that due to the occurrences during the battle of Esztebnekhuta, it was not possible to re-erect the regiment anytime soon. The officials, however, stated that if the battalion's men would again show their bravery on the battlefield and so proof that they were worthy to be pardoned by the emperor, the High Command could be willing to change its mind.[87] Although the unit's officers and men were highly disappointed by this decision, the battalion managed to proof its loyalty again only some days later. On the 20th of July 1915 Italian forces captured the Monte San Michele near Görz, which was crucial for the defence in that sector of the Austro-Hungarian front. Subsequently the batallion was ordered to carry out a counterattack and take back the mountain at any cost. The attack, which began in the morning of the following day, ended in a disaster for the 11th replacement battalion, since nearly all but 204 soldiers of the unit, which had in the morning of the day consisted of 800 officers and men, were either slain or wounded.[88] Despite these terrible losses, the battalion's soldiers managed to put the enemy to flight and take back the Monte San Michele before the end of the day.[89] This bravery again impressed the commander of the k.u.k. 93rd infantry division as well as the commander of the k.u.k. 5th army, who some months later, in December 1915, decided to write another proposal to the k.u.k. High Command. In his report General Boroević informed his superiors about the battalion's outstanding performance during the past six months and, with reference to the successful counterattack on the Monte San Michele, asked his superiors to honour the men's spirit and to re-erect the IR 28.[90] To the surprise of everybody, the High Command didn't turn down the application this time, but forwarded it the military chancellery of Emperor Franz Josef together with a statement of Archduke Friedrich, in which the Archduke declared that he had no objections against the re-erection of the unit.[91] Since the Emperor as well didn't have any doubts, he finally gave the order to re-erect the IR 28 from the remains of its 11th replacement battalion on the 22nd of December 1915.[92] Shortly after that the k.u.k. Ministry of War officially

87 IR 28 – Majestätsgesuch Hptm Knobloch auf Wiederformierung, AOK Op. 11983, 1915 July 7, ÖStA Wien/KA/AOK.

88 XI. Marschbataillon/IR 28, Namentliche Verlustlisten für den Zeitraum 21. Juli bis 25. Juli 1915, KM VG Nr. 19505, ÖStA Wien/KA/KM/Verlustlisten.

89 93. ITD – Bericht über Stände, moralischen und physischen Zustand der Truppen, 1915 July 30, ÖStA Wien/KA/GB/93. ITD.

90 IR 28 – Antrag auf Wiederaufstellung, AOK Op. 17859, 1915 December 18, ÖStA Wien/KA/AOK.

91 IR 28 – Antrag auf Wiederaufstellung, 2, AOK Op. 17859, 1915 December 18, ÖStA Wien/KA/AOK.

92 Wiederaufstellung des IR 28 – Allerhöchstes Handschreiben, MKSM 69/6/14/11 ex 1915, 1915 December 21, ÖStA Wien/KA/MKSM.

gave the order to re-establish the unit's home garrison and to enlarge the badly-beaten replacement battalion to the size of a regiment in the course of the following months.[93] The IR 28 itself, after a short interlude in Montenegro[94], stayed on the Italian front for the rest of the war, where the unit, again, fought with great courage.[95]

Meanwhile the field court of the 28th infantry division, which had been ordered to determine the cause of events during the battle of Esztebnekhuta, had also finished its investigation and presented its verdict in December 1915, which greatly surprised the Austro-Hungarian High Command. In its final statement the court pointed out that according to the testimonies of more than 200 officers and men, who had been eyewitnesses of the battle of April 3[96], the IR 28 had obviously fulfilled its duty that day and only a handful of men had surrendered to the enemy without proper cause.[97] The court further stated that the Russian attack on the units' left flank had not only been successful because the defenders had been outnumbered by the rate of 1 to 5, but also because most of the men had been insufficiently trained replacements who hadn't been able to handle their rifles properly. After that, according to the verdict, the Russians had simply blocked the valley's exit south of Esztebnekhuta and had captured or slain the rest of the regiment's soldiers in a short time. The court concluded that the main causes for the military setback had been the Russian surprise attack, the numerical superiority of the enemy and the lack of training of the last replacement battalion's men. A disloyal behaviour of at least some of the regiment's soldiers could, however, not be ruled out completely. The judges argued that since the majority of the men were still being held in Russian captivity, it was not possible to decide whether all of them had done their duty or not.[98] The court therefore recommended to interrupt the investigation until the prisoners had returned home after the end of the war[99], a proposal, which unfortunately could not be carried out due to the dissolution of the Austro-Hungarian monarchy in October 1918. Nevertheless the k.u.k. Ministry of War was impressed by the verdict as well as by the

93 Anordnung zur Neuformierung des IR 28, MKSM 69/19/1/2 ex 1916, 1916 February 7, ÖStA Wien/KA/MKSM.

94 Tagebuch Oblt idR Klemens Mayr, 22-61, ÖStA/KA/Nachlässe, B/318:1, Nachlass Mayr

95 Josef Fučík, Osmadvacátníci. Spor o českého vojáka I. světové války, Praha 2006, 219-387.

96 Das Infanterie-Regiment Nr. 28 wurde ungerecht beschuldigt, Wiener Allgemeine Zeitung, 1926 April 22, 1.

97 Obslt Florian Schaumeier, Obstlt Theodor Praschak, Ehrenangelegenheit, KM-Präs 14/627/1 ex 1916, 1916 December 29, ÖStA Wien/KA/KM-Präs.

98 Ibid.

99 Ibid.

performance of the regiment's 11th replacement battalion and planned to fully rehabilitate the unit, but soon faced unexpected problems.

Since the whole investigation had been declared a military secret, the public in Austria-Hungary remained distrustful or even hostile towards the Czechs since they still believed they were traitors. The High Command knew that in this atmosphere a rehabilitation of the IR 28 could not only lead to unrest among the public, but could also cause severe political problems, since especially the German nationalists opposed all concessions regarding the Czechs and could be expected to protest against what in their eyes would look like an act of mercy for the unit's soldiers. Due to the fact that it wasn't possible to publish the documents regarding the fate of the IR 28 before the end of the war, it was evident that this unfavourable situation would not change in the foreseeable future. At the same time the High Command didn't want to admit that the regiment had been punished without a proper cause in the first place, which is why the Austro-Hungarian authorities tried to find a different way of explaining to the public why the unit had been re-erected only six months after it had been disbanded. Subsequently the High Command stated to the press that the IR 28 had been disbanded due to the fact that its soldiers had deserted to the enemy, but had later been re-erected since its 11th marching battalion had performed on the Italian front in an exemplary manner and so had restored the unit's honour.[100] Although the authorities knew that this statement was false and would further damage the regiment's reputation, they nevertheless decided that it was the best way to settle the whole affair. The attitude of the authorities, however, greatly insulted the Czech soldiers as well as the Czech public who knew that they were being accused of crimes they hadn't committed. Due to this fact the Czech-German national conflict within the Austro-Hungarian monarchy did not, as the government had hoped, subside, but increased over the course of time and later contributed to the dissolution of the Habsburg monarchy in November 1918.[101]

Conclusion

The dissolution of the IR 28 shows us clearly how paranoid and hostile the Austro-Hungarian authorities had become towards the Czechs in the course of World War One. Despite the fact that the defeat suffered by the

100 Anfragebeantwortung, 8. Mai 1918, k.k. Hof- und Staatsdruckerei (Hg.), Stenographische Protokolle XXII. Session des Reichsrates, Anfragebeantwortung 621.

101 Josef Kalvoda, The Genesis of Czechoslovakia, New York 1986, 377-434; Křen, Thechen und Deutsch, 306-382.

k.u.k. forces in the Battle of Esztebnekhuta on the 3rd of April 1915 did not have any negative effects on other parts of the front, the importance of the event was greatly overestimated by the military authorities. In their eyes a Czech-dominated unit had not only surrendered, but willingly deserted to the enemy during battle, which is why, at lest in their opinion, the Czech soldiers of the k.u.k. army could no longer be trusted. This assumption was obviously fuelled by the behaviour of some of the commanding officers, who were afraid that they could be held responsible for the fatal strategy errors they had made in the battle of Esztebnekhuta. Their decision, to let the Czech soldiers take the blame for their own mistakes, had quite dramatic consequences since the false statement of the commander of the k.u.k. IIIrd corps, who reported to the High Command that the IR 28 had surrendered to the Russians, finally led to the disbandment of the unit. It remains, however, unclear why the High Command had the IR 28 struck from the register of the k.u.k. army in such a hurry without at first trying to determine the cause of events during the battle. Since the military authorities reacted differently in similar cases, it is evident that the High Command was obviously not interested in finding out what had really happened during the battle of April 3, 1915, but was delighted to be able to let the Czech IR 28 take the blame for the failure of the counterattack on the mountain range near Bartfá, an operation, which shouldn't have been started in the first place.

The result of the investigation of the military court of the k.u.k. 28th infantry division, which finally cleared the regiment of all charges, naturally caused a great dilemma for the High Command, since it now became obvious that the unit had been disbanded without proper cause in the first place. At the same time the authorities could not ignore the outstanding performance of the IR 28's 11th replacement battalion on the Italian front, which had caused the commanders of the k.u.k. 93rd infantry division and the k.u.k. 5th army to openly demand the re-erection of the unit. The High Command therefore had to find a way to rehabilitate the unit without loosing its own face, which was quite a difficult task. In the end, as was pointed out already, the authorities found an unorthodox solution for their dilemma. While on one hand the regiment was finally re-erected in December 1915, the authorities on the other hand declared the reports of the military court a secret and so ultimately prevented the public from ever learning about the real circumstances of the battle of Esztebnekhuta. At the same time the High Command reported to the press that the IR 28 had, indeed been disbanded in April 1915 for having deserted to the enemy, but had later been re-erected due to the outstanding performance of its 11th replacement battalion on the Italian front. Owing to this statement, the public remained distrustful towards the Czech soldiers, although the majority of them continued to do their duty in the Austro-Hungarian army until the end of the war. Due to these circumstances the stories of the "treacherous Czech soldiers" have, unfortunately, survived until today in collective memory as well as in Czech[102] and Austrian[103] historiography. I therefore hope that this short research paper will be able to help changing this unsatisfactory situation.

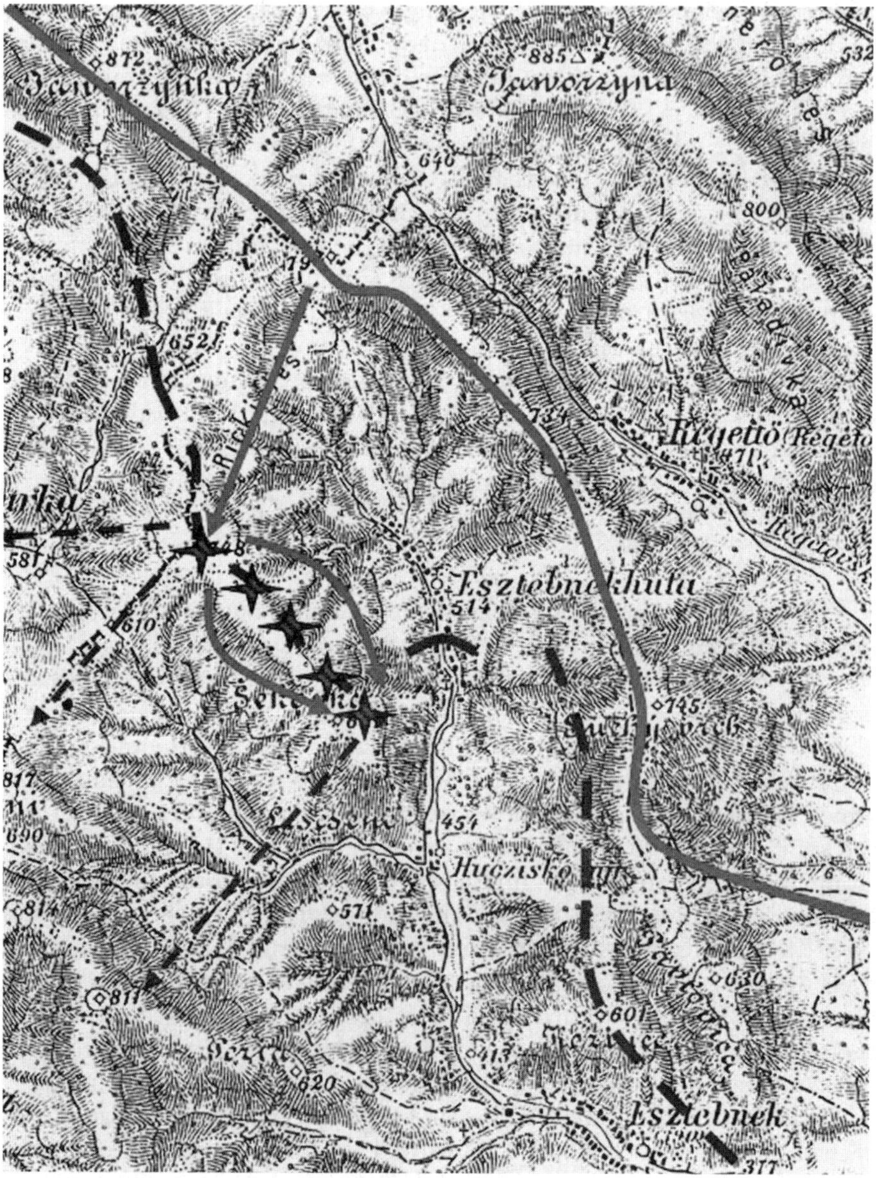

Battle of Esztebnekhuta - Phase 1

102 Pavel Augusta – František Honzák, Československo 1918-1938, Praha 1992, 1-2.
103 Anton Wagner, Der erste Weltkrieg. Ein Blick zurück, Wien [2]1993, 219.

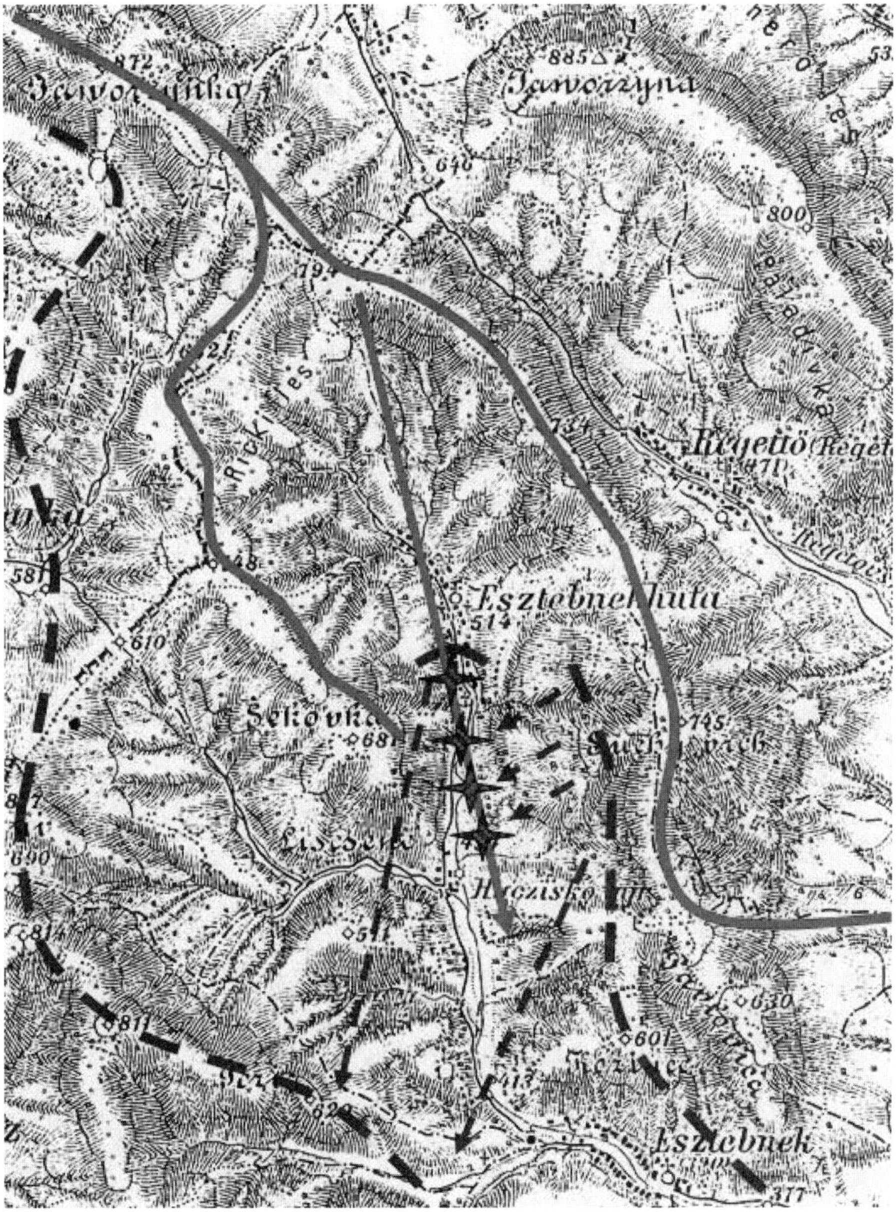

Battle of Esztebnekhuta - Phase 2

Europa Orientalis

hrsg. vom Institut für Osteuropäische Geschichte an der Universität Wien

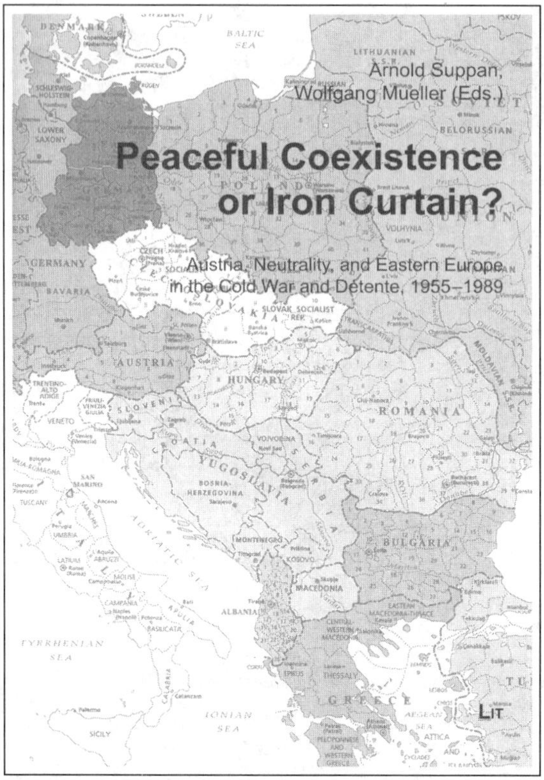

Arnold Suppan; Wolfgang Mueller (Eds.)

"Peaceful Coexistence" or "Iron Curtain"

Austria, Neutrality, and Eastern Europe in the Cold War and Détente, 1955 – 1989

In the history of the Cold War and détente, reference is seldom made to the international relations of the small states. This volume undertakes the task of reassessing comparatively, on the basis of newly declassified sources from Western and formerly Eastern archives, the preconditions and various developments of bilateral relations across the Iron Curtain, between the USSR, Eastern Europe, and neutral but capitalist Austria. While the Soviet attitude saw neutrality as a valuable model for Western Europe and Austria as a showcase for the „peaceful coexistence" between East and West, this small country and its communist neighbors developed their own kind of *Ostpolitik* long before the bigger political actors had ushered in European détente.

Bd. 7, 2009, 536 S., 39,90 €, br., ISBN 978-3-8258-1978-1

LIT Verlag Berlin – Münster – Wien – Zürich – London

Auslieferung Deutschland / Österreich / Schweiz: siehe Impressumsseite